Children Learning Language

THIRD EDITION

Rita C. Naremore

Indiana University

Robert Hopper

University of Texas

1817

HARPER & ROW PUBLISHERS, New York
Grand Rapids, Philadelphia, St. Louis, San Francisco,
London, Singapore, Sydney, Tokyo

Sponsoring Editor: Jane Kinney
Project Editor: David Nickol
Art Direction/Cover Coordinator: Heather A. Ziegler
Cover Design: Joan Peckolick Design
Production: Willie Lane

Children Learning Language, Third Edition
Copyright © 1990 by Harper & Row, Publishers, Inc.

Library of Congress Cataloging-in-Publication Data

Naremore, Rita C.
    Children learning language / Rita C. Naremore, Robert Hopper. —
3rd ed.
        p.   cm.
    Rev. ed. of: Children's speech / Robert Hopper, Rita C. Naremore.
2nd ed. c1978.
    Includes bibliographical references.
    ISBN 0-06-042898-8
    1. Language acquisition.   2. Children-Language.   I. Hopper,
Robert.   II. Hopper, Robert. Children's speech.   III. Title.
P118.H65   1990
401'.93—dc20   89-24441
                                                                   CIP

89 90 91 92 9 8 7 6 5 4 3 2 1

Contents

Preface

We hope that you will enjoy reading this book. Our goal has been to translate the discoveries of researchers into everyday language and to try to show people who work with children how these discoveries can be translated into everyday practice. We have tried to avoid jargon; when we use a term, we define what we are talking about and give examples. We do not use extensive footnotes. Rather, we briefly identify our sources by author and year in the text. If you wish to pursue an idea, you can look up the cited work in the bibliography at the back of the book. In addition, each chapter contains suggestions for further reading on the topics in the chapter. Reading in depth will begin to teach you more about the fascination which children's speech holds for researchers and teachers.

Readers familiar with our prior editions will notice that we have changed our title to reflect the focus of this edition more accurately. We have also added new chapters about prelinguistic communication, conversation, and written language and updated the other chapters extensively. This is truly a *new* edition, reflecting changes in our thinking as well as changes in research. One important change in research in the years since the first edition appeared has been a shift toward studying the development of meanings in children's language. This shift is reflected throughout the book. A second important change has been the emergence of pragmatics, or usage, as a major concern of child development researchers. In many ways this is not a change for us, since our first edition was one of the first published works to advocate the importance of pragmatics in children's speech. It is with some proprietary pride that we point out the focus on language use in all of our chapters. To strengthen this focus, the materials that suggest day-to-day experiences for teachers have been substantially increased in this edition, and we have added to each chapter suggested activities to give you an opportunity to interact with children for yourself.

The world has changed for us as well since the first edition. We thank families and friends who have supported us. Brian and Jay were young children when we started writing this book. Now they are adults. Christine, Brian's sister, is almost through school, having learned how to talk in her own way— a way quite different from the paths Brian and Jay used. We are now surer about what we don't know. We will not soon understand all the complexities of how children learn to talk. Perhaps that will make the tone of this edition less impatient than the first. However, there is still one thing we can get on a soapbox about: Children are neither half-formed humans nor little adults. Children must be understood in terms of what they are, not what they aren't yet.

Read this book. Disagree where you want to, and share with us any insights you gain from it. Then if you really want to understand children's speech, listen to children.

R.C.N. and R.H.

Children
Learning
Language

Chapter 1

The Child's Garden of Eloquence

*C*hildren's communication development attracts widespread attention these days—for many good reasons. Recent research has brought startling advances in what we know about children's speech, language, and learning abilities. Teachers and clinicians welcome these new insights because with such information schools and clinics can be made more effective and humane. These advances are no less relevant to parents. As we learn more about normal communication development, we can define better what is not normal—which improves prospects for intervention with children who have speech or emotional handicaps. And, of course, parents also are concerned because their children must learn so many communication skills in the preschool years. Finally, all Americans should be aware of research in this area. If the "American dream"— a just society in which there is equality of opportunity for all citizens— is to be realized, we must know how to help all children learn better and, perhaps even more important, communicate more effectively.

There are many reasons for being fascinated by how children communicate. Young children exhibit a vivacity in communicating and learning that can serve as a model for everyone. Whatever the stuff of life is, children seem to have an overflow supply. Just watch a group of 4-year-olds play—they never seem to slow down. The same boundless energy and creativity children show in playing is unleashed in the more important task-game of learning to communicate.

We say task-game because parents and teachers take it more "seriously" and pay more "conscious attention" to children's speech than the children do. Kids are most interested (and probably learn most) while playing. Listen at cribside to a 2-year-old waiting for sleep or a 3-year-old playing alone with dolls. Children play with sounds and words, putting them together to create and also to re-create events of the day. They seem to create because the act of creation is a delightful experience. Here is a monologue spoken by 2½-year-old Brian Hopper, playing in the bathtub.

> Chim chiminey chiminey
> Chim chiminey chiminey
> Here come some
> I be right there
> I want someone to wash me
> wiff my wash cloff
> washy washy cloth
> I got it all full *[referring to washcloth, which he put in mouth; he then spat several times]*
>
> No
> Well, hard
> Chim chiminey chiminey
> Chiminey
> I love you
>
> With that
> At the other page, she can get it
> A store
> An hour, an' a page
> Honey, can't wash me *[in falsetto]*
> No no, and we let it out
> And she doesn't want me to remember you
> Washy washy
> Oh the bizzin of the bees *[alteration of "Big Rock Candy Mountain"]*
> Oh the bizzin of the bees
> Oh the bizzin of the bees
> Oh the bizzin of the bees
> Oh the bizzin of the bees
> Mix mix mix
> Don't like that water
> Chim chiminey, I'll poo soo
> Chim chiminey
> Some more
> *[Pause]*
>
> Oh the bizzin a the bees
> Oh the bizzin a the bees
> Oh the bizzin of the bees
> Oh the bizzin a the bees
> 2, 3, 4, 5, 6, 7 *[singing]*
> you guys
> Would you like my boat?

[Several unintelligible sounds] some more
I think that's about enough
Now let's put my washcloth in

Chim chiminey
Mix
Mix a orange juice
It's a washy
Now
Wait to see what she
Oh, happy, really

Chim chiminey chiminey
Hey chiminey boy
Hey, four como
Hey chiminey chiminey
Um *[pause]*

Hey, Mommy
I already called

This child, while playing, is also learning to speak a native language. It takes a lot of learning to speak a language. Imagine waking up one morning to find yourself in some strange culture where everybody spoke a language you did not understand. Adults (especially those who teach) would be overwhelmed by the enormity of what they would have to learn in order to communicate.

The child's problem is even more severe than that of the misplaced adult, for if you woke up tomorrow in a strange culture, you would at least know about spoken communication from your previous experience. The human child has to learn that *communication is happening through speech.*

In spite of these problems little children routinely succeed in learning to speak long before school age, usually with no formal instruction. And, as shown by the preceding example, children enjoy speaking.

We must point out, lest we be accused of taking too narrow a view, that we are both parents and thus have learned that children are not always totally charming communicators. But regardless of how an adult may feel about any single child at any given moment, the world of children's speech permits us to reexamine part of youth beyond memory. Children's speech (if we listen carefully) reveals to us a great deal about how people learn, how people motivate themselves, how people create, and more.

A child's speaking is artistic, educational, and rhetorical-persuasive. Through learning to talk, children learn how to function in society. And as they learn, they create beauty. The samples of children's speech you will read in the following chapters are cut flowers from the child's garden of eloquence.

FROM A CHILD'S VIEW

Our book is titled *Children Learning Language*, and the next two sections of this chapter ask you to consider the words *children* and *language*.

Words such as children, child, kid, and baby signal a stage of life and ordinarily a position in a family unit. A child is a young person, and a lot of things "go with" being in the stage of being young, for example, (1) having older, larger people take care of you, (2) being watched for "mistakes," such as falling down or chewing on electrical cords, (3) playing games, such as "peek-a-boo," (4) crying out at night, (5) being encouraged to make noises (and especially to speak) at some times, such as in front of grandparents, and yet (6) being required to be silent (and especially not to speak) at other times.

None of the readers of this book is a "child" in the sense of our title. (We remain our parents' "children" beyond their own lives, but that sense of "child" does not concern us here.) However, each reader was once a child. At the beginning of human life each of us is a child. At some point each of us stops being a child permanently and becomes some sort of grown-up. "Child" is a stage of human life—the first stage. All of us are "alumni" of childhood.

What is the experience of childhood from the child's perspective? What is childhood like? How well can you remember? Most of us have many stereotyped assumptions about children that we routinely use, not always wisely. For example, how do grown-ups talk to children? Watch a typical middle-class, adult male encounter a 3-year-old child. A smile comes to the adult's face—a beaming, condescending smile. A greeting, "How are you doing today, my little one?" is delivered with exaggerated rising pitch. It is a tone of voice adults use with someone stupid or with a pet. Few adults (or children) stop to think about it, since they hear adults talking to children in this way so often.

Look back through the cobwebs. What was it like for you when you were, say, 4 years old? Can you remember when you entered kindergarten at age 5? What kinds of events do you remember from your childhood? Was it a tranquil, happy time? Do you recall feeling rage? Many (by no means all) people say that their childhood was pleasant and carefree. Yet few people can remember more than three events before the age of 5. And it's often difficult to tell whether events that are remembered are really recalled in original form or are reconstructions from what others have told us about the events. One feature of "first memories" is that the stories have been told a number of times, and each retelling may make the event more removed from the original childhood occurrence. A curtain is gradually drawn over our early life that makes it difficult or impossible to remember much about how it was. How do we accomplish this forgetting of childhood and why?

In his book *I'm OK, You're OK*, Thomas Harris argues that people forget so much of childhood because it is too painful to remember. Childhood, he says, is a time when you are 2 or 3 feet tall and unable to do much of anything for yourself. Grown-ups, on the other hand, are 6 feet tall, competent, and always pretty sure they know what's correct. In this setting children nearly always build up a significant number of "not-OK" feelings about themselves, because they see that they can't do things as well as or know as much as grown-ups. We never really get these experiences out of our minds, says Harris; we just try not to remember them. They are repressed. Every now and then, however, when we feel insignificant or clumsy compared to people we think of as OK, this not-OK feeling reasserts itself.

We don't want to exaggerate the difficulties of childhood or sentimentalize its pleasures. Consider the following: When we ask a group of students which they like better, childhood or the present, about 90 percent usually respond that they prefer childhood. However, if we then ask how many would like to return to this stage that they liked so much, few would choose to do so.

Here are a couple of things you might do to understand a child's experiences. First, imagine that you cannot understand what people are saying. Watch a foreign movie and pretend you are in that verbal setting. Play a tape recording backward and consider what it would be like if everyone you heard talking sounded that way to you. Next, sit on the floor and look at a chair. Imagine that you would like to climb up onto the chair but that it would take you about two minutes of climbing to get there. Think of how it would feel to put your hands on the chair and try to push yourself up with your elbows until you could swing your leg up over the seat. If there is a tree house in your neighborhood, try climbing up to it and imagining that it is a chair; imagine how you would feel sitting at that height at the dinner table, surrounded by other tree houses that held people twice your size.

These activities may help you explore the question "What is childhood really like?" If you think about that question only in terms of how children's behavior and knowledge differ from that of grown-ups, the answer may not be too helpful. While reading this book, try to think about what children are like in ways that do not have much to do with what grown-ups are like.

When children do things differently from the ways adults do them, adults often assume this is because children haven't learned how to do them right yet. In a trivial sense that is true. But children know and feel many things. Their thoughts and feelings might be strange in an adult, but they are right for kids. Children are not born blank, but show evidence of thinking right from the start. Children are also not little adults. If you went to an alien culture and listened to the people talk and watched them act, would you decide that they didn't know how to behave because they were different from you? Probably not. But do you assume a similar thing of a child?

And how does it all feel from the child's perspective? Suppose some people invite you to dinner. They remind you to wipe your feet as you come in the door. Then they remind you to wash your hands. They force you to eat the brussels sprouts. They give you milk, but they drink wine. They prod you to clean your plate. You would be appalled at their rudeness. But that kind of behavior would not be considered rude if the person invited to dinner were a child, because it is assumed that it is in some way helpful for children to be reminded "They don't know how to be grown-ups yet."

To understand what a child is like, watch children's television. Mister Rogers' Neighborhood is especially attuned to 3-year-olds, Sesame Street appeals to 4- to 6-year-olds, and Electric Company and cartoon shows appeal to 7- to 10-year-olds. These are only some examples. When watching these shows, ask yourself, "If I liked this show better than anything else on television, what kind of person would I be? If I were the ideal audience member that this show appeals to, what kinds of entertainment or learning would I prefer?" Look for clues. Assume that the child might be different from you and that the difference is acceptable. We promise you that what you see will be more than worth the effort. Perhaps you will observe as a child, rather than recycling adult stereotypes of childhood.

Having considered a child's eye-and-ear view of the world, let us turn to that aspect of childhood that is this book's focus: children's *language*.

SPEECH AND SPEAKING

Language learning occurs in a human-centered, biological world, a world of interacting talking bodies. Each talking body lives in its own bag of skin, pretty much unaffected by other bodies, except when it senses another body: We see each other, touch each other, hear each other, and *speak to each other*. In speaking to others, we describe, we argue, we tell stories, and much else. Spoken language is a primary communication system for humans.

Just think of all the things you manage to do when you use language:

1. *You make sounds* in English, sounds subtly and systematically different from those in any other language.
2. *You express meanings* of English concepts and words.
3. *You structure sentences* using numerous systematic components such as word order.
4. *You accomplish actions* in talking.
5. *You accompany speech with visual displays*: gestures and facial expression.

All of these are things that are related to each other within "conversation" or "talking."

In conversation we take turns speaking to each other, and the nature of the game is that once people begin to be in conversation with one another, they stay in conversation until something stops it. That's the experience of using language. It seems to flow without effort, as the best piano music seems to flow. The analogy seems apt, for we know piano virtuosity to be a complex and difficult art. Speaking a language may be no less complex and difficult, yet almost every child learns to talk!

AN ECOLOGICAL MODEL OF SPEAKING AND LISTENING

We suggest an ecological model of conversation with interlocking coding systems that seem like "layers" of activities. Each time we speak and listen, we show fine-grained knowledge and timing about four systems of signs: sounds of English, meanings in English, sentences or utterances in English, and actions in our lives as members of a speech community. We know something about each of these systems that allows us to participate in talk with other people. Yet we don't know about sounds and meanings and sentences and actions in the same way we know about math lessons or piano lessons. We do not understand our own speech actions, yet we know how to operate a multilayer system for ordering speech in time.

As Figure 1.1 illustrates, each speaker's turn at talk requires that a number of ordering constraints be respected all at once. The speaker must utter sounds in a language, make sense in a language, perform speech actions (such as telling stories or making promises), and more. Suppose a conversation proceeds at 80 words per minute, which is slow in English. Suppose that there are three sounds in each word, that each

$$===T==i==m==e==>>$$

Speaker 1's turn				Speaker 2's turn		
B		E	B			E
E	Sounds	N	E	Sounds		N
G	Meanings	D	G	Meanings		D
I	Sentences/	S	I	Sentences/		S
N	utterances		N	utterances		Speaker change recurs
S	Speech actions		S	Speech actions		===>
	Visual display			Visual display		

$$======T==i==m==e=============>>$$

Figure 1.1   Layers of the Speech Ecology

word may be ambiguous in meaning, that five words make the average sentence, and that there are dozens of different speech actions that might be performed within a minute of conversation. Given these conservative estimates, speakers must sort and organize thousands of units in coherence-building, language-layered turns.

Most of our readers are surprised when they consider the complexity of language use, especially given the smooth way that talkers accomplish transitions between turns at talk. In ordinary experience we just find ourselves speaking without having to give it much thought. We experience conversation as a whole, as a single ecology. But researchers rarely study speaking as a system, as an ecology. Most often they study special aspects of speaking, just one of the layers in Figure 1.1. In fact, the layers in the figure are actually layers in the *study* of speaking; we hope these descriptions also denote realities.

Figure 1.2 extends the ecology model by displaying layers of the study of speaking and listening. The central term for the system is still "conversation," at the left of the figure. Conversation unfolds in time through alternations of speaker turns. Each of these turns is a complex, layered activity that is orderly in its sounds and structures. Our model's terms for the layers are in the middle column, and the terms for the study of each layer are at the right. The word *etc.* appears on the figure to indicate the primitive state of our understanding. New layers may be added to the model and old ones changed or deleted.

"Studies" of the layers are each the basis for a chapter in this book about children's speech. During our survey of what is known about children's speech, we shall summarize work in each of these areas and others. But before narrowing our inquiry to details about language and use, let us consider some basic questions about the speech ecology, the entire system of human interaction.

WHERE WE ARE GOING

The goal of this book is to explain how children learn to talk. First, children's language use must be considered as a biological event. The human being's unique heritage is to be the speaking animal. Children talk

	Layer	Study of layer
Conversation	Sounds	Phonetics, phonology
	Meanings	Semantics
	Sentences/utterances	Syntax
	Speech action, sequences	Pragmatics
	Etc.	

Figure 1.2   Layers of Conversation and Studies of These Layers

almost as naturally as they stand up and walk and almost as naturally as they grow toenails and baby fat. Chapter 2 examines communication development in the context of nonhuman communication systems and the human biological endowment.

Second, children's language use must be considered in terms of its role in the system of interaction, its sequential structuring across speaker turns. This is described in Chapter 3. Chapter 4 places the biological child in the interactional environment with a description of communication prior to language.

Third, various aspects of the act of learning to talk must be examined. In one sense, acquisition of speaking ability is a single developmental matrix of events. In another, it is a collection of specific aspects of development, each having its own history. Each aspect may be studied separately. Part Two of this book summarizes significant research in several areas: development of the sound system (Chapter 5), development of meaning (Chapter 6), development of language structure (Chapter 7), and development of pragmatics (Chapter 8).

Fourth, in Part Three we place the child's language in a larger world, the world of thought and learning. Chapter 9 considers the relation of the child's cognitive development to the child's overall communication behavior. Chapter 10 surveys ideas about how children learn language. The remaining chapters address some practical questions: How can family members and educators help children learn to speak and listen? How can problems of cultural and individual language differences be handled in classrooms? How can we help children suffering from speaking and listening problems? Chapters 11, 12, 13, and 14 apply this information to current educational problems, to issues of language diversity in society, to problems of children whose language development is not proceeding normally, and to issues of speaking and writing.

This plan organizes the material we want to cover in the book and provides a structure to help you remember the material. The danger in this structuring is that you may occasionally lose touch with the "stuff" of children's language use—the actual sights and sounds of children's communication. Remember that our target is the phenomenon, more than the theory. Our target is the experience, not the jargon. To this end, we ask that throughout the book you examine your experiences talking and listening to children and that you listen to tape recordings of children's (and grown-ups') speech.

Study hint: As you read later chapters, keep a journal in which you record samples of conversational interaction as precisely as you can. With real-life events it is essential to make your notes immediately, lest details be distorted by later recall. Transcriptions of tape recordings may, of course, be considerably more precise than recall of talk.

PART
One

THE CHILD AND THE ENVIRONMENT

In the three chapters that follow, we will examine the child's biological endowment for language learning (Chapter 2) and the interactional environment in which language occurs (Chapter 3). Chapter 4 can be viewed as an extended example of what happens in the earliest interaction of the child and the environment. This section of the book sets the stage for everything that comes later. As you read it, keep in mind the following observations:

1. Normal children are born with a sensory system (sight, hearing, taste, touch, smell) and a brain that seem to be "set" for language learning.
2. The environment in which the child learns language provides much more than sounds, words, and sentence patterns for the child to learn.
3. The child is a language learner from birth.

Chapter
2
Child Speech as a Biological Process

*C*hildren's communication development is considered in terms of biology because children's talk is as much a part of their natural development as growing two sets of teeth. In this chapter we examine some biological concepts that have applications to human communication development, we view the process of learning to talk in light of nonhuman communication systems in nature, and we survey our human "biological endowment" for language.

DIFFERENTIATION

Each of us begins life as a single-celled organism, or zygote. The cell divides to form a small collection of cells, each of which is precisely like the original cell. Some of the cells are inside the group; others are outside. In these different surroundings, inside cells and outside cells become less alike. So begins the process called *differentiation.* There is no complete explanation for differentiation. A human embryo starts out as a single cell, becomes a group of identical cells, and eventually develops into an organism consisting of millions of cells of many varieties. Some cells "specialize" to make blood, others to constitute tooth enamel, and so forth. The types of cells that develop in a growing person are not a matter of chance. The zygote is coded to become a fully functioning human being. Further, the characteristics of each individual—eye color, skin color, and many other features—are specified in the individual's genetic structures. We inherit these genetic structures from our ancestors.

Just as certain physical characteristics are genetically coded, certain behaviors are also a result of heredity. Such hereditary, or innate, behaviors are often called *instinctive.* Baby ducks, for example, follow moving objects the size of their mothers; this behavior seems to be genetically determined, just as are physical characteristics such as the structure of the duck's webbed feet. Each species of animals performs certain unique and inherited behaviors: Dogs bark, spiders spin intricate webs, and birds go through elaborate courtship rituals. In the sense that webs are unique to spiders, human language appears to be unique to people.

The relationship between our biological heritage and our language behavior will be discussed throughout this book. For example, some aspects of communication development unfold in a manner that recalls the differentiation of complicated life forms from single-celled zygotes. Processes of differentiation can be seen in the development of language structure (syntax), the sound system (phonology), and the meaning system (semantics). The concept is introduced at this point to indicate that the capacity and the process of learning to communicate, even in structural form, resembles the growth of life itself.

The differentiation of speech and language forms is unique to humans, but many other animals communicate. Comparing human communication with other communication systems in nature reveals further information about child speech as a biological process.

COMMUNICATION IN NATURE

Although human beings are not the only communicators, their language is among the most impressively complex systems we have discovered. These are some things human communicators can do:

1. *Express emotions.* Human speech can express varied emotional states. When a stage actor screams, we know that he is communicating terror. A mother's coo to her baby carries a readily understandable emotional message. Infants can express emotions— they can let us know how they feel—long before they can talk. As we grow, we learn to use language to express more precise emotions.

2. *Refer to and describe events and objects.* Human beings can point out and describe anything from a tree to tranquility because human language assigns arbitrary fixed meanings to words and constructions—meanings that have no necessary connection with the objects to which they refer. This makes description an easy task once the code is learned. Many of the child's first sentences are descriptive: "Red truck," "Ball all gone," "Big tree."

3. *Combine sounds into complicated structures,* with each structure (phrase or sentence) being a meaningful unit. The human capacity for syntax, which is probably human beings' most remarkable

communication ability, will be discussed in Chapter 7. At this point we note only that sentences are complex structures, and the learning of these structures by children is a major aspect of their communication development.

Each of these abilities is used many times each day. Humans may be the only creatures who have all three, yet no one of the abilities is unique to human beings; each exists in some form in other organisms. All mammals can express emotion. A dog is easily understandable when he growls at the mail person, whines to be let outside, or barks happily at other dogs. The ability to describe also occurs among nonhumans. The best example is the well-known "dance of the bees." Bees that have found food dance around the hive to describe to other bees the distance and direction of the food source. The ability to combine smaller units into larger ones to obtain more complex meanings also occurs in other animals. Some birds, for example, combine smaller song segments into larger ones in a manner similar to the human combining of sounds and phrases into sentences.

MONKEY SEE, MONKEY DO?

The question of how animals communicate has led some researchers to ask whether human language can be taught to nonhumans. Because apes are closer to humans in evolution than any other animal, they have been the subjects of the most interesting of these teaching experiments. Most attempts to teach language to apes have been undertaken within the framework of learning theory, on the premise that nonhumans might learn the human language system with carefully administered reinforcement. If all such attempts fail, then evidence mounts that language is unique to human beings.

It is obvious that chimpanzees communicate with one another and that they can even communicate with humans. Jane Goodall's wonderful book *In the Shadow of Man* tells how a patient observer was able to make sense out of many chimpanzee social behaviors. Reading this book, it is easy to forget that Goodall is describing nonhumans. Chimps show jealousy, sexiness, authority, affection, and fear in quite precise ways.

People have known about this sociability of chimpanzees for generations. There have been numerous attempts to teach chimpanzees to talk to people. Some ambitious researchers have even raised chimp babies along with their own children, giving them equal attention and stimulation. The researchers grew very attached to the chimps and much communication took place, but almost none of the communication was verbal. It was rare for chimps in these studies to utter single words, even rarer for them to combine words as very young children do routinely.

These failures to teach apes to talk seemed to close off the question.

But in the late 1960s two innovative attempts to teach chimps to use language proved remarkably successful. Both research teams taught the chimps some form of visual language, noting that chimps are clever with their hands, but not too handy with their mouths. Besides, the chimpanzee's oral cavity is too flat for making human language sounds. Hence the idea of using hand manipulation of symbols seemed promising.

Beatrice and Alan Gardner (1969) were leaders in this line of research. They raised a baby chimp named Washoe in their home much as other experimenters had done, but instead of talking with Washoe, they "signed" to her using the symbols of American Sign Language. American Sign Language, used by many deaf humans, is clearly a language, but it uses the hands to send almost all messages. Washoe picked up vocabulary quickly. After four years of teaching she used a vocabulary of about 150 signs. She also learned to use combinations of two or three signs quite often. This may not seem too remarkable, since a large teaching effort was expended on Washoe, but it far surpassed any earlier chimpanzee language learners. Also, Washoe was occasionally observed to create *new* words of her own, a feat never before observed in nonhumans. For example, for the concept "funny" Washoe invented the symbol of pressing her index finger against her nose and snorting. Washoe also showed that conceptual classes were meaningful to her in some sense. It was common for her to confuse the signs for "cat" and "dog" or for "comb" and "brush," showing that she classified these sets together. She also referred on one occasion to some meat as "food," showing abstraction ability.

It is not easy to answer the question, "Does Washoe use language." She does communicate and play with language. She invents new uses for it. She combines symbols, although there is no clear evidence that she combines them in definite order. By contrast, we shall show in future chapters that word order plays an important part in early human syntax. A possible answer is that Washoe is a language user, but not quite as facile a language user as the human child. Washoe is still serving as the subject of language studies in a different lab. Perhaps time will answer our questions about her abilities.

A second major chimpanzee project was supervised by David Premack (1971). Unlike the Gardners, Premack started with an adult chimpanzee. Premack's project sounds more structured than the Gardners', since learning was based on careful reinforcement schedules. The chimp, Sarah, used a "language" invented by Premack. He paired symbols arbitrarily with concepts, which is the way words work (for example, the word for banana does not look like one). The language was expressed by placing tokens, on which the symbols appear, on a magnetic board.

Premack's experiments allowed much greater control over the chimpanzee and showed more precisely which kinds of operations can be performed. For instance, same-different comparisons and logical categorization were shown convincingly. Sarah could look at tokens meaning "apple" or "watermelon" and categorize them into the class "fruit." But Sarah didn't seem as inventive or playful as Washoe and was less inclined to be funny. Sarah would not play with the symbols just for fun, as Washoe seemed to sign-play. Her knowledge of her token language might be compared to the French or Spanish learned by school children who have never spoken the language outside the classroom. Sarah became linguistically competent, but not much of a communicator.

In summary, Washoe and Sarah lead us to believe that chimpanzees can perform some types of linguistic tasks, but they cannot use language with the facility of humans. However, these experiments and other observations show that human beings did not invent language from ground zero. The capacity to communicate is shown by members of a number of species. Language is a product of evolution. The recent cases of the linguistic apes show that this evolution has more continuity between beasts and people than we used to think.

Unfortunately for both humans and their ape friends, the animal language experiments have not been without controversy, and their outcomes have sometimes been tragic for the apes involved. While some scientists see the attempts to teach language to apes as valid investigations into the nature of the capacity for language, others are adamantly opposed to such research. When those who favor such research are in positions of political power, grant money to support the research (and to feed and house the apes) is plentiful. When the opponents are in the ascendancy, however, the grant money dries up and the research is discontinued. Chimpanzees who have learned to trust and communicate with human beings have been sold to medical laboratories as test animals. Others have been left to languish in their cages, signing to their keepers who do not understand the language the chimps have been taught to use. Eugene Linden has reviewed the outcomes of much of the research in his book *Silent Partners*, and he shows us a dark side of humanity that may cause many of us to believe that we are not ready to know whether apes can learn language. We are not ready to know, because we are not prepared to deal with the implications if the answer is yes. Nevertheless, the attempts continue, as Penny Patterson works with Koko, her now famous gorilla, and Duane and Sue Savage Rumbaugh work with pygmy chimpanzees. We can only hope that our learning about ourselves will keep pace with our learning about the apes.

THE CONTRIBUTION OF THE HUMAN BRAIN

People who doubt that chimpanzees will ever learn language cite the unique structure of the human brain. Humans do appear to have specialized neural mechanisms related specifically to language learning and use. These mechanisms are so powerful that it would be difficult to prevent a normal child from learning language! What is the nature of this powerful biological endowment?

First, the actual shape of the brain is related to language functioning. The brain consists of two sides or *hemispheres*, known as the left and right cerebral hemispheres. In most adults the left hemisphere is slightly larger than the right and contains some neurological structures that are different. This physical difference reflects a functional difference. In about 90 percent of the adult population the left cerebral hemisphere controls (or is dominant for) language. (People who are left-brain dominant will also be right-handed. People who are left-handed are either right-brain dominant for language or have no clear dominant hemisphere for language.) The dominant language hemisphere contains several areas that control specific language functions. For example, the back, or posterior, area of the hemisphere appears to be specialized for the tasks of recognition and comprehension of language. The front, or anterior, region of the hemisphere controls the planning and execution of speaking or writing tasks. For normal language functioning to occur, these specialized areas must not only be intact and healthy, they must also be neurologically connected with one another. The dominant and nondominant hemispheres must also be connected, since the "language" hemisphere depends on information from the other hemisphere for part of its functioning.

It is important to remember that this much-simplified account applies to the adult human brain. No other species has been found to have a brain structurally specialized for language in the way the human brain is specialized. Furthermore, the brains of young children also appear to be less structurally specialized, although there is some argument about this. What does appear to be the case is that if the language areas of an adult's brain are injured (as a result of accident or stroke), it is unlikely that the adult will recover language functioning. If the same thing happens to a young child, say at age 2 or 3, other areas of the brain appear to take over control of language functioning, and language ability is usually recovered. Some researchers account for this by saying that the child's brain is more plastic, or adaptable, than that of the adult. This adaptability is one more piece of evidence showing how powerful the human endowment for language is.

GROWING UP COMMUNICATING

Just as communication patterns developed in early humans, they develop in each growing child. The ways in which the child's development shows itself demonstrate further that using language to communicate is a natural consequence of being human. Think about the shape of a person's mouth and throat, for instance. Language sounds are usually classified according to the positions of the articulators (tongue, teeth, lips, various parts of the mouth) when a sound is made. It would be difficult for other animals, whose mouths are shaped differently, to make the same sounds. As mentioned earlier, attempts to teach chimpanzees to talk failed partly because of the shape of their mouth.

Almost all children speak. We expect it of them and classify them as abnormal if they fail to do so. We expect children who are exposed to language to speak regardless of the environment in which they are raised. If a child's parents are deaf and speechless but the child is physiologically normal, he or she will learn how to speak like any other child. And children may not need much practice to learn to talk. Although the sounds babies make, particularly in the "babbling" stage, suggest speaking practice, this "practice" may be of little importance in learning to talk. Children who seldom babble may speak just as well as those who babble a great deal. Lenneberg (1966) reported the case of a 14-month-old child who had been unable to make any sounds for six months because of a throat operation. The day after his throat was repaired, the child made sounds typical of his age group without having babbled. No practice was required.

To some extent the development of communication seems associated with physical and motor development. Table 2.1 indicates that the development of communication skills parallels the development of motor abilities. For example, at about age 4 months the child coos and chuckles and can hold his or her head up when in a sitting position. We caution you not to expect particular behaviors to emerge at exactly the age listed in the table. Children are not trains; they do not run on regular schedules. A child who does not coo until 6 months is not retarded. The important point is that at about the same time that a child coos, she will be able to support her head. The behaviors seem to emerge about the same time. Both seem to result from growth in the brain and nervous system. In sum, communicative development seems closely tied to the general biological development of the human animal.

LINGUISTIC UNIVERSALS

If learning how to talk is the same for all people, what accounts for the uniqueness of each language? It is true that languages sound very different from each other. But there are also ways in which all languages are the same. Aspects of grammar that appear in all languages are called *linguistic universals.*

Several linguistic universals have been discovered in the area of sound systems. All languages recognize a difference between vowels and consonants, and all use syllables. Although no two languages are made up of identical sets of sounds, there does seem to be one set of

Table 2.1   SIMULTANEOUS DEVELOPMENT OF LANGUAGE AND COORDINATION

Age in Months	Vocalization and Language	Motor Development
4	Coos and chuckles	Head self-supported; tonic neck reflex subsiding; can sit with pillow props on three sides
6 to 9	Babbles; produces sounds such as "ma" or "da"; duplication of sounds common	Sits alone; pulls self to standing; prompt unilateral reaching; first thumb opposition of grasp
12 to 18	Small number of "words"; follows simple commands; responds to "no"	Stands momentarily alone; crawls; walks sideways when holding on to a railing; takes a few steps when held by hands; grasp, prehension, and release fully developed
18 to 21	From about 20 words at 18 months to about 200 words at 21; points to many more objects; comprehends simple questions; forms two-word phrases	Stance fully developed; gait stiff, propulsive, and precipitated; seats self on child's chair with only fair aim; creeps downstairs backward; has difficulty building tower of three cubes; can throw a ball, but clumsily
24 to 27	Vocabulary of 300 to 400 words; forms two- to three-word phrases; uses prepositions and pronouns	Runs, but falls when making a sudden turn; can alternate quickly between standing, kneeling, and sitting positions; walks stairs up and down, one foot forward only
30 to 33	Fastest increase in vocabulary; forms three- to four-word sentences; approximates word order, phrase structure, and grammatical agreement of language of surroundings, but many utterances unlike anything an adult would say	Good hand and finger coordination; can move digits independently; manipulation of objects much improved; builds tower of six cubes
36 to 39	Vocabulary of 1000 words or more; forms sentences using complex grammatical rules, although certain rules not yet fully mastered; grammatical mistakes less frequent; about 90 percent comprehensibility	Runs smoothly with acceleration and deceleration; negotiates sharp and fast curves without difficulty; walks stairs by alternating feet; jumps 12 inches; can operate tricycle; stands on one foot for a few seconds

Source: Adapted from Eric Lenneberg, The natural history of language, in F. Smith and G. Miller (eds.), *The Genesis of Language* (Cambridge, Mass.: MIT Press, 1966), Table 1, p. 222.

sounds from which all languages draw subsets. This set of sounds is best classified in terms of places of articulation in the human mouth. The sound system will be discussed in Chapter 5.

There are also linguistic universals in the area of sentence structure (syntax). All languages have structural categories corresponding to noun phrase, verb phrase, and object. All languages construct sentences by showing grammatical relationships among these basic categories, but the way in which the relationships are established varies. In English, for example, most relationships between parts of sentences are shown by word order, but in Russian they are indicated by word endings and word order is less constrained.

The existence of linguistic universals provides further evidence that people are born with a capacity to learn language. These universals might be something that people simply have the capacity to learn without being taught, just as birds learn how to fly (instinctively). Some scholars feel, for example, that the child is innately programmed to look for the relationship between subject and predicate in a sentence. Thus the child needs to learn only that in English this relationship is expressed through word order. Whatever the form of the child's knowledge about language, it cannot be denied that humans are born with unique capacities for learning to speak.

WHAT DIFFERENCE DOES ENVIRONMENT MAKE?

At this point you are probably ready to ask, "If human communication is innate, that is, if children will talk no matter what we do, why should we worry so much about how parents and educators teach language skills to children?" You may also be seized by a feeling of helplessness; "If that's the way it is, there is no way we can improve things for our children." Don't despair. How we teach our children *does* make a difference.

To analyze the effects of what we do to children, we must consider the concepts of heredity and environment. The two are usually presented as opposites, but they are not as separate and contradictory as some theoretical discussions would indicate. In reality, heredity and environment are two sides of the same coin.

Take the example of the developing zygote used at the start of this chapter. At first all the cells are alike, but there is a genetic coding in each that foretells many characteristics. This is the extreme case of heredity. But the actual differentiation of cells, which brings the genetic changes, comes about because of where each cell happens to be in the organism (its environment). In this case the relationship between heredity and environment is more one of interaction than of opposition.

As another example, consider the baby duck, which instinctively follows its mother soon after birth. If some other object of the right size moves by at this time, the duckling will follow it and will never learn to follow the mother. If neither mother nor any other object passes by during the "critical period" for this learning, it never will learn to follow as normal ducks do.

Rats with identical genetic histories but raised in radically different environments often show behavioral differences. Environmental differences that persist through many generations favor certain naturally occurring mutations and thus alter the animals' genetic structure. Whole animals, just like individual cells, change in response to the environment. Change that takes place in one animal's lifetime is called *learning,* whereas change that requires adaptation over several generations is more likely to be called *genetic.* Both adaptations, however, are part of the biological scheme of evolution. Seen in this light, the distinction between innate behavior and learned behavior seems arbitrary (Alland, 1967). It may be more realistic to speak of three classes of behavior:

1. *Innate.* Such behavior remains the same generation after generation no matter what we do; for example, sexual behavior that serves to multiply a species.

2. *Innate-learned.* The ability to perform such behavior is also transmitted genetically, but the behavior appears only in response to environmental conditions. One might say that the environment must "trigger" innate-learned behavior. Communication patterns, from bird songs to human language, fall into this category.

3. *Learned.* This type of behavior results from a single animal's successful adaptation to a set of conditions. It is not transmitted genetically. The abilities to write, to read, and to speak eloquently seem to fall into this category.

Thus the child really has two kinds of biologically endowed abilities that help communicative development: (1) an innate capacity, which might include some form of knowledge about linguistic universals, and (2) strong general learning abilities relative to other animals. His or her learning strategies are important to mastering the purely learned behavior associated with actual use of language.

The content of the child's environment, then, is important in two ways. First, the innate capacity to learn language behavior *must be triggered by the environment.* Just as the baby duck will not learn to follow without something to follow, the child will not learn to talk unless there are models around from which to learn. Second, environment is all-important in learned behavior such as reading and writing. In this area nothing is transmitted biologically, and each generation must learn anew.

Seen in this light, our roles as teachers and parents are vital. This view also makes it clearer what we must teach. There is no need to teach a child to talk; his biological heritage ensures that he will grow up talking. Our job as teachers and parents is to teach children to talk effectively, in ways that benefit the individual and society alike. The child's language learning environment will be discussed in greater detail in the next chapter.

RATIONALISTS VERSUS EMPIRICISTS

In recent years a battle has raged between two schools of thought in child speech development. Empiricists, or behaviorists (for example, Skinner, 1957), maintain that the mind is practically a blank slate at birth and that only experiences (stimuli) are important to the individual's behavior. Scholars in this camp hold that the child's environment is all-important in learning to speak. They emphasize the role of the language the child hears and the responses of adults to the child's attempts to talk.

Rationalists, or nativists (for example, Chomsky, 1968), maintain that genetic structure determines that the individual will speak and that environmental variation is of little importance. Most rationalists argue that the only environmental factor necessary for the child to learn to speak is exposure to some language. They regard such environmental factors as the mother's correction of the child's mistakes or her responses in general as relatively unimportant to learning. This position may be summarized thus: Although environmental factors can affect the quality of the language learned by the child, a "bad" environment cannot prevent the child from learning to speak if there is some language in the environment.

Scholars in each camp expend much energy trying to discredit the other. This battling is unfortunate because the influences of heredity and environment are allies, not enemies. Both heredity and environment stimulate adaptive mechanisms. The best research will combine the strengths of both the rationalist and empiricist positions and give us a better picture of communication development.

ATTENTION, PERCEPTION, AND CONCEPTS

Squabbling over whether children learn to talk over a period of time or just start talking of their own accord might obscure the deeper problem of what it is children must know to start talking. As we will discuss in later chapters, some theorists argue that children must know the grammar of the language to start talking. In one sense that is true, but children do not know the adult grammar of the language when they start talking. Instead they know something that makes the learning of the grammar both necessary and possible. That something results from the process of *categorization.* Categorization is the ability to sort reality, which is chaotic and usually without categories except those into which human beings organize it for purposes of interpretation or explanation. Categorization is the core process behind human perception.

When a human comes into contact with events, the human pays attention, perceives, and then conceptualizes. This three-stage process takes continuous wholes and sorts them into organizing categories. Let us discuss visual perception as an example.

When the light from an object that you see hits your eyes, the light hits millions of tiny receptor cells. A complex image is presented. The task of perception is to ask, "What's going on here?" Perceptual processes answer that question by destroying most of the information that comes into your eye before that information gets to your brain. This happens through a process called inhibition. When the light rays hit your eyes, millions of tiny images of color, size, and texture result. These images are passed into the nervous system. In the nervous system these images are grouped into clusters, and a sort of poll is taken to find out what kinds of information are there. The information that doesn't fit into the clusters is not preserved. This happens all over the nervous system, and images are greatly simplified before the information gets to the brain. You simplify each message you receive by sorting it into categories.

A convenient example of how sorting messages into categories makes things simple is found in the way words appear in books. Consider the following:

Shewenthometonurseherbackache.

You may have trouble making sense of the preceding sentence when it appears as one giant word. But if it is segmented into words visually—sorted into categories—then you can understand it easily:

She went home to nurse her backache.

Here's a fact that may surprise you—when we speak, the sounds we say are really more like giant words than like neatly divided-up written sentences. There are no pauses between most words, *but our perceptual system simplifies these giant sound sets by dividing them into small units!*

Why must messages be simplified? To help make sense of them. Simplification "captures" a message. Simplification gives closure, understanding. Speech perception is categorical, because this perceptual skill makes language easier to interpret.

Another way to describe what happens in your magnificent perceptual system is to use the terms of gestalt psychologists. Gestalt theories point out that we never perceive individual items in a vacuum, but only *items-in-contexts,* foregrounds against backgrounds. "What other way is there to perceive things?" you might ask. Well, you might perceive only contexts and never individual items. Or you might perceive only single items at a time, but never be able to place them in contexts. Both of these ways of perceiving would be so limiting that they are hard to imagine, but pointing to these absurdities we realize how useful (and complex) our perceptions are.

When you perceive a sentence placed in time, space, and other situational factors, you are differentiating that sentence from the rest of the environment. When your perceptual system divides a sentence into words and sounds and ideas and motives, it is differentiating parts of the sentence from each other and from the total setting. This skill of differentiation recalls the discussion with which we began this chapter.

Biological differentiation forms complex organisms. Perceptual differentiation creates *concepts.* Humans are speaking animals because humans are conceptualizing animals. The ability to segment a whole into parts and perceive each of those parts against the whole makes language possible. In fact, it is possible to argue that language has developed simply because language structure gives convenient ways to use our perception system.

To summarize, our perception system, through differentiation of items in contexts, underlies the formation of concepts. Items and concepts are formed against background information. Concepts connect our perceptions with each other, giving our world coherence. These concepts and coherences are the sources of meaning. Our attention-perception-conceptualization system is where meaning is nurtured. As individual meanings develop, so does the possibility for communication. The growth of meaning will be treated in detail in Chapter 6, and the developing human perceptual system will be further discussed in Chapter 4.

SUMMARY

Several principles of developmental biology can be applied to speech development. Growth in the ability of children to use adult communication patterns depends on the same kinds of developmental processes that affect other aspects of the human organism. Our communication system is remarkable, but many of its building blocks are echoed elsewhere in our natures. The onset of language behavior in children is synchronized with motor development, and language itself is founded on the basic psychological abilities of attention, perception, and conceptualization.

Although human communication abilities are biologically based and genetically transmitted, environment is also important to speech development. Destructive environments can harm even genetically determined behavior, and even though children can learn to speak in almost any environment, only in supportive, teaching environments will they learn to read, write, or speak eloquently.

SUGGESTED READINGS

Alland, Alexander. *Evolution and Human Behavior.* New York: Natural History Press, 1967. Alland explains in readable language the principles of evolution and genetics and gives examples of the effects of these principles on animal and human behavior.

Lenneberg, Eric. *Biological Foundations of Language.* New York: Wiley, 1967. Lenneberg collects evidence from many areas of developmental biology to support the thesis that language behavior is species-specific to humans. His data range all the way from diagrams of the oral cavity to charts measuring brain growth to case histories of aphasic children.

Linden, Eugene. *Apes, Men, and Language.* New York: Pelican, 1974. Linden conducts an exhaustive survey of the ape communication experiments, presenting the data and drawing his conclusions from them.

Geschwind, N. Specializations of the human brain. In W. S.-Y. Wang (ed.), *Human Communication: Language and Its Psychobiological Bases.* San Francisco: Freeman, 1979. Geschwind presents a fascinating and readable account of how the human brain is organized to perform its various functions.

SUGGESTED PROJECTS

1. Interview a group of your classmates, asking them to tell you what kinds of behavior would cause them to believe that apes could use language. Using the criteria derived from these interviews, review the data from the ape language studies and present your evaluation of the results.

2. Pursue the question of whether the right cerebral hemisphere has language capabilities, and if so, what these capabilities are. (Hint: Consult the journal *Brain and Language.*)

Chapter
3

Conversation: The Language-Learning Environment

*I*n Chapter 2 we discussed the biological endowment that makes language learning possible. Several times in that chapter we mentioned that children must be "exposed" to language in order to learn it. In saying this, we are not implying that a child could learn a language by sitting in a room listening to a radio. Such passive exposure would be grossly insufficient. Children learn language as active participants in interactions with others. They are exposed not only to sounds and sentence structures, but also to human interaction, to people doing things as they speak. The interactions that allow this learning to occur are everyday conversations. In this chapter we will explore the nature of conversation and the child's role in early conversational exchange.

CHILDREN'S SPEECH AS CONVERSATION

Sociologist and critic Kenneth Burke describes the human condition as an "unending conversation" which is already going on when we are born:

> Imagine that you enter a parlor. You come late. When you arrive, others have long preceded you, and they are engaged in a heated discussion, a discussion too heated for them to pause and tell you exactly what it is about. In fact, the discussion had already begun long before any of them got there, so that no one present is qualified to retrace for you all the steps that had gone before. You listen for a while, until you decide that you have caught the tenor of the argument; then you put in your oar. Someone answers; you answer him; another comes to your defense; another aligns himself against

you. . . . However, the discussion is interminable. The hour grows late and you must depart. And you do depart, with the discussion still vigorously in progress. . . . (1973, p. 94)

A child is born into a world of speech events that can best be called "conversations." Children's speech occurs overwhelmingly in conversations—especially in conversations with caretaker-adults. This insight has changed much of the flavor of our thinking about children's speech (Dore, 1979, 1985). Children do not first learn to talk, then speak in conversations. Rather, each child enters and participates in conversations early in life. In fact, Lieven (1978) writes that one of the most striking features in the protocols of children's speech with which many investigators have been struggling over the years is that, with very few exceptions, they are conversations. The development of children's speech, then, is a history of children's conversations. We have discovered the importance of the conversational format in studies based upon tape recordings of speech between children and their caretakers.

We use the term *conversation* as a general term to refer to the entire speech ecology. As we saw in Figure 1.2, conversation is divided into several aspects, or layers, each of which can be studied separately. In this book we summarize work in each of these areas and others; but first let us consider some overarching questions about the entire human conversation.

Conversation is talking, back and forth; I take a turn and you take a turn. Turns in conversation may be as short as a single word and as long as a long story. Turn length is locally managed by the participants, that is, each speaker-listener decides how long to speak during the speaking itself. How do speakers know when to begin a turn or to pass the turn to the next speaker? This is only one of the things about conversation that children must learn. In a real sense, the child who learns to speak is learning, first of all, to take turns in a human conversation. Within the conversations children enter, they learn how to speak and listen, as it were, "on the job." Children don't go to school to learn how to speak and listen, although mastery of conversation is as difficult and complex as any school subject.

Nineteenth-century philosopher Adam Muller wrote, "conversation is the first of all delights because it is the soul of all other delights." Conversation involves us in primordial activity that underlies other communicative activity. A public speech, for example, is a conversation with certain restrictions on the taking of turns; so is a debate, so is a dramatic performance, a job interview, a classroom reading-group, and a courtroom trial. Most immediate to our purposes are those conversational encounters that children experience with their care-givers and their peers. Recent researchers have observed that children's conversations contain a curriculum of language examples, repetitive drilling, problem-solving tasks, clues about group membership, sound play, and a lot of fun.

In this chapter we describe the development of children's speech in a holistic way as development of a conversation. We raise the following topics:

1. How children take turns in conversations
2. How children arrange conversational turns into sequences
3. How children repair problems in conversation
4. How conversation between the child and adults forms a scaffolding for learning to speak and listen

LEARNING TO TAKE TURNS IN CONVERSATION

The most fundamental "fact" of conversation is that speakers take turns. Speakers alternate speaking and ordinarily just one speaker talks at a time. How do speakers take turns so smoothly? How do children learn that this is how conversation is done? How does a given speaker signal the passing of a turn? How is the next speaker chosen? These are all issues that vex scholars considerably, but here is a summary of findings, based mostly on the research of Sacks, Schegloff, and Jefferson (1974).

Speakers generally arrange their conversational turns so that there is neither a large gap nor a large overlap between turns. That's obvious. But *how* we do this is less obvious. We must signal each other that it is time to take and yield turns. Consider this example, an unremarkable exchange of greetings:

SUE: Hello.
GEORGE: Hi, how are you?
SUE: Fine.

It is remarkable that these three speaker turns usually occur one right next to each other, with no pauses and no overlap between turns. The "facts" of turn-taking are so "obvious" that adults no longer notice them. But consider a greeting exchange involving an infant:

SUE: *[Addressing infant.]* Hello! *[Pause.]*
SARA:
SUE: Hi, Sara. *[Speaks slowly; offers big smile.]*
SARA:
MOTHER: Hi, Sue. *[Speaking for child.]*
SUE: How are you? *[Touches child.]*
MOTHER: Say, "I'm fine."

Adult-child greetings are interesting. The child is greeted, usually by name, and sometimes the adult's hand is extended to tickle or shake hands. This is displaying to the child a *summons* to enter conversation by taking a turn at talk and fitting that talk to the previous greeting. We notice, when speaking to infants, that they do not take turns talking, although they may smile or vocalize in response to our turns. We may not notice that we *cue* the child in various ways that there are "slots" when turns at talk may be taken. For instance, when greeting a child, adults often say things that offer the child a turn at talk and pause to give the child a chance to take a turn. When the possible turn is not taken in response to the first greeting, the greeting may be offered repeatedly, displaying that there is a slot for a fitting next turn to be taken. Frequently, a mother or other care-giver then responds "on behalf of" the child, as in the last example.

These seem to be some of the ways that we teach children about the turn system for conversation. We give them slots to talk in and demonstrate the kinds of speech that might go in these turns. After the child takes a turn, the adult takes a turn and fits that turn to the "child's turn." Consider this conversation between Robert Hopper and his daughter, aged 18 months.

DAD:	Did Christine eat breakfast?
CHRISTINE:	Yeh.
DAD:	Eggs?
CHR:	Egg.
DAD:	With Brian?
CHR:	Maya. *[Brian.]*
DAD:	And Mom?
CHR:	Mom.
DAD:	And Dad?
CHR:	Daddy.
DAD:	And Christine?
	[Pause.]
CHR:	Ti-tee. *[Christine.]*
DAD:	Christine was there, sure.
CHR:	Ti-tee 'ere.
DAD:	Christine was in her pajamas.
CHR:	Ti-tee nammies.
DAD:	Right, and she ate egg.
CHR:	Egg.

This is a pretty ordinary parent-child conversation. It doesn't have a lot of content. The child has a limited vocabulary and a limited grasp of the sound system. But the child and parent *take turns* flawlessly. The child has already learned something about the game of conversation— that one person speaks at a time and as soon as one person stops talking the other starts. There is only one short pause in this example, and this follows the use of the child's own (hard-to-say) name. The rest of the talk flows as rapidly as a ping-pong match, suggesting that even a very young child, a child with little to say, already has figured out how to take turns in the human conversation.

At first, turn-taking is quite slow. It takes a couple of seconds for a 1-year-old to figure out when the last utterance has ended. Between the ages of 2 and 6 the child gradually sharpens and quickens turn-taking skills. A study by Garvey and Berninger (1981) found that interturn gaps of 3-year-olds ranged from 1.1 to 1.8 seconds, while those of 5-year-olds ranged from 0.8 to 1.5 seconds. This timing change reflects the child's increasing competence with the turn-taking system, a competence that is aided and structured by the conversational environments in which the child participates.

ARRANGING TURNS IN SEQUENCES

As children enter the human conversation, they need to learn not only to take individual turns, but also to arrange these turns so they form sequences. This can be observed in Hopper's dialogue with his daughter in which he elicits answers to questions. If the child vocalizes after the question, the adult commonly "hears" the child's utterance as the second part of a question-answer sequence.

Just as questions get answers in response, so many other kinds of *first pair parts* are followed in adult speech by matching *second pair parts*. If a projected second part is not supplied, something is noticeably missing. Thus questions take answers matched to the question, and an invitation is ordinarily followed by an acceptance or rejection of the request. If one speaker makes an assessment, a second might confirm or agree with the assessment, for example:

MOTHER: He looks very nice today.
DAUGHTER: Yes.

If you agree with another person as does the daughter in this example, you build your turn to display that agreement. In other words, you set up a second part to follow a recognized first part.

To get a sense of what goes in a first position and what goes in a second position, consider the human greeting, something that speakers of most languages do upon first meeting acquaintances. If you walk up to somebody and say "Hi," you've accomplished the first part of something, and that something is an exchange of greetings. If a greeting occurs, a return greeting predictably occurs. We hardly notice this, but we do notice if the greeting is not returned. In other words, not only does a greeting illustrate how we take turns, as discussed earlier, but it shows that a certain kind of first turn often leads to a certain kind of second turn. This introduces the notion of an *adjacency pair*, which is two "matched" turns spoken by different speakers but placed one right after the other. Paired greetings show adjacency pairing, and so do a statement and agreement and an invitation and acceptance/rejection.

We can reexamine how adults structure conversations with children to see how the notion of adjacency pairs is introduced. An adult, by supplying an easy first pair part and by responding to what the child says as though it were a second pair part, offers a recognizable structure for mastery of both the turn-taking system and a system of sequencing.

REPAIR OF PROBLEMS IN CONVERSATION

Competent adult conversationalists have learned to take turns and to string their turns together with those of other speakers into adjacency pairs and longer sequences. They also have learned to monitor talk for communicative failure and to *repair* these problems in conversation. Schegloff, Jefferson, and Sacks (1977) distinguish between *self-initiated repairs,* or repairs initiated by the current speaker, and *other-initiated repairs,* or those initiated by the other speaker. An example of a self-initiated repair is:

A: Do you like his sist— I mean, his brother?

An other-initiated repair would be:

A: Do you like his sister?
B: His sister?
A: His brother.
B: Yes, I like him a lot.

Self-initiated and other-initiated repairs occur differently from each other. When a speaker repairs her own utterance, the repair usually is produced in the same turn with the error to be repaired, that is, the speaker has first chance at repairing errors. The other speaker does not get a chance to indicate there's a problem until the next turn. For this reason, self-initiated repairs are much more frequent than other-initiated repairs, both in child and adult speech.

Self-repairs also have a simpler structure than other-repairs, as shown by the examples above. The speaker who is repairing her own utterance knows what the problem is and merely has to show some disjunction, such as by cutting off the voice or by saying "I mean," before producing correction. These "flags" display to hearers that something unusual, some change, is projected (Goffman, 1978, p. 212).

Other-initiated repairs are more complex than self-initiated repairs in two ways. First, in a self-repair the speaker knows what the problem is when the repair is initiated. In other-initiated repair the initiator of the repair must *locate the problem and display that understanding.* In the example above this is done by repeating some of the wording of the turn to be repaired ("His sister?"). Notice that the repeated wording ends with an upward slide in pitch, marked by a question mark. This distinctive pitch contour leads to labeling this kind of repair initiation a *question-repeat.* Some other ways of locating a problem are (adapted from Garvey, 1979; McTear, 1985):

1. Nonspecific request for repetition

A: Do you like his brother?
B: What?
A: Do you like his brother?

2. Specific request for repetition (with partial repeat)

A: Do you like his brother?
B: His what?
A: His brother.

3. Request for clarification

A: Do you like his brother?
B: Which one?
A: Jethro.

The second way that other-initiated repair is more complex than self-initiated repair is also shown in these examples. In self-initiated repair the speaker usually both initiates the repair and makes the actual correction. In other-initiated repair the initiator usually indicates there's a problem, but does not correct it. Rather, the initiator lets the original speaker make the correction. (The "corrections" are spoken by speaker A in the third turns of the examples above.) In this way an initiation-by-other and a repair-by-self form an adjacency pair, one that takes "time out" from the business at hand (in the examples above the business at hand is a question about "liking") in order to clarify the business (to figure out the identity of the subject of the question). When the repair is completed by the original speaker, the speakers return to the conversation at the point where the repair was initiated. We repeat the first example of an other-initiated repair arranged to show this *time out sequence,* sometimes called a *side sequence.*

A: Do you like his sister?
B: His sister?
A: His brother.
B: Yes, I like him a lot.

The fourth turn in this sequence is an answer to the question in the first turn, and this adjacency pair is sandwiched around the adjacency repair of initiation-correction.

You may be surprised by the complexities of the repair system. They are considerable, and yet children master the repair system at quite a young age. Garvey (1977) reports that children between 3 and 5 years of age routinely responded appropriately to repair initiations. Garvey notes that these sequences show the child's comprehension of syntax and semantics (see later chapters), as well as knowledge of conversation. This is one of many examples from recent research that demonstrate that a child's language abilities develop as a coherent (and coherence-making) whole rather than as separate registers for syntax, phonology, and so forth.

Children's early mastery of repair procedures is all the more remarkable because the speech of adults to children does not necessarily treat the child's repair initiations as they would those of adults. For instance, Johnson (1979, reported in McTear, 1985, p. 167) reports that while children between $1\frac{1}{2}$ and 3 years responded to two-thirds of requests for repetition with an appropriate repetition, only 28 percent of mothers' responses to children's requests for repetition provided that repetition! For example:

> J: Dolly.
> MOM: The dollies. *[Pause.]* They're called puppets.
> J: Hm?
> MOM: They're puppets.
> J: Hm?
> MOM: See, you put your hand in.
> J: Hm?
> MOM: Remember, we've got the owl at home?

In this instance the mother treats the child's first "hm?" as a request for repetition, but treats subsequent instances as occasions to elaborate. How does the child learn the difference?

Adding to the mystery of how children learn how to accomplish repairs at the very beginnings of language development is the fact that most adults are fairly "unconscious" of repairs, especially self-repairs. We simply don't notice them when they happen. In fact, most researchers who transcribe children's speech seem not to notice self-repairs, and they don't appear on transcripts (McTear, 1985, p. 188). Children, as usual, are better listeners than the researchers are; Clark (1978) indicates that children make self-repairs by 18 months of age.

It is perhaps instructive to ask what kinds of errors children correct and whether awareness of different sorts of errors increases with age and development. Children around age 2 seem to perform mostly phonological repairs. By age 5 or 6 they self-correct morphology and syntax (Rogers, 1978; Karmiloff-Smith, 1979). McTear found that the most frequent self-corrections of two 4- to 5-year-olds involved grammar. For instance at 4 years 7 months:

> HEATHER: Where's the old witch in this *[pause]* on this book? Where's the old witch in this book?

At 4 years 10 months:

> HEATHER: Well, I hurt me *[pause]* I hurt myself.

Also, McTear reports the emergence between ages 4 and 5 of "pragmatically occasioned" repairs, those not aimed at grammar, but at getting specific tasks accomplished. At 4 years 6 months:

> SIOBHAN: I could *[pause]* could I cut them out?

In this instance the child begins by making an offer, then changes it to a question, apparently for rhetorical purposes.

At 4 years 9 months:

SIOBHAN: Just put them up *[pause]* up there alright the crayons?

In this instance the child self-corrects not because there is a problem with the original sentence, but to continue directing the other to act.

These last two examples lead us to some other complexities in conversational repair. We sometimes "repair" speech that was "correct" to begin with, that is, speech that displayed no errors. Also, there are many errors that go uncorrected in adult speech and child speech. Repair cannot all be explained one simple way. Children learn repair in conversation, on the fly, usually without paying a lot of attention to it.

Teachers and parents often believe that it's "their job" to correct children's speech and think their corrections are more consistent than they actually are. Sometimes this leads to arguments and hard feelings. Not all "repairs" lead straightforwardly to correction; some lead to problems. (See the correction of "Nobody don't likes me" in Chapter 10, for instance.) This leads us to the question of what the role of adults is in teaching children about human conversation.

CONTRIBUTION OF ADULT-CHILD CONVERSATION TO LANGUAGE DEVELOPMENT

A number of researchers have described the speech of mothers to children, for speech of mothers to children is thought to be an important contributor to speech development. Snow (1977) reports that mother's speech to children, or *motherese,* is simple and redundant. It contains many questions and imperatives. It contains few past tenses, coordinations or subordinations, and disfluencies. It is pitched higher and has an exaggerated intonation pattern.

Most Anglo-American researchers agree that motherese is a simplified register of talk, a sort of teaching register, that presents to the child a clear set of formats for dialogue. Some researchers have claimed that repetitive, simplified caretaker speech is essential to speech development. Opponents argue that motherese is spoken only in some Anglo-American, middle-class cultural settings and that the impact of such speech patterns is questionable. The motherese debate will be discussed several times in the present text. Motherese is raised as a topic here because it occurs largely in dyadic turn-taking conversational settings. We will expand on the topic in the next chapter, so our discussion here will be considerably simplified.

The mother's turns to the prelinguistic child (discussed in Chapter 4) seem to be instances of early motherese. One characteristic of motherese is that it seems to change with the speech of the child. Brown (1973) proposes that effective mother's speech displays models of what the child's speech is soon to become, and it therefore provides the child with achievable developmental exemplars. Phillips (1973) argues that motherese begins only when the child responds reliably to speech. Snow (1977, p. 37) suggests that mothers are only able to produce motherese in actual interaction with the child, demonstrating that something strongly adaptive and interactive happens between caretaker and child during prelinguistic and early speech development.

Not only are caretakers showing the child some possibilities for grammar and wording, thus "fine-tuning" the child's grammar toward adult rules for speech, adults are also carefully fitting their speech to that of the child. Wells (1982) notes that the most effective caretakers use their turns to add new and contextually relevant material to the conversation. Thus, motherese not only exemplifies "how to speak," but exemplifies the usefulness of speaking (simplified from Wells, 1982, p. 7):

> CHILD: Birds mummy.
> MOTHER: Um.
> CHILD: Jubs *[= birds]*.
> MOTHER: What are they doing?
> CHILD: Jubs bread.
> MOTHER: Oh, look. They're eating the berries, aren't they?
> CHILD: Yeh.

Wells notes about this instance that in spite of the child's limited resources, "there's a real conversation going on there, even though it's the mother who is doing most of the work." Wells compares this mother's work to teaching a child to catch a ball by throwing the ball so it happens to land in the child's cupped hands, then rushing to catch the ball wherever it goes when the child "throws" it.

Part of this mother's work involves the use of pitch to sound interested in what the child is saying. Part of it involves the mother's willingness to follow up on a topic (the birds) introduced by the child. The mother invites the child to expand on this topic by asking "What are they doing?" When the child responds again, the mother expands further.

What is the child doing? The child's responses seem minimal at first, but note that the child is displaying considerable skill in turn-taking. As Wells notes, the child "knows the game of conversation and how to play his part in it" (1982, p. 8).

THE MOTHERESE DEBATE

A number of researchers who have studied middle-class children in England and the United States agree on some characteristics of motherese, and most researchers believe that caretaker-child dialogue is of instructional importance to the development of child speech. The topic remains controversial, however. There is not that much agreement on just which characteristics of motherese do the most teaching or on what is taught. Furthermore, there seem to be many settings around the world in which children develop speech without benefit of motherese dialogues.

Ochs and Schieffelin (1982) contrast Anglo-American middle-class child-raising practices with those in two other cultural settings, one in New Guinea and one in Samoa. In these other cultures mother-child dialogues do not seem to play a central role in children's speech development. Among the Kaluli of New Guinea babies are rarely addressed as if they were conversational partners, aside from being greeted by name. Mothers and children rarely spend time alone or make eye contact with each other. Children's babbling is not believed to have any communicative significance; thus mothers do not re-do children's nonword vocalizations into words or expect babies to imitate their vocalizations.

In Samoa, as among the Kaluli, the child grows up in a group setting and is not directly addressed by other speakers. Rather, adults make the child the topic of much talk and the child overhears this talk.

These cross-cultural accounts suggest that there may be no need to treat the baby as a dyadic conversation-partner during early development. There may be many roads to development and no one best way. Perhaps motherese is simply an Anglo-American custom, a window-dressing felt by mothers to be of developmental importance, but really unessential. Or, perhaps what the child learns from it has less to do with language than with the child's place in society.

What seems to be essential in all the cultural settings described by Ochs and Schieffelin is that the child is learning how to be a member of a certain kind of social group. In Anglo-America the focus of socialization is on the dyad, or the two-person mother-child dialogue. In other cultures the group is of central importance; the child develops in a network of relationships. For instance, in Samoa, described as a hierarchical society, young children's requests are addressed not to the mother (or primary caretaker), but to an older child, who relays these requests to the adult caretaker. In all cultures the child learns "how things are done with speech around here." (We return to this theme in Chapter 9, which describes the development of pragmatics.)

One lesson from the foregoing is that the dyad, which is thought by many Anglo-Americans to be the primary unit of conversation, may not have this status everywhere. In fact, group size is an important situational factor that seems to affect how speech is done. Perhaps the lesson of the Ochs and Schieffelin descriptions is less "the importance of culture" than "the importance of group size." For example, when there are two people in a conversation, and one person stops talking, it is clearly the other person's turn to talk. Thus, there's sort of an obligation to talk next. By contrast, when there are three or more persons in a scene, one often has the option to say nothing.

Wells (1982) reports a finding of relevance here. Wells's data are perhaps the most "naturalistic" and candid speech data gathered to date. He equipped children with radio microphones that picked up sound throughout the day rather than following the more usual procedure of recording children and parents in laboratory settings. Wells, like Ochs and Schieffelin, found group size to be of great importance. For instance, expansions of children's speech by caretakers, which many people think are important developmental stimuli, were found by Wells to be rather uncommon in caretaker-child dyads. These expansions, ironically, occurred when caretakers and children were in groups and seemed to have a function of explaining to overhearers what was occurring. When one realizes that in lab rooms a camera operator or other researcher is present in most instances, it is possible that it is the presence of a third party that actually elicits some of the expansions that we believe are an important part of motherese.

The final moral of this story: In spite of an explosion of research about children's language learning in the last two decades, we are still learning about its complexities. The motherese controversy has sparked some of the most useful recent investigations, but the actual effects of motherese are far from known.

What we do know is that children are guests at a "conversation" that is going on among members of the children's social group before they are born. They grow up to be part of that conversation and participate in it throughout their lives. And, that conversation continues after their lives are over.

SUMMARY

Children's language use is to be treated in later chapters of this book in terms of many specific aspects of its development—the sound system, the meaning system, and so forth. But child speech develops holistically, within actual conversations. The young child is not just learning to speak; the child is getting things done in conversations.

Primary to being in conversation is learning to take turns, which children do in preverbal games such as peek-a-boo. Adult-child speech, at least in our society, frequently centers around offering children speaking turns and then treating whatever the child speaks as if it fills a turn or speaking slot.

Children learn in conversation not only to take turns, but to string these turns together into sequences. These include two-part sequences (adjacency pairs) such as greeting-greeting, question-answer, and invitation-reply.

Children also learn some techniques for repairing problems in conversation, and from a very young age children correct their own errors (especially in phonology) without adult assistance. In children's speech, as in adult speech, self-initiated repairs occur more frequently than other-initiated repairs.

Caretaker-child dialogue, or motherese, is a characteristic speech pattern in middle-class, Anglo-American settings. Many researchers contend that caretakers who speak motherese aid the child's development by providing a simplified model and many opportunities to participate actively in speech communication. It is unclear just which aspects of motherese are most helpful to children and how much of it children find useful. In some other cultures development proceeds normally in different conversational settings—settings in which the child is primarily an overhearer in group conversations.

SUGGESTED READINGS

Wells, G. *The Meaning Makers.* Portsmouth, England: Heinemann, 1986. Wells makes a strong and eloquent case that children learn language through interaction. He gives many examples of child-child and adult-child dialogues.

Bruner, J. *Child's Talk: Learning to Use Language.* Oxford: Oxford University Press, 1983. Bruner presents a variety of approaches to the study of children's conversations and postulates the existence of a language acquisition support system in the interactions between children and adults.

SUGGESTED PROJECTS

1. Tape record a child aged 2 or 3 in interaction with his or her parent in a natural setting. Then tape record the parent talking with you (maybe discussing the child's development and abilities.) Transcribe the two tapes, and identify the differences between the parent's language to you and to the child.

2. Tape record a group of children (no more than five in the group) interacting in a normal, free play setting. Then, choose two of the children and tape record an interaction between you and each child (maybe about a favorite television show or an activity the child recently participated in). What kinds of differences do you find in the child's conversation in these two settings? Why do you think these differences occur? (Hint: Read Wells, 1986, for some ideas.)

Chapter
4

Preverbal Communication

*S*arah is talking with her 3-month-old daughter, Marcia, while she dresses the baby to go out. Marcia is lying on the bed; Sarah is standing.

SARAH: What a fat baby you are. Just look at that fat tummy. *[Tickles baby.]*

MARCIA: *[Gurgles.]*

SARAH: You like that? Let's get this shirt on now. *[Puts shirt over baby's head, briefly covering her face.]* Peek-a-boo. There's Marcia. There's the baby. *[Covers and uncovers baby's face.]* There's Marcia.

MARCIA: *[Watches mother's face closely.]*

SARAH: *[Looking at baby.]* Peek-a-boo, Marcia. Peek-a-boo.

MARCIA: *[Vocalizes, looking at mother's face.]*

SARAH: Can you say peek-a-boo? *[Looks aside for baby's socks.]* Where did I put your socks? Here they are.

MARCIA: *[Looks at socks mother is holding up.]*

SARAH: *[Checks to see where baby is looking.]* Here are your socks. See the socks? *[Wiggles socks in the air; checks again to see where baby is looking.]* Look. These are your pretty socks. We'll put them on your feet. *[Captures one of baby's feet; begins to put sock on.]*

MARCIA: *[Looks at her feet, both of which she is kicking. Vocalizes.]*

SARAH: That's right. We've got one sock on. Now let's put on the other sock. These are nice new socks. And it would help if you didn't kick.

This real-life interaction between a mother and her baby taken from a longer tape recording is typical in many ways of the interactions infants engage in. In this chapter we review research related to infant communication behaviors prior to the onset of language and discuss relationships between preverbal and later linguistic communication. We suggest that the infant's preverbal communication experiences provide foundations for later social communication and linguistic interaction. We consider what the infant brings to the early transactions between the infant and the environment and what the environment contributes. This chapter is a first attempt to combine the biological perspective of Chapter 2 and the environmental perspective of Chapter 3.

INFANT CAPABILITIES

As recently as 20 years ago, one of the authors was advised by a well-meaning grandparent not to take a new baby out, because the light would hurt the baby's eyes, which were still developing. Most people believed babies were barely able to see or hear and needed to be kept in dim, quiet environments until these senses had matured. While there is much to be said for the soothing qualities of dim, quiet environments (for new parents as well as new babies), infants have, in fact, remarkable visual and auditory skills.

The discovery and examination of these skills by adult researchers required considerable ingenuity and patience. Infants have a limited repertoire of controllable and observable responses—direction and duration of gaze, sucking, head turning. The limited set of responses and infants' tendency to cry in the middle of experimental procedures demand fortitude and patience from investigators. Nevertheless, experimenters have gathered convincing evidence indicating that newborns are equipped to begin interacting with their environment at birth.

Visual Perception

In a group of experiments designed to challenge the prevailing view that newborn infants do not perceive objects or patterns, Fantz (1967) demonstrated that newborns prefer pattern to color and have definite pattern preferences. Fantz studied 18 babies under 5 days old. He provided several objects at which they could look: a schematically drawn face, a bull's-eye pattern, a section of newsprint, a plain white circle, a fluorescent yellow circle, and a red circle. Eleven of the babies looked longest at the face pattern, 5 at the bull's-eye, and 2 at the newsprint. None chose to look at the colors. This is not because babies cannot see colors, however. Chase (1937), in an experiment using a moving spot of color on a different colored background, demonstrated that infants from 15 to 70 days old can make a wide variety of color discriminations.

Given our concern with communication, it is reasonable to ask what infants might perceive about the most important of social stimuli, the human face. While many people have interpreted the results of studies like that of Fantz to indicate that infants are born with a preference for the human face, this does not really seem to be the case. More recent research suggests that before they are 2 months old, infants pay more attention to the borders or outlines of a stimulus than to its internal features (Maurer and Salapatek, 1976). After 2 months, however, the human face does appear to have a special status for infants. In fact, soon after infants begin to scan visual stimuli systematically, they seem to recognize the human face (both in photographs and drawings). Several studies have shown that infants prefer to look at photographs of human faces rather than line drawings, models, distorted faces, or faces with scrambled features (Haaf and Brown, 1976; Lewis, 1969; Kagan, 1967). This interest in faces and this apparent understanding of what faces are supposed to look like seem important for infants' ability to recognize people and to discriminate facial expressions.

The key socializing role played by the mother in our culture makes it logical to ask when the infant recognizes the mother. Bigelow (1977) demonstrates that infants as young as 5 weeks are able to discriminate between their mothers and strangers when both auditory and visual cues are present. Based on visual cues alone, this discrimination occurs around age 3 months. Barrera and Maurer (1981) report that 3-month-old babies are able not only to discriminate between a photograph of a stranger and a photograph of the mother, but also to distinguish among the faces of unfamiliar people. By around 7 months babies also appear to be able to recognize one face in several poses (Cohen, DeLoache, and Pearl, 1977). This research into children's visual perceptions of faces indicates that as early as 2 months of age, infants are beginning to learn something about the identity of objects.

These discriminations and recognitions, not only of faces but also of other objects, are beginning steps in the infant's development of the concept of *object permanence*, or the idea that things exist in the world independently of our perception of them. The concept of object permanence is a key precursor to the ability to use words to represent ideas. (See Chapter 9 for a more complete discussion.)

One further aspect of the infant's visual perception deserves comment here, and that is the infant's ability to discriminate among facial expressions denoting emotion. Facial expression is a powerful signal of emotional state in our culture and is thus a key part of our communication system. Although only a few of the common facial expressions used in communication have been studied with infants, and although several of the existing studies are methodologically flawed, we can draw some tentative conclusions. Maurer and Salapatek (1976) and Caron, Caron, Caldwell, and Weiss (1973) report that the eyes are the most examined facial feature for infants looking at a human face. This is significant because the eyes serve to indicate emotion as well as to indicate the aspects of the environment a person is attending to. An infant who looks at the mother's eyes will not only receive clues about how she feels, but also will be able to tell what she is looking at by following her gaze. By 6 months infants can discriminate smiling from frowning faces (Barrera and Maurer, 1981) and "surprised" from "happy" faces (Browne, Rosenfield, and Horowitz, 1977).

To summarize, infants bring to their interactions with the environment a variety of visual perceptual skills. Around 2 months of age infants begin to regard the human face as a particularly interesting stimulus. By 3 months they show an ability to discriminate between the faces of their mothers and the faces of strangers, to recognize the same face in different poses, and to discriminate among some facial expressions. It seems fair to say, then, that the infant by age 3 months is visually able to begin to identify other people in the environment.

Auditory Perception

There is some evidence suggesting that infants are sensitive to sound even before birth. Bernard and Sontag (1947) placed a speaker close to but not touching the abdomens of a group of pregnant women. They discovered that sounds broadcast through the speaker caused the fetal heartbeat to increase sharply.

Spelt (1948) used this information to set up a study in which he conditioned unborn babies (the mothers were past the seventh month of pregnancy) to respond to a vibrator placed against the mother's abdomen after he had paired the vibrator with a loud sound. Spelt first ascertained that the vibrator placed on the mother's abdomen did not cause the fetus to move. He then made a loud sound (banging two pieces of wood together) just beside the mother. This sound caused the baby to move. He then combined the vibrator and the sound, turning the vibrator on for a few seconds and then making the noise. After 15 to 20 such pairings, the babies began to move in response to the vibrator alone. This study indicates not only the responsiveness of the fetus to sound, but also its capability for associative learning. (It is important to remember that the babies in this study were past the seventh gestational month—a stage at which babies are often born and at which they can survive outside the mother's body.)

Since this early work a considerable body of research has accumulated attesting to the abilities of human infants to perceive sound, especially to discriminate among speech sounds. Obviously, if children are to learn to speak, they must be able to perceive the characteristics that distinguish one sound (such as "peach") from another sound (such as "beach").

We will describe the first, ground-breaking study in this area (Eimas, Siqueland, Jusczyk, and Vigorito, 1971). This study investigated the ability of infants at 1 and 4 months of age to discriminate between [ba] and [pa]. The two sounds differ in terms of voicing. (See Chapter 5.) Eimas and his colleagues used a "habituation paradigm" to study the child's sucking behavior during the presentation of the sound stimulus. To understand the habituation paradigm, think of what happens when you first walk into a kitchen where someone is baking a cake. At first you are sharply aware of the smell of the cake baking, but after you've been in the room for a while, you don't notice the smell as much. You have habituated to the smell (you no longer sense it as strongly). This same habituation phenomenon can be observed with other sensory input, such as touch or sound.

Eimas and his colleagues observed that babies sucking on pacifiers increased their rate of sucking when a new or novel stimulus caught their attention and then decreased their sucking rate when they habituated to that stimulus. They wired the pacifiers so that sucking rate could be automatically recorded. They then exposed the infants to a recording of either [ba] or [pa] which had been generated by a computer. When the infants first began to hear the repeated syllable, their sucking rates increased as they attended to the sound. After about three minutes their sucking rates decreased, indicating that the infants had habituated to the stimulus. At the end of five minutes those infants who had been hearing [ba] were given the signal [pa], and those who had been hearing [pa] were given the signal [ba]. Sucking rates immediately increased, indicating that the infants perceived a new and different stimulus.

Although this is a highly simplified description of this research, it should be sufficient to give you some idea of how researchers have investigated infant speech perception. The study by Eimas and his colleagues has been followed by many others investigating infants' abilities to make a variety of speech-related discriminations, all of which indicate that infants at astonishingly young ages seem able to perceive differences among the sounds we make when we speak. This is not the same as saying that infants know anything about language or speech, however. Learning about the systematic combinations of sounds used to make the words of a language and the meanings associated with those sounds takes the baby much longer. What we have learned from the work in auditory perception is that the human auditory system is set up to make speech and language learning possible. As the infant interacts with the environment and has more and more exposure to the sounds of a language, the capabilities of the auditory system become shaped and focused.

MOTHER-INFANT INTERACTION

As we discovered in the preceding section of this chapter, babies are not passive in their earliest encounters with the environment. Their visual and auditory systems are actively taking in and being shaped by environ-

mental stimulation, and their cognitive growth during this stage is phe-
nomenal. Communication between the mother and the infant is important in preparing for the child's early use of language.

One caveat is in order as we begin this discussion. When we discuss
mother-infant interaction and its importance for the child's later linguistic communication, we are speaking in terms of our own culture. The
descriptions we provide are not universal. As we pointed out in the previous chapter, there are cultures in which infants receive little verbal
stimulation and still learn to talk. There are cultures in which quite different assumptions are made by adults about infant capabilities, and the
infants in those cultures still mature into competent adults. In other
words, we are not saying that the kinds of mother-infant interactions we
describe here are necessary if children are to learn language. Rather, we
are saying that these are the kinds of interactions that lead to the kinds
of early language use we observe in children in this culture.

Putting the Infant in a Social Context

Perhaps the first thing to notice about mothers and their babies is the
extent to which mothers treat babies as social beings. (This is also true
of fathers, grandparents, and other significant adults. We use the term
mother here both because the mother is usually the primary emotional
bond for the infant in our culture and because most of the available research involves mothers.) From the beginning mothers talk to babies as
though the babies could understand. The mother engages in pseudo-
conversations in which she takes both her own turns and the baby's. Any
sound or movement made by the baby is treated as though it had meaning. This can be seen in the interaction reported at the beginning of
this chapter and is perhaps even clearer in the interaction below, which
occurred in the presence of one of the authors. Karen, the mother, is
driving the car with her fussy 5-week-old son strapped into the car-seat
beside her.

BABY: *[Makes a fussy, whiny sound.]*
KAREN: I know, sweetie. You're ready to eat and Mommy kept you
out too long. It's a tough life, isn't it?
BABY: *[Whimpers.]*
KAREN: You think so? We'll be home soon and we'll get you changed
and fed and you'll feel much better.
BABY: *[Continues to fuss.]*
KAREN: Yes, sweetie. I hear you. We're almost there now.
BABY: *[Cries briefly.]*
KAREN: I know. You're absolutely right. It's just terrible. *[Speaks to
adult in back seat.]* You know, sometimes I wonder what
I'm agreeing with when I tell him he's right.

Karen is aware of her infant's limitations and of the apparently illogi-
cal nature of her behavior in talking to him as she does. However, she

is used to obeying conversational rules in speech and automatically behaves the same way with her infant. We certainly could not maintain that the infant in this interaction is in any way an intentional, knowing conversationalist. The baby is fussing because he is hungry. The mother, however, treats the situation as a conversation and acts as though the baby were a reciprocating conversational partner. As Snow (1977) puts it, the mother *imposes* the rules of conversation on the interaction.

Many researchers, having observed mother-infant interactions, have discussed the apparent reciprocity existing in these interchanges (Bakeman and Brown, 1977; Trevarthen, 1977; Jaffe, Stern, and Peery, 1973). Trevarthen (1977, p. 238) says that "human infants are endowed with a specialized mechanism for human behavioral exchange." Newson and Newson (1975, p.440) state that "the infant's action sequences are temporally organized so that they can mesh—with a high degree of precision—with similar patterns of action produced by his human caretaker." Condon and Sander (1974), in an often cited study, claim that the infant's movements are synchronized with the speech behavior of others in the environment. In other words, these researchers are attributing to the infant the capacity to interact in some more or less equal fashion with adults. They seem to imply that the infant's behaviors are organized into something like turns, which are timed to synchronize and not overlap with the behaviors of the mother.

Some of these studies are not entirely convincing, due to design flaws and overly subjective procedures used to code the infants' behavior. In a sense, the reciprocal behavior of the infant is in the eye of the beholder. It is much more likely, especially in the early months of the infant's life, that the infant is not synchronizing his or her behavior with the mother's, but rather that the mother is synchronizing with the baby. The resemblance of these early mother-infant interactions to conversations is primarily due to the fact that the mother, through her own vocal and gaze behavior, makes them look that way. This is not to say that the baby is not aware of and focused on the mother's behavior. As Hayes (1984, p. 143) writes, "Mutual facial gaze and nonoverlapping vocalization have fundamental significance for human communication, and the mother seems determined to structure her interactive behavior in a way which maximizes the opportunities for her infant to acquire these basic conversational rules."

At least for the first three months, and probably for the first six months of the infant's life, then, it seems reasonable to say that the mother is attempting to fit her behavior to the more or less autonomous behavior of the infant, to create conversation-like interactions. In the process of doing this, the mother is not only showing the child something about conversational rules, she is also defining for the infant those situations and behaviors which will be meaningful. As Cairns (1977, p. 3) puts it, "the mother . . . determines what kinds of initiations the child can make, and how often, by arranging the circumstances in which he is placed."

This assignment of meaning goes even further, as the mother appears to impose what Keenan (1974) calls a "domain of relevance." Mothers talk about what they think their babies are paying attention to; they constantly check to see where the baby is looking and then look back at the baby. Schaffer (1977) suggests that the mother spends so much time looking at the baby because she is trying to figure out the regularities in the baby's behavior and to learn to predict the baby's timing and responses. As Hayes (1984, p. 147) comments, "the combination of careful monitoring interspersed with periods of co-orientation provides the foundation for the infant eventually to realize the relevance and the meaning of his or her experiences for another. These are essentially the processes of intersubjective awareness, shared meaning and communication."

The Beginning of the Language Game

In the second half of the infant's first year, games and other structured interactions become frequent and important carriers of language-related information. Under the guidance of the mother (or other adult) the child enters into a variety of self-contained, rule-governed activities (games such as peek-a-boo and ride-a-horsie, book reading) involving limited, repetitive language use, turn-taking, and predictable outcomes. The adult's support is gradually removed from the activity as the child's ability to carry it alone increases. Bruner (1975a) has called this process "scaffolding." Wertsch (1979) refers to these activities, in which the child behaves under the guidance of an adult as though he or she understood the situation, as "language-games." To clarify the nature of these interactions, we will describe in some detail observations made by Bruner and his colleagues (Ratner and Bruner, 1978; Ninio and Bruner, 1978).

First, Bruner describes the progress of the peek-a-boo, or disappear-reappear game, as played by Jonathan and his mother from the time Jonathan was 5 months old until he was 14 months. They began playing the game with a toy like a jack-in-the-box, consisting of a clown and a cone shape mounted on a stick. The clown could be made to disappear into and then pop out of the cone. The constituents of the game and the language associated with each constituent are presented in Figure 4.1.

Bruner reports that Jonathan entered into the game gradually. At first he simply attempted to grab the clown. At 6 months he would vocalize as he tried to grab. By 7 months, however, he seemed to appreciate the rhythm of the game. He would wait for his mother to give the appropriate utterance at each point, looking at her, at the clown, and back at her, smiling and vocalizing at appropriate points. During this time the mother also began to expand and diversify her language at appropriate points in the game. At 7 months she added the phrase "Where is he?" to the search component. At 8 months she added "Is he in there? Can you see him?" and at 9 months "Where's the clown?" These phrases

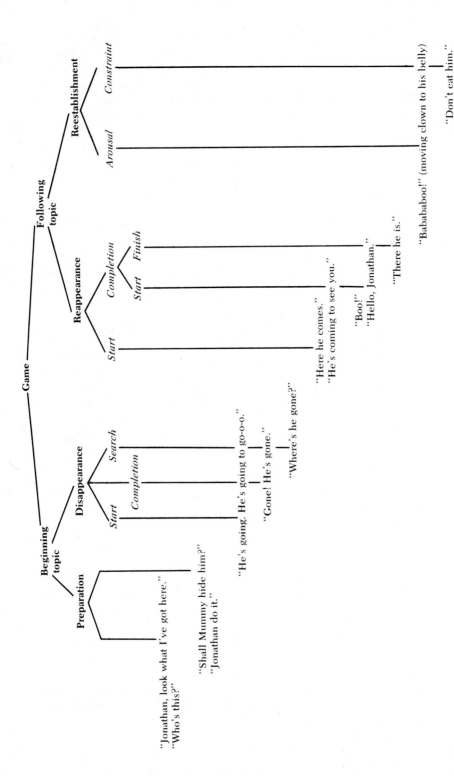

Figure 4.1 Constituents of the Clown Game. (*Source:* Adapted from J. Bruner, 1975.)

became an expected part of the game for Jonathan, who would wait to hear them, smiling and vocalizing. Around 8 months Jonathan began to attempt the role of agent—the person who makes the clown disappear. At first his efforts were clumsy, but as he learned the motor skills involved, his mother gradually gave him control. During this time the language aspect of the game was condensed to two constituents, "gone" at disappearance and "boo" at reappearance. Jonathan began to vocalize along with his mother on at least one constituent of every game. Between 9 and 14 months Jonathan appeared bored with the clown game, although he and his mother continued to play peek-a-boo, first hiding other objects and then themselves. Then, at 14 months the clown regained interest. At this point Jonathan could participate either as agent, controlling the clown, or as experiencer, watching the action. He and his mother would negotiate their roles. He had some limited control of the language needed, saying "boo" as the clown popped out and "all gone" as he stuffed it back into the cone. Jonathan had learned to play two roles in the game, had learned some language to use in the game, and had learned where to fit this language in. The mother's gradual giving up of control is an excellent example of scaffolding a routine and then tracking and supporting the child's development within it.

A second example of prelinguistic interaction leading to language use by the child can be seen in Bruner's description of book reading by another child, Richard, and his mother, when Richard was between 8 and 18 months old. Bruner characterizes the major components of the activity and the language associated with each as follows:

1. *[Attention.]* Mother says "Look" or "Look at that" to get the child's attention.
2. Child gazes at picture or points.
3. *[Query.]* Mother says "What's that?" or "What are those?"
4. Child vocalizes.
5. *[Feedback and label.]* Mother says "Yes, that's an X."

These components make up a sequence carried out repeatedly with children's picture books. The mother is not reading stories—that is a different activity which begins much later. Rather, she and Richard appear to be participating in a labeling game, using books as props. At the outset of this activity the mother would accept any sound Richard made in response to her query as a label and would reword it accordingly. If he said nothing at all, she would provide a label for him. By the time Richard was 14 months old, he had begun to use recognizable words. At this point the mother began to require responses to her queries that sounded more like words. She appeared to remember which words he knew and expect him to recall them, as in the following sequence, between a different mother and her child:

MOTHER: *[Pointing to picture.]* What's that?
CHILD: Chicken.

MOTHER: That's not a chicken. Come on, you know what that is. What says "quack quack"?

CHILD: Duck.

MOTHER: Right. That's a duck. See, he's in the water.

Not only did Richard's mother change her expectations as he demonstrated greater competence, she also began to ask for and give new information. After he had learned labels, she began to ask "What's X doing?" or "What does X say?" As Bruner (1983, p. 84) puts it, "the game shifted from labeling to prediction." The mother in this activity is providing the child with a clear, predictable structure for turn-taking. She is teaching and giving the child an opportunity to practice labeling. As the child matures, she is increasing her demands—probably to keep the child's interest as well as to give him more information about the world and to push his developing competence. Discourse and dialogue are providing a rich learning environment for the still linguistically unsophisticated child.

THE MANIFESTATION OF INTENTIONAL COMMUNICATION

Although the child in the first year of life remains linguistically unsophisticated, this period of development is characterized by the child's increasing ability to function as a full-fledged participant in communicative interactions. During this time the child's behaviors are increasingly interpretable. While at 6 months the child who wants a cookie may sit on the floor and cry, at 10 months he or she will point toward the cookie box and vocalize. This pointing behavior is certainly more communicative than undifferentiated crying, but, as Sugarman (1984) argues, the pointing and vocalizing still cannot be taken as evidence that the child *intends* to communicate. Certainly, the child wants to have a cookie, but it is not clear that the child intends to indicate this to anyone else. The intention to communicate is clear only when the child, in Sugarman's terms, "marks behaviorally, if globally, what action or reaction is expected of whom regarding what thing" (p. 28).

Perhaps another example will serve to clarify this distinction. Melissa, age 8 months, was playing with a spoon which she was banging on a metal pot lid while her mother tried to talk on the telephone. Her mother took the spoon and put it in her lap while she continued to talk. Melissa, sitting on the floor at her mother's feet, looked up at the spoon, reached for it, and then began to pull on her mother's skirt in an attempt to move the spoon closer to her. She did not look at her mother, but kept her attention entirely on the spoon. Compare this situation to the behavior of 13-month-old Amy in a similar context. When Amy's mother removed a toy hammer with which Amy was attempting to smash a plastic cup, Amy first looked at her mother and pointed to the hammer. Then, still looking at her mother, she attempted to uncurl her mother's fingers from the toy. This proving unsuccessful, she sat back, looked at her mother's face, held out her hands, and vocalized. The difference in the behavior of the two little girls is that Amy was trying to use her mother as an agent to get the toy and Melissa was not. Amy's behavior is what Sugarman calls a *person-object coordination.* She was, essentially, asking that the hammer be given to her. Melissa tried to get the spoon that had been taken from her by herself, without involving her mother in the act.

Sugarman explains these two behavioral sequences in terms of the child's general cognitive development. As she points out, a characteristic of early cognitive development is the increasing complexity of behavior. (See Chapter 9 for discussion of this development.) One aspect of this complex behavior is tool use, or the use of one object to achieve a goal involving another object. Tool use is seen when Melissa pulls on her mother's skirt to move the spoon closer to her so she can reach it. Sugarman calls such behaviors *object-object coordination.* Such coordination indicates the child's understanding that an object can be used as an instrument to achieve some end. The use of tools as instruments usually appears near the end of the child's first year. Sugarman hypothesizes that the child's understanding that objects can be used as instruments is soon followed by the understanding that people can serve as instruments as well, that is, the child becomes capable of person-object coordination. This conceptualization is important because the coordination of people and objects in the child's communicative behavior occurs just prior to the child's ability to use language to communicate.

This tie between cognitive development and communicative behavior prior to language was perhaps most clearly demonstrated by Bates, Camaione, and Volterra (1975). They identified two clearly communicative acts performed by young children just prior to the onset of language. They called these acts *protodeclaratives*, characterized as the use of an object to gain adult attention, and *protoimperatives*, characterized as the use of an adult to gain a desired object. Several other researchers, among them Lock (1979) and Trevarthen and Hubley (1979), have confirmed these findings.

Sugarman (1984), after studying normal children raised at home and in institutions, concludes that this signaling of intentional communication is a necessary, but not sufficient condition for the development of language. In other words, the child's development of intentional communication is a stage of cognitive development that must be achieved before language appears. However, this stage of cognitive development alone will not ensure that language use will appear. She suggests that the kinds of social interactions between a child and a primary caretaker described earlier in this chapter may also be necessary for the child's language development, and that in the absence of a history of such interactions, language development will be delayed even though cognitive development occurs on schedule.

If Sugarman's ideas, which are shared by Bruner (1975b) and Halliday (1975), about the importance of preverbal communicative interaction for the development of language should be borne out by future research, our theories of language acquisition will need considerable modification. We will be forced to conclude that the cognitive endowment that the child brings to the learning process must be accompanied by a very special kind of exposure to language. If language development is to be the culmination of the sensorimotor period of development, then the child must experience language use in interaction with another person who can interpret and respond to the child's behaviors as though these were meaningful from the beginning. The presence of facilitative preverbal communicative interactions may constitute the environmental support for language development.

SUMMARY

Infants communicate with the people in their environments from birth, using vocalizations, crying, eye movements, and gestures. In fact, the human infant is a remarkably competent organism, seemingly "wired" to focus on aspects of the environment that will facilitate the growth of communication skills.

The environment provided by caretakers in our culture also seems designed to facilitate the child's communication. From the beginning we treat a baby's acts as though they were intentional, and we establish interactions organized into turns. As soon as the child is capable of taking an active role in our turn taking, we play a variety of communication games to support further development.

The preverbal stage culminates in the development of person-object coordination, shown by the child's attempts to use other people as instruments. This stage of cognitive development appears to be a necessary precursor to the use of language to communicate.

SUGGESTED READINGS

Bullowa, M. (ed.). *Before Speech*. Cambridge: Cambridge University Press, 1979. This is a collection of research reports and summaries describing the communication behaviors of infants in the period prior to speech, with an introduction designed to give the reader a perspective for approaching the research.

Golinkoff, R. (ed.). *The Transition from Prelinguistic to Linguistic Communication*. Hillsdale, N.J.: Erlbaum, 1983. This book is concerned with how children move from the stage of no language production to a stage in which language is produced.

SUGGESTED PROJECTS

1. Interview a group of mothers who have babies under 12 months old. Ask them what kinds of things their babies communicate to them and how this communication occurs. Compare the results of the mothers' observations with the research findings presented in Bullowa, *Before Speech,* cited above.

2. The literature in child psychology contains many studies of children who do not have the kind of prelinguistic communication opportunities described in this chapter. Summarize the findings of this literature, and try to devise a plan for helping these infants to compensate. (Hint: Start with Brauwald's chapter in Golinkoff, *The Transition from Prelinguistic to Linguistic Communication,* cited above.)

3. This chapter emphasized the importance of mutual gaze, joint attention, and facial expression in mother-infant interaction. What do you suppose occurs between blind infants and their mothers? Summarize the literature in this area. (Hint: Start with C. Urwin, "Communication in infancy and the emergence of language in blind children," in R. Schiefelbusch and J. Pickar (eds.), *The Acquisition of Communicative Competence,* Baltimore: University Park Press, 1984.)

PART
Two

THE LANGUAGE SYSTEM: WHAT IS BEING LEARNED

It is artificial and in some ways misleading to divide language into segments as we do in this part of the book. Unfortunately, if we don't, we have an exceptionally difficult time talking about it. Language is *sounds structured meaningfully and used to communicate.* In the next four chapters language is broken apart into sound (Chapter 5), meaning (Chapter 6), sentence structure (Chapter 7), and pragmatics (Chapter 8). All of these parts must be learned by the child, and we can trace development in each part.

To keep from getting caught up in the parts and losing sight of the whole, remember this as you read: Children do not learn language by acquiring one system at a time. Sound, meaning, syntax, and pragmatics are all being learned at once, and children are not aware of them as separate aspects of language as they learn.

Chapter
5

Development of the Sound System

*O*ne of our many language-related abilities is the ability to recognize that another person is speaking a foreign language. Indeed, we can often tell just from the sound what language it is. If you do not speak French or German, it is likely, nonetheless, that you recognize the sounds of these languages. A language's pattern of sounds is one of the things we must learn if we are to speak it. In this chapter we shall explore children's acquisition of the sounds of their language. We consider first what the child has to learn and second what happens in the learning process.

PHONEMES

Every language is made up of a limited number of sounds, the building blocks of language. They are put together in various combinations to make up the words of the language. Approximately 43 sounds make up all the words used in English. Other languages have different numbers of sounds. Spanish, for example, uses about 24. Some languages share sounds. For example, English and Spanish both use the sound we represent by the letter *p*. Some languages have different sounds. Many Spanish speakers have difficulty hearing the difference between the vowel sounds in the English words *leave* and *live* because these are not separate sounds in Spanish.

The sounds used to make words are called *phonemes*. Phonemes are the smallest sound segments in language that signal changes in meaning. Since meanings are different in each language and are signaled differently, all languages do not share all the same phonemes. English and

Spanish, for example, sound different because they use different sets of phonemes.

PLACE AND MANNER OF ARTICULATION

There are many ways to describe language sounds. A physicist might describe sounds in terms of acoustical properties such as frequency of vibrations. In analyzing phonemes, however, it is easiest to classify sounds according to where and how they are articulated. Make the sound /p/. Notice that the sound happens when you bring your lips together and release a puff of air. Thus the *place of articulation* is the lips; the *manner of articulation* is to stop air and then release it.

Table 5.1 classifies the consonants of English according to place and manner of articulation. At the top of the table sounds are classified according to place of articulation. *Bilabial* sounds are made with the lips (e.g., /p/ and /b/). *Labiodental* sounds are made by contact between the lower lip and upper teeth (/f/ and /v/). Many sounds are made by contact between the tongue and some part of the mouth. *Dental* sounds are made with the tongue and teeth (/th/ as in "think"). *Alveolar* sounds are made with tongue and alveolar ridge, the part of the mouth behind the top teeth (e.g., /t/ and /d/). *Palatal* sounds are made by raising the tongue toward the palate, or roof of the mouth (e.g., the initial sound in "yes" and "yellow"). Behind the palate is the velum, or soft palate. Sounds made by contact between the back of the tongue and the velum are called *velar* (e.g., /k/ and /g/). Even farther down the throat than the velum are the vocal cords. *Glottal* sounds are made only with the vocal cords (e.g., the initial sound in "happy" and "how").

The terms in the first column of Table 5.1 refer to the manner of articulation. *Stop* sounds are made by closing off the flow of air completely, then releasing it. As you can see by looking across the table, stop sounds can be made at many locations in the mouth. *Fricative* sounds are made by narrowing the opening of the mouth so that the flow of air is not entirely blocked, but is obstructed. Fricatives produce a hissing noise due to the turbulence of the air passing through the small opening. Consonant sounds that combine the properties of stops and fricatives are called *affricates.* Affricates are made by cutting off the air flow completely, as in a stop, then releasing it through a very small opening, as in a fricative. Affricates are accompanied by the hissing sound typical of fricatives, as can be heard by pronouncing "church" and "judge." Sounds made by closing the mouth at some point and allowing air to escape through the nose are called *nasals.* Nasals are classified according to where the closure in the mouth occurs. Some consonants are much like vowels in that no closure occurs in the mouth. These are the *liquids* (/l/ and /r/) and the *glides* (/w/, /wh/, and /y/). Glides are so much like vowels that they are often called *semivowels.*

Consonant sounds are classified according to place and manner of

Table 5.1 PLACE AND MANNER OF ARTICULATION IN ENGLISH CONSONANTS

	Bilabial	Labiodental	Dental	Alveolar	Palatal	Velar	Glottal
Stop	p b			t d		k g	
Fricative		f v	th	s z	sh zh		h
Affricative				ch j			
Glide	w wh				y		
Liquid				l	r		
Nasal	m			n		ng	

articulation. Vowel sounds are classified according to the height of the tongue in the mouth (high, mid, or low) and the location in the mouth of the highest point of the tongue (front, central, or back). One main difference between consonants and vowels is that for vowels there is never a closure in the mouth and for consonants there often is. Vowel classification is shown in Table 5.2. The vowels are classified as high, mid, or low and as front, central, or back. For example, /i/ as in "beat" is a high front vowel, and /a/ as in "hot" is a low back vowel.

DISTINCTIVE FEATURES

Suppose you decide to describe the sound /p/. You could say several things about it. First, the sound is a consonant, not a vowel. Second, it is articulated by bringing the lips together (bilabial). Third, it is articulated as a stop. To summarize, /p/ is a consonant and a bilabial stop.

Table 5.2 ENGLISH VOWELS

	Front	Central	Back
High	/i/ as in "beat"		/u/ as in "boo"
	/ɪ/ as in "bit"		/ʊ/ as in "good"
Mid	/e/ as in "bait"	/ʌ/ as in "much" /ə/ as in "arrest"	/o/ as in "boat"
	/ɛ/ as in "bet"		/ɔ/ as in "ball"
Low	/æ/ as in "bat"		/a/ as in "hot"

The sound /b/ also has all of these features, but it is different from /p/ in *voicing*. If the vocal cords vibrate when a sound is made, the sound is voiced. If you put your fingers lightly over your throat where the Adam's apple is and make the sounds /p/ and /b/, you should feel the vocal cords vibrate on /b/, but not on /p/. The sound /b/ is voiced; /p/ is not.

The description of a sound in terms of all the articulatory features we have discussed is called a *distinctive feature analysis* (Table 5.3). Distinctive features provide an economical way to describe and compare sounds. The table tells us, for example, that the only difference between /p/ and /b/ is the voicing feature.

Not all articulatory features are distinctive in a given language. For example, /t/ can be made with the tongue against the alveolar ridge or with the tongue against the teeth (if the tongue touches the teeth, /t/ is said to be dentalized). You can make /t/ with the lips rounded or not rounded. You can also make /t/ *aspirated* or *unaspirated*. An aspirated sound is one that is accompanied by a puff of air. You can feel this if you hold your hand about an inch away from your lips and pronounce "toy." Now, with your hand still there, pronounce "stop." The /t/ in "toy" is aspirated; in "stop" it is not. All these features of articulation can vary, and yet the sound produced will still be recognized by speakers of English as /t/. We do not usually distinguish between aspirated /t/ and unaspirated /t/, but in some Arabic languages these are regarded as different sounds, just as /t/ and /d/ are regarded as different sounds in English. The point here is that in every language some sound differences are *distinctive*, that is, they distinguish one phoneme from others, and other differences are *nondistinctive*. As mentioned earlier, aspiration is nondistinctive for English speakers. This means that we do not have two words that are different because one has an aspirated /t/ and one has an unaspirated /t/. However, other sound features are distinctive for English speakers. For example, as noted previously, voicing is a distinctive

Table 5.3 DISTINCTIVE FEATURE
ANALYSIS OF FOUR
CONSONANTS

Features	p	b	f	t
Consonant	+	+	+	+
Vowel	−	−	−	−
Labial	+	+	−	−
Dental	−	−	+	−
Alveolar	−	−	−	−
Palatal	−	−	−	−
Stop	+	+	−	+
Fricative	−	−	+	−
Voiced	−	+	−	−

feature in English. To speakers of languages in which voicing is not a distinctive feature, "beat" and "peat" might sound like the same word.

Many other sound features are distinctive for speakers of English. An oversimplified view of the theory has been presented here (for more information, see Chomsky and Halle, 1968), but one note should be added here. We have defined distinctive features in terms of how sounds are articulated. Most theorists today say that that account is incomplete and that distinctive features are based on the acoustics of the sound as well as on how sounds are articulated.

SOUND ACQUISITION

The child seems to learn the phonemic system of the language by discovering distinctive features, which is a process of *differentiation.* Phoneme differentiation does not begin until sounds are used meaningfully—in words. The first distinction the child makes is usually between vowel and consonant. One example of this, which appears early in children's speech, is the distinction between /p/ as in "pit" and /a/ as in "father." Using this distinction, the child can say "pa" or "papa."

Once begun, the process of differentiation proceeds rapidly. The next distinction made may be between nasal and nonnasal consonants, for example, distinguishing /p/ from /m/.

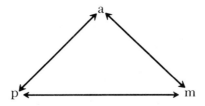

Now the phonemes /pa/ and /ma/—and usually the words designating the child's parents, "papa" and "mama"—are available for use. Both /p/ and /m/ are made with the lips, so the child soon makes a labial-nonlabial distinction in the form of using /f/ or /s/ in contrast with /p/ and /m/. Whatever the sounds first used (they may vary from the examples given here), the child can make three or four sounds, and the "first words" can mean a variety of things. Valued objects such as baby bottles or cookies may be named "ba" or "sa" or some other easy-to-say form.

The child may not make any vowel contrasts until several consonants have been mastered. The first vowel distinction is likely to be between *wide-open mouth* (e.g., /a/) and *narrow opening* (e.g., /i/).

Jakobson and Halle (1956) say that these first few consonant and vowel contrasts are language universals (in the sense discussed in Chapter 2). Some support for this view is found in the fact that many languages use words similar to "mama" and "papa" to refer to parents.

More important than the universality of particular sounds is the idea that the differentiation process for learning these sounds may be universal. It may spring from general rules of sound that describe all languages. In other words, all languages have the basic kinds of sound contrasts discussed for English: between stops and nasals and fricatives for consonants; between wide and narrow for vowels. This universality explains why children might make these distinctions first.

This does not mean that all languages have the same phonemes, nor does it mean that all children learn each contrast at the same age. Normal children vary in *rate* of acquisition, but *order* of learning of certain contrasts seems to be the same. As children develop more sound contrasts, they progress further into a specific language such as English or French and further away from the early universal contrasts. The sound contrasts could be arranged hierarchically, with broad, universal contrasts, such as vowel versus consonant, occurring first and fine, language-specific contrasts, such as voiced versus unvoiced sounds, occurring later. Jakobson and Halle's theory explains the acquisition of the broad contrasts for many children, but it is important to remember that there may be individual exceptions to these patterns.

It is also important to note that the child seems to be discriminating not so much among phonemes (such as /b/ and /p/) as among features (such as voicing). That may sound like a minor distinction, but if the child learns a feature, he or she has learned something much more general than a one-phoneme distinction. Learning a voicing feature involves learning not only the difference between /b/ and /p/, but also the differences between /f/ and /v/, between /k/ and /g/, and between /t/ and /d/. Thus most theorists say that the child learns the sound system at the feature level. This obviously has some implications for speech therapy. There is some evidence (McReynolds and Huston, 1972) that teaching features (such as voicing) brings changes in behavior more readily than teaching each phoneme separately.

Distinctive feature analysis alone is not enough to specify all that children must learn about the sounds of their language. As we mentioned earlier, not all the articulatory features of sounds are distinctive for any given language. Features that are not distinctive (that do not serve to identify different words in the language) are specified by linguistic rules. For example, aspiration is not a distinctive feature for speakers of English. A general phonological rule of English states that all initial voiceless stops are aspirated, that is, in words such as "tin" and "pin" the first sounds are aspirated. There are no contrasting words that begin with unaspirated /t/ or /p/. When the child learns to say "tin," he or she must learn that /t/ is voiceless (to distinguish it from "din") and must learn that it is an alveolar stop rather than a fricative (to distinguish it from "sin"). However, the child need not learn that in this particular word /t/ is always aspirated in English. Having mastered the general rule, the child does not have to be concerned about every particular instance of the sound.

Another rule of English is that stop sounds are always unaspirated after /s/. A child learning to say "stop" or "spat" need not learn for each individual word that the sound coming after /s/ is unaspirated. It will always be so. All that must be learned is the rule. There are no contrasts between words beginning /s/-aspirated stop and those beginning /s/-unaspirated stop, so the child does not learn this through a series of contrasts, as he or she learns distinctive features. The child must, instead, somehow acquire knowledge of the system of rules that governs how we put sounds together to make words in English. We have given only a hint of what some of these rules are like. We know little about how the child learns these rules and the order in which they are acquired. However, it is clear that the child who is going to speak English must abide by them.

EARLY WORD FORMATION

As most parents can tell you, children often have difficulty with the sounds of the language when they are first learning to make words. The whole idea of "baby talk" is based on this fact, so when a mother says "Bwing Mommy the wabbit," she may be imitating the mistakes made by the child. Some children quickly overcome these early difficulties, but others continue to have trouble with certain sounds even after they have started school.

The kinds of mistakes children make in their early words can be described systematically. According to Franke (1912), children's first words are one-consonant forms. The consonants /m/, /b/, and /p/ are among the first to appear, and they are used in consonant-vowel or consonant-vowel-consonant forms. Although children in the first stages of word formation may be able to articulate as many as eight consonants properly, they will seldom use more than one in any individual word. It is as if the child cannot change place or manner of articulation within words. This phenomenon can be seen clearly in one of Franke's examples of children's pronunciation of the German word *"baum"* (tree). Of three children observed, one said "maumau," one said "bau," and one said "maum." Although the three pronunciations are different, they have in common the fact that a word with two consonants was changed to a one-consonant form by dropping one consonant or substituting for it.

Children's tendencies in sound omission or substitution in early word formation reflect this one-consonant tendency. When a word the child is trying to say has more than one consonant, all consonants except one are likely to be eliminated. Sometimes the child substitutes this one for the others. Thus the English word "bug" becomes "gug" or "down" becomes "nown." This process is known as *assimilation,* referring to a change in one sound to make it more like another.

Several factors influence which consonant in a word will be retained. Franke argues that the middle consonant is most likely to be retained (the /n/ in "pencil," for example), followed by the first, then the last. Another factor influencing consonant retention is difficulty of articulation. Consonants that are hard for children to make (for example, /r/) will be dropped or substituted for in children's early speech. Finally, in a word with many syllables, only stressed syllables are likely to be retained. Thus "elephant" may become "ef," or "banana" may become "na" or "nana."

The distortions little children produce when they try to say some words are not simply a result of the fact that some sounds are too hard for them to make. By the age of 2 many children are able to articulate clearly all the sounds of the language. However, there is more to making words than this. Putting sounds together is not the same as saying sounds in isolation, and children must learn which sounds to use and how to put them together before it can be said that they have learned the sound system of a language. This suggests that the process of babbling, which used to be considered essential to speech development, does not ensure that children will be able to articulate clearly when they begin to make words. When infants lie in their cribs making sounds, they may make a large range of sounds, even the /r/ and /l/ sounds, which are quite difficult for many 4-year-olds. But the fact that a baby can make a sound in isolation while babbling does not mean that he or she will be able to use the sound in combination with other sounds to make words. Deaf children babble for several months, just as hearing children do, yet young deaf children will not develop spoken language unless they can be helped to hear it. We'll return to this issue later in the chapter.

We have used the vocabulary of speech clinicians to discuss the mistakes children are likely to make: substitutions, distortions, omissions, and so on. Actually, children are ordinarily not substituting one phoneme for another when they use /w/ instead of /r/. Rather, they are making an error on one feature of /w/, which does not quite produce /r/, although it isn't /w/. The adult typically guesses that the children say /r/, but actually the contrast is on a subphonemic (feature) level. What may appear to be strange distortions in children's speech will often become comprehensible if analyzed in this way. Consider, for example, a child who has the following set of pronunciations:

adult	pat	child says	bat
	tack		dack
	come		gum
	bag		bag (correct)
	date		date (correct)

This child appears to have trouble putting a voiceless stop (/p/, /t/, /k/) in the initial position in a word, even though these sounds occur in other positions. The child also maintains correct place of articulation, even though errors are made in voicing. This description makes two things clear. First, the child is not incapable of making voiceless stops altogether. In fact, they are made correctly in some positions. Second, although three different substitutions are being made (/b/ for /p/, /d/ for /t/, and /g/ for /k/), only one feature (voicing) is incorrect. This pattern, although hypothetical, is not unlike the pattern one might see in a child who is still developing the sound system of English.

SUPRASEGMENTAL PHONOLOGY

To this point our description of phonology and phonological development has concentrated on the sounds the child makes and what can be determined by segmenting the speech stream into phonemes. For obvious reasons this is called *segmental phonology*. There is, however, another level to the sound system. There are *suprasegmental* characteristics such as pitch and stress. It is harder to describe these suprasegmental features of the sound system than to talk about segmented descriptions of the sounds themselves, yet these characteristics are quite important to the ways in which sentences are interpreted. Adults, for instance, communicate irony, or meaning opposite to what they say, entirely through suprasegmental features. We will briefly discuss two broad areas of suprasegmental phonology, pitch and stress. Readers are referred to Lehiste (1970) for a deeper explanation.

Pitch refers to the tonal quality of speech in roughly a musical sense. Vocal folds vibrate and the mouth parts resonate in ways analogous to parts of musical instruments. Each speaker establishes a sort of fundamental frequency, which others adjust to as a pitch departure point. From that fundamental frequency, speech varies up and down in tone; these variations can be distinctive features, thus cuing differences in meaning. In some languages the tone of words is distinctive; Chinese languages are often this way. In English the tonal quality of a word doesn't ordinarily signal changes in meaning, but the intonation pattern of an entire phrase or sentence definitely cues many changes in meaning. Hence intonation can carry meaning in English.

Intonation results partly from the way we breathe. There is only so much air in the lungs. When the air begins to run out, the frequency of the voice is lower. That explains why most speakers of most languages use an intonation pattern that lowers at the ends of sentences. There are many specific kinds of meanings cued by intonation. Questions in English, for one example, usually end with rising intonation. This difference by itself is usually quite sufficient to show a listener that an utterance is a question. For instance, think of the sentence "She went to the bank" with and without a question mark at the end. If you read it with a question mark, the intonation contour rises on the word "bank." This change probably would be interpreted by a listener as transforming the sentence from a declarative statement to a question. Similarly, if you imagine an exclamation point at the end of a sentence, you read it with a different intonation (also a different stress pattern, which will be discussed below). Punctuation marks are not precise markers of stress or intonation. We use them to get you to think in a way that will enable you to examine the intonation patterns used in such contexts.

In a number of places in this book (most notably near the end of Chapter 6) we describe ways young children use intonation to supplement other information, especially syntactic information that they lack the linguistic maturity to produce. The early appearance of intonation patterns in children's speech may indicate that these suprasegmental features are particularly salient characteristics of language for young children.

A second major suprasegmental indicator is the stress given to parts of words and sentences. *Stress* indicates emphasis, the relative importance of a word or syllable. Every word has a characteristic stress pattern, emphasizing one syllable. This is marked clearly in most dictionaries. Similarly, certain words are stressed in sentences. Nouns seem most often stressed in English, which may help to explain why many of the child's first words are nouns. In fact, many researchers have described early child speech as "telegraphic" in the sense that only the stressed words seem to be present (Brown and Bellugi, 1964).

Children certainly seem sensitive to stress and intonation patterns in language. In fact, they show this kind of sensitivity as early as any other. You can get a very young child to smile by saying something like "You are a complete creep" in a cooing intonation, especially if your speech is accompanied by smiles.

Intonation and stress are suprasegmental features that sometimes indicate information about emotional states of the speaker. In performing such functions, suprasegmentals may interact with nonverbal features such as gestures and facial expressions. In fact, some authors classify most suprasegmentals as *paralanguage* (which means "beside language"). Paralanguage includes suprasegmental phonemes and some other sounds that are not words, such as laughter, crying, sighs, and whines. It is not of much importance whether such matters are discussed as phonology or nonverbal communication, so long as observers of child speech attempt to get a feel for the messages the child is working out using these tools of language.

In Chapter 11 we discuss dialects of English and some issues that dialect diversity raises for education. It might be argued that many dialect variations in English are as different from each other in suprasegmental phonology as in any other ways. For example, so-called black English seems distinctive from other American varieties largely because of rapid rates of speech in colloquial styles, melodic pitch patterns sometimes including falsettos uncommon in other dialects of English, and a few stress patterns (for example, "*Dee*-troit" and "*tee*vee"). Similarly, southern drawls are characterized largely by slow speech rates that lengthen certain sounds (the drawl) and by some stress patterns ("You are in a *heap* of trouble!").

BABBLING

You may have noticed that our account of phonemic development began with the utterance of meaningful words. Most theorists agree that uttering sounds within meaningful speech contexts requires a different level of skill from that required by uttering the sounds in isolation. There seems not to be a clear continuity between the early (prespeech) sounds the child makes and later phonemic development. But the child does not make first sounds in the context of meaningful speech. The child performs many behaviors early in life that show learning about the system before speech appears. The major question is "Just what is the child learning about sounds during the first year and a half, and how much does this learning affect later phonemic development?"

The first thing that must be noted is that the child is apparently not born without knowledge about sounds. A newborn infant reacts to sound differences that are a lot like differences among phonemes. (See Chapter 4.) In the first month of life the child already makes vocal sounds other than crying. During this period the child can also make some distinction between speech sounds and nonspeech sounds. Woolf (1966), for example, showed that vocalizations were more effective in stopping crying than inanimate sounds. If that is so, the child must be able to tell the difference between speech and nonspeech.

The newborn infant not only discriminates speech sounds from nonspeech sounds, but also discriminates among speech sounds. As we pointed out in Chapter 4, the best way to show this is to set up an experimental situation in which the infant sucks on a pacifier while a tape recorder plays a repeated sound, say /ba/. The child's sucking on the pacifier increases with the occurrence of the sound at first, but decreases as the child habituates to the sound. When the sucking has slowed, if the sound /pa/ is played, without a change in any other conditions, the sucking frequency is likely to increase again. The increased sucking that accompanies the new sound shows that the child can indeed make a distinction between the two sounds. This distinction, you may have noticed, corresponds to just one distinctive feature, voicing. Researchers (e.g., Eimas et al., 1971) have demonstrated in this way that 6-week-old infants can discriminate according to place of articulation in consonants and tongue height in vowels. There have also been demonstrations that children can distinguish between rising intonation and falling intonation in speech sounds. In fact, Lieberman (1967) showed that children actually vary the fundamental frequency of their own voice in the direction of that of either a male or a female who interacts with them.

It is significant that children make these discriminations primarily when dealing with speech sounds and are less able to discriminate non-speech sounds, say musical tones or other kinds of noises. Something about the sound structure of the language seems to dovetail with the categories of the child's perception, even in earliest infancy. We might say, then, that the child is born with some perceptual headstart toward learning sound systems of language.

We next examine what sort of learning about sounds is happening during the months when the child is making babbling noises. First, we should be more precise about what babbling is like. At about the end of the first month of life, the child begins to make some cooing sounds (mostly back vowels like the /u/ sound in the word "coo"). These continue and become more differentiated until roughly the age of 6 months, when the stage called babbling begins. Babbling is distinguished from cooing by the degree to which the babbles sound like the syllables of words. You can tell that a baby is moving into babbling when the baby begins to put consonant sounds in front of the vowel sounds that were being cooed previously. Eventually, even more syllable-like patterns emerge (consonant-vowel-consonant, for instance). A bit later (around 10 or 12 months) the child begins to use the sounds of babbling as an object of play. Repetitive sequences emerge. The child will say a sound over and over or work up some rhymes or run through a contrast or two.

This activity has impressed many observers because it seems a lot like the practicing of scales on a piano. The child appears at this point to be practicing the little units of language in preparation for putting them into words and sentences. This appearance led early theorists to assume that the child was practicing talk during the babbling phase. Roman Jakobson, the originator of distinctive feature analysis, was among the first to point out some problems with this position. There are some discontinuities between babbling and true speech. The first sounds to be babbled are not the first sounds to occur in words. The child cannot put all (or even most) of the babbled sounds into words for a number of years. Further, there is a period of silence in most children between the time at which they stop babbling and the time at which they begin to speak. Finally, and most telling, it seems that children do not need to babble in order to talk any more than children need to crawl in order to walk. Many children babble little, and there is no evidence that these children's speech is in any way delayed as a result. Even children unable to babble because of throat surgery suffer no handicaps in learning to speak after the vocal apparatus is returned to normal. Therefore, Jakobson and a number of other researchers have taken a strong position that babbling is simply a period of vocal play having little effect on the later differentiation of phonemes.

We do not totally deny the importance of babbling. There do seem to be some things the child is learning during babbling. For instance, pitch and stress patterns that sound much like sentences often emerge at about 12 months. It surely can't be hurting the child's expertise with the phonemic system to be playing with the motor apparatus in these ways. Further, some researchers (most notably Oller, Wieman, Doyle, and Ross, 1976) present evidence of important ties between babbling and speech, including patterns of consonant-vowel clustering and some substitutions of one sound for another.

One last piece of research complicates the picture still further. Olney and Scholnick (1976) studied what adults could perceive in children's babbling. It is important to ask what adults perceive because if babbling is practice for speech, then adults are presumably the teachers. Adults, so the reasoning goes, provide some feedback or reinforcement for the most speechlike of child sounds, encouraging children increasingly toward the sounds of the language. If this happens, one must presume that adults can perceive differences in the children's babbling, just as piano teachers can observe distinctions when students play scales.

Olney and Scholnick played tapes of children's babbling for college students. The students were asked to make judgments about the language the child was learning (there was one child of American parents and one of Chinese parents) and how old the child was (there were recordings at 6, 12, and 18 months). It turned out that the college students were able to discriminate ages, but could not tell which language the child was preparing to learn. They could not tell the difference between the babbles of the child learning English and the one learning Chinese. Hence the children must have been following some developmental sequence in their babbling, but that progress may not have been oriented toward the language they were learning.

In sum, the role of babbling is still unclear. The child is undoubtedly practicing and playing with sounds and intonations. This includes practice of consonant-vowel combinations sounding much like words. The practice is responded to by adults and probably has some effect on later language habits. However, the strong discontinuities between babbling and meaningful speech make it difficult to say that babbling is important sound practice for talking and language.

SUMMARY

Children seem to acquire the sound system by learning a system of contrasts called distinctive features, beginning with the major contrast between consonants and vowels and proceeding through finer and finer contrasts until they have learned all the important sound features of the language. This learning by differentiation is accompanied by the acquisition of the rules that govern the use of nondistinctive sound features.

When they are learning to talk, children often distort the sounds of words. Such distortion is attributable to several factors, among them that children appear to have difficulty changing the place or manner of articulation of consonants within a word and that some sounds are harder for children to articulate than others.

Babbling seems a somewhat separate process from learning to speak, although the child probably learns about intonation, a distinctive feature in English, during the babbling experience. In addition, the child learns to put vowels and consonants into combinations, a skill that comes in handy later.

SUGGESTED READINGS

Chomsky, N., and M. Halle. *The Sound Patterns of English.* Cambridge, Mass.: MIT Press, 1968. This widely read book has influenced a number of scholars. It contains a fairly readable discussion of the concept of distinctive features. Some aspects of the Chomsky-Halle approach are disputed by others.

Lehiste, U. *Suprasegmentals.* Cambridge, Mass.: MIT Press, 1970. Lehiste has assembled a wide array of information about suprasegmental phonology in this volume.

Lewis, M. M. *Language, Thought and Personality in Infancy and Childhood.* New York: Basic Books, 1963. Lewis provides a thoughtful and readable account of sounds children make. The account is based largely on observations of his own children.

Ferguson, C. A., and Farwell, C. B. Words and sounds in early language acquisition. *Language 51,* 439-491, 1975. This is a detailed and readable discussion of the processes of phonological development in young children.

SUGGESTED PROJECTS

1. Find a child who is at the babbling stage. Tape record the child's vocalizations, and make a list of all the sounds you hear.

2. What do you think might be the relationship between perception and production in children's phonological development? Do children produce sounds incorrectly because they hear them that way? Prepare a position paper on this issue. (Hint: You will find some useful material in G. Yeni-Komshian, J. Kavanagh, and C. A. Ferguson, *Child Phonology,* vol. 1, *Production;* vol. 2, *Perception,* New York: Academic Press, 1980.)

Chapter 6

Development of Meaning

O ne of the least understood aspects of children's development is how meanings come to be attached to language structure. We do not understand the nature of the semantic system that the child is acquiring, there has been little research into the process of this acquisition, and much of the research we have is contradictory.

WORDS AND OBJECTS

When we think about meaning, probably the first thing that comes to mind is the idea of *definition*, that is, the idea that words have referents in the real world, that words stand for things. We assume that the first words uttered by children are names of things. In fact, we assume that both adults and children carry around in their heads kinds of "dictionaries," in which words and their meanings are somehow connected. With each word we match up a set of semantic markers or features. The set of semantic features that goes with a particular word corresponds in some ways to a dictionary definition of that word. For example, the semantic markers of "dog" might include "furry," "four legs," "barks," "wagging tail." The acquisition of the set of semantic markers for a given word may be described as a process of *concept* development.

As Quine (1964) has expressed it, the child who is developing concepts must develop *individuated* terms. To develop individuated terms, the child must have some conception of the permanence of recurring objects. She must realize that the moon she sees in the sky tonight is the same moon that was there last night and that there are not 2 moons or

60. The child must also realize that the apple he is eating for lunch today is not the same apple he ate for lunch yesterday, but another apple. The child does not truly use individuated terms until he can understand the difference between "that apple," "not that apple," "an apple," "some apple," "another apple," "these apples." In this sense it could be said that the child's word "mama" does not become a label for the child's mother until the child learns the difference between "my mama," "not my mama," "my mama in a different dress," and so forth. To say that the child understands these various uses of a word implies that the child has developed a concept to go with a certain label.

Saying that a child has developed a correspondence between label and concept is quite different from saying that a child has developed a correspondence between label and thing. When we speak of the concept "chair," for instance, we are not speaking of one particular chair, but rather of some quality of "chairness" that is shared by and unique to all chairs. The child must develop a set of working concepts in order to classify properly all the objects in his or her world.

We may observe the progress of this development in children's speech. For example, a young friend named Andrew first applied the word "car" only to the family Volkswagen, indicating a narrow sense of "car." After a time Andrew began to apply the word to all cars, trucks, and tractors, and soon he was using it to label anything that moved on wheels. At this point Andrew's concept of "car" was too broad. It needed to be refined. He soon learned to distinguish trucks and used the word "tuck" to label these. Later he used the word "bus" to label another set of vehicles. The point here is that Andrew had to learn that not all moving things with wheels are called by one word. He had to learn which of these things could be properly grouped together under one label. It is not so easy to put the meaning of the concept "car" into words so that it can be distinguished from truck or bus. The child seems to develop such concepts through experience.

This process of concept development has been the focus of a good deal of research, and the research has caused us to change many of our ideas about children's development of word meaning. Consider the following examples of children's interactions with their mothers.

When Susie was 10 months old, she pulled her mother by the hand over to the refrigerator, pointed up, and said, "ka ka." Her mother responded by reaching up and getting the box of animal crackers, customarily kept on top of the refrigerator, and saying, "Oh, would you like a cracker?" When Billy was 13 months old, he was kneeling on a chair in the living room, looking out the window. A fire truck drove past. He bounded up and down excitedly saying, "tuck, tuck," and looking back at his mother. She replied, "Yes, that was a fire truck." Perhaps the most obvious, and the most taken for granted, aspect of these mother-child interactions is that the children were using language to describe objects and that their mothers recognized this and confirmed their labelings.

Indeed, children's early language is not meaningless. Yet if children use language to convey meaning, then one must ask how these meanings are learned: Where do the meanings expressed in children's early language come from? The answer is to be found not only in the study of children's language behavior, but also in the study of their general development before language appears. When children first begin to talk, they express what they know about reality—about the physical and social events in their environments. Dan Slobin (1973), in discussing the prerequisites for learning language, writes that children must be able to "cognize the physical and social events encoded in language." In other words, children must be able to organize reality into conceptual categories so that they can communicate.

It is difficult for us as adults to understand what it means to "organize reality." Some analogy can be drawn to a simple game. Imagine that you have in front of you a pile of blocks in a variety of shapes, sizes, colors, and textures. You are told that a small, smooth, round, yellow block is called a "grop"; a large, red, square block is a "feep"; and an oblong, blue, sandpaper-covered block is a "nam." Your task is to divide all the blocks into appropriate piles, based on what you can derive from these three examples. You might try any number of ways to do this. The blocks could be grouped by size, color, shape, texture, or any combination of these. Only by repeated trial and error, with feedback from the person who knew some "right answers," would you be able to organize the pile of blocks into appropriate classes. This is like the task faced by children, except that they have to decide how to classify not just a pile of blocks, but *everything*. A child who encounters a dog for the first time and hears an adult say "doggie" while pointing to the animal has not learned the meaning of "doggie." The relevant characteristics that distinguish dogs from cats or other mammals, other brown objects, or other things with four legs have not been specified. It is precisely these characteristics used to categorize or group things and events in the environment that children must learn if they are ever to use language normally. The meanings we convey when we use language are arbitrary organizations we impose on reality. Children must learn about these organizations before they begin to talk, and children's early word use reflects how they are organizing reality. Andrew's use of the word "car" shows one attempt on the part of a child to match up words and organizations of reality.

Bowerman (1976) reports that her daughter Eva used the word "moon" first to refer to the real moon, but subsequently applied it "to such diverse referents as a half-grapefruit seen from below, flat shiny green leaves, lemon slices, mounted steer horns, a chrome dishwasher dial, hangnails, etc." No adult would ever think of lumping together such a motley collection of objects and calling them by any label more specific than "things." Yet, as Bowerman points out, all these things were shaped like the moon, whether round, semicircle, or crescent, and in addition shared one or several other attributes of the moon, "including flatness, shininess, yellowness, being seen at an angle from below, and having a broad expanse as a background" (p. 13).

Apparently, children begin their attempts to organize reality by choosing some small sets of characteristics on the basis of which they group objects and events. Nelson (1974) writes that a young child carries around a set of concepts, or organized categories, referring to aspects of the environment. These concepts arise from the child's experience. They may overlap with those referred to by adult language, but the definitions attached to the words the child uses will initially reflect the child's own concepts, and these concepts will determine whether the child's word is applied correctly or incorrectly from the adult point of view.

The question then becomes "From where do children derive the set of characteristics on which they base concepts?" Searching for answers to this question, Eve Clark (1973) reviewed several diary studies, in which parents recorded their children's early communication attempts. The diaries showed that the children's first utterances seem heavily perceptual, that is, based on sensory characteristics of objects. These organizations of sensory input, or *percepts,* might be responsible for the kind of overgeneralization of "moon" that Eva showed. Clark found that the most frequently used basis for perceptual categories is shape and that other relevant attributes of reality include sound, size, movement, texture, and taste. She found no early categories based on color. Clark argued that these perceptual categories are universal, that is, regardless of the language being acquired, there is something about children's nonlinguistic experience with the environment, and perhaps about the human sensory system itself, that causes children to organize reality around these characteristics.

Nelson (1975) also studied children's early words, but she concluded that rather than reflecting perceptual categories, the first words refer to categories based on action schemas (organizations built around movement, change, and manipulation). In her study of the first 50 words used by 18 children, Nelson noted that "the one outstanding general characteristic of the early words is their reference to objects and events that are perceived in dynamic relationships: that is, actions, sounds, transformations—in short, variations of all kinds" (p. 269). This finding—that words for active or manipulable objects are used sooner than words for static or immovable objects—has been noted by other researchers as well.

On the face of it, there appears to be disagreement about exactly what kinds of early, nonlinguistic experience lead to the meanings children express in their earliest words. Clark argues that reception of sensory input from hearing, seeing, feeling, and tasting is enough to provide the child with data to organize into categories. Nelson and others hold that active experience with the environment, movement and participation, provide the basis for early categorization. In fact, there may not really be a controversy. Bowerman (1974) argues that much of the child's perceptual organization of reality may be based on actions the child performs on objects rather than on passive observation. A child may learn about shape as much by feeling, touching, chewing, and manipulating items of various shapes as he or she does by simply seeing them. The important thing to note about both viewpoints is that they place the locus of meaning in the child's early experience with the environment, before any language has been learned. Prelinguistic children are not passively waiting for the appearance of words. They are active, developing, learning organisms, and language is a continuation of a concept development process that begins in earliest infancy.

DEVELOPMENT OF SENTENCE MEANINGS

Up to this point we have discussed only individual words and their relation to prelinguistic cognitive development. Yet when you put words together to make a sentence, you make a statement that is somehow more than the sum of its parts. The *total sentence meaning* is evaluated by speakers and listeners. For example, we would not readily accept the sentence "The paper bit the car" because such an event is unlikely in the extreme. The sentence would be regarded as odd by a listener, even though the structure is perfectly adequate. Children's development of the ability to handle meanings of word combinations as well as meanings of individual words may have its roots in early cognitive development. Complex concepts come to be expressed as elaborate sentences. How can we describe this process? Perhaps it will be useful to return to the beginning.

Before acquiring language, a child must discover that objects exist as separate entities in the environment and that they exist permanently apart from the child's own ability to see or touch them. Concepts of cause and effect, space, and time must also be acquired. Once the child can make these distinctions in reality, they can be reflected in language by distinctions between actor and action or action and acted upon in multiword utterances. The concept ordinarily precedes the expression.

To give an example of this reasoning, suppose 10-month-old Michael is pulling on the string of a pull-toy. As he pulls, the toy moves toward him. When he first learns to pull on the string, he has no idea that there is any connection between his pulling and the movement of the toy. It is only through experience with many actions and many objects that he learns the effects of his actions on objects. At some point in children's development, they must arrive at the concept that actions have *agents,* or causes, and may have corresponding *recipients,* which feel the effects of the actions. Until children have learned this about the nonlinguistic environment, it is unlikely that they will code such relations in language. After all, why should they?

The realization that children's early utterances are reflections of meanings acquired in the course of prelinguistic cognitive development has caused researchers to take a new approach to analyzing them. The previous approach, in which only the grammar of the utterance was described, has given way to a semantic approach. The first attempt at such analysis was that of Bloom (1971), who pointed out that a description of a child's sentence structure alone does not always give a full picture of what the child said. Bloom argued that structural descriptions of children's two-word sentences are inadequate because they fail to take semantics into account. For example, she noted that the sentence "Mommy sock" was said twice by a child in one day's observations. On the basis of structure, or linguistic evidence, the repeated sentences are the same. But if you look at the context, you see that in one case the child was picking up the mother's sock ("Mommy's sock," possessive) and in the other the mother was putting the child's sock on him ("Mommy is putting on my sock," descriptive). There are many more situations in which "Mommy sock" might occur. The child might pick up one of the father's socks in the presence of mother ("Mommy, here's a sock"), or might bring the mother his own sock to identify it ("Mommy, this is my sock") or to ask the mother to put it on him ("Mommy, put my sock on me"). If you take only syntax into account, all these instances of "Mommy sock" look the same. Yet attention to the semantic dimension reveals five distinct speech events.

Researchers investigating children's early utterances have identified the set of semantic relations that appear most often in children's early language. These are shown in Table 6.1. As you can see from the table, it is not really possible to look only at the words uttered by the child and tell what the child means. An utterance like "doggie chair," for example, might mean "Put the doggie in the chair" or "This is the doggie's chair" or even "The doggie is biting the chair." In spite of this apparent ambiguity, parents and other adults who interact with young children are remarkably good at figuring out what the child means. We use the context

Table 6.1   SEMANTIC RELATIONS IN CHILDREN'S EARLY UTTERANCES

Semantic Relation	Examples
Agent + action	Daddy go, baby cry
Agent + object	Throw ball, eat cookie
Agent + object	Baby toy (meaning "The baby dropped the toy.")
Action + location	Sit chair, go outside
Entity + location	Doggie chair (meaning "The dog is on the chair.")
Possessor + possession	My hat; mommy key
Entity + attribute	Water hot, bad doggie
Demonstrative + entity	That radio (meaning "That is a radio.")

Source: Adapted from R. Brown, *First Language: The Early Stages* (Cambridge, Mass.: Harvard University Press, 1973).

(if we are playing a game listing all the things doggies can bite, the utterance "doggie chair" probably means "doggie bite chair"). We also use the child's word order as a clue to meaning (while "daddy go" implies that daddy is the actor, "go daddy" probably means something like "go to daddy" or "go where daddy is"). Young children seem to catch on to English word order early, and it is one of the first aspects of language structure they employ with any consistency.

The research perspective of using word order and context to interpret children's meaning gives children maximum credit for knowing precisely what they mean in early cryptic or telegraphic utterances. Following Brown (1973), this perspective is labeled *rich interpretation.* In effect, we treat children as though they meant what we would mean. This seems to work in ordinary situations. We should remember, however, that adult categories of meaning may or may not correspond to the children's categories. While rich interpretation is an everyday occurrence among those who speak to children, it is a dangerous practice for researchers who are trying to determine children's knowledge of semantic relations. The danger is that in rich interpretation the meanings of utterances are assigned to children by adults. What could constitute objective evidence that these are, in fact, the children's meanings?

Eventually, the child does learn the structural alternatives available for expressing all these different meanings. How the child comes to associate various structures with their total meanings goes beyond the domain of semantics into the domain of syntax, the topic of the next chapter.

To summarize, it appears that children begin to use words applying to general categories, or organizations of reality, and that these categories are defined in terms of one or more perceptual features. The categories gradually become more refined through the addition or subtraction of features, until they resemble adult concepts. This implies that the child must somehow learn which perceptual features are most relevant to language as adults speak it. The process of semantic development is one of the child's comparing perceptions to the language's representations of reality and of refining the categories to conform with the adult model.

At the same time that children are learning about the concepts to which words refer, they are also learning about the relations between people, things, events, and actions in the environment. It is this set of relations that is coded in children's early word combinations.

SEMANTIC MEANING AND PRAGMATIC MEANING

We have been talking about a kind of meaning that speakers use to make perceptual and conceptual sense out of their world. We call this kind of meaning *semantic meaning.* It is concerned largely with how objects and events relate to each other in language. Semantic meanings are relationships between words and sentences and what these language units symbolize. For instance, the semantic meaning of the word "moon" consists of relationships between perceptual-conceptual attributes (shape, size, color, etc.) and the notion of "moonness." Semantic meaning relates language to concepts.

There is a different set of meanings in language called *pragmatic meanings*. Pragmatic meanings involve speaking to fill some function. For example, a child might say "moon" in order to get a pat on the head from mother or to express a desire to handle the object. Pragmatic meaning relates words to people. Morris (1946) makes this distinction between semantic and pragmatic meanings in regard to language in general, and Dore (1975) makes a similar distinction in regard to child speech.

In the earliest stages of language use, children seem to express two pragmatic meanings: asserting, or declaring, and requesting. Bates, Camaione, and Volterra (1975) observed these communicative functions even prior to speech. As we saw in Chapter 4, they labeled these functions protodeclaratives, defined as the child's use of something in the environment to gain the adult's attention, and protoimperatives, or the child's use of the adult to get something in the environment. We can see both functions in the following interaction between Kyle (aged 12 months) and his mother.

Mother is sitting in a chair at the kitchen table. Kyle, who has recently begun to walk, is making his way around the room. He comes upon a cookie which he had previously stepped on. He picks up one piece of it and takes it to his mother.

> KYLE: Uh, uh. *[Holding the piece of cookie out to his mother.]*
> MOTHER: What have you found? Oh, it's a squashed up cookie. Give it to me. *[Takes the cookie.]*
> KYLE: *[Goes back to the cookie pieces, picks up another piece, and returns to his mother.]* Ka. Mama. Uh, ka. *[Puts the cookie piece in his mother's lap.]*
> MOTHER: Oh, thank you. More cookie.

This sequence is repeated until all the pieces are picked up, and the mother is holding them. At this point Kyle is standing beside his mother looking at the pieces. He reaches for them, and his mother closes her hand around them.

> MOTHER: No, Kyle. These are all dirty. Let's throw them away.
> KYLE: *[Trying to open his mother's hand.]* Ka. Ka. Uh, ka.
> MOTHER: No, no. Let's throw these away.
> KYLE: *[Takes his mother's hand and starts to walk toward the refrigerator, trying to pull her with him.]* Mama. Uh, ka.
> MOTHER: Oh, you want another cookie, do you? Well, let's get rid of this one first.

As this episode demonstrates, Kyle is quite capable of bringing the broken cookie to his mother's attention and of asking for another cookie. He can do this even though he still does not have many recognizable words. As he develops a conventional vocabulary and begins to combine words, he will become more skilled at performing these two speech acts. It will be some time, however, before he adds to his repertoire of pragmatic meanings. Clark and Clark (1977) point out that, rather than adding new functions, children at the two-word stage are busy elaborating on the two original ones. Table 6.2 shows some examples of these elaborations.

As you can see, there seems to be an overlap between what we called semantic relations in Table 6.1 and what we call elaborated pragmatic meanings in Table 6.2. This was not set up intentionally to confuse you. In fact, children's early meanings are closely tied to what they are trying to do with language, and their limited expression of their organization of the world is slotted into these communicative intentions.

The developmental sequence in which meanings find expression through language, from "protowords" to syntax, can be viewed in the following example. Mother and child are in the kitchen. A fresh batch of oatmeal cookies is cooling on the stove. The child points and says:

1. Ga!
2. Kooko!
3. Cookie!!
4. Ga cookie!
5. Mommy cookie
6. Gimme cookie
7. May I have a cookie?

Obviously, the *form* (1 through 7) the child selects to say will differ according to the stage of development. Forms are what change as devel-

Table 6.2 ELABORATED REQUESTS AND
             ASSERTIONS

Requests	
For action	Give cookie, more milk
For information	Where daddy go?
Refusal	No more milk

Assertions	
Presence of object	That airplane, see baby
Denial of presence	No soap, all gone juice
Location of object	Daddy outside, mama work
Possession of object	My shoe
Quality of object	Good juice, nice kitty
Ongoing event	Baby sleep, house fall down

Source: Adapted from Clark and Clark, 1977.

opment of language unfolds. The major point is that utterances 1 through 7 all express similar sets of semantic-pragmatic meaning. The only thing that changes is the set of forms through which expression occurs. Let us discuss each of the stages implied by the preceding list.

1. *Preword stage.* The child may vocalize, but meanings are basically expressed nonverbally and through intonation. The most probable function of "ga!" is to get the mother's attention. The reference to the cookies (semantic meaning) is provided through pointing behavior. Pragmatic behavior appears mostly in the exclamatory urgency of the information pattern. Intonation is critical here, and it serves as a primary carrier of pragmatic meaning throughout early development (Dore, Franklin, Miller, and Ramer, 1976).

2. *Nonstandard word stage.* This term was coined by Bruner (1975b), who observes that parent and child commonly establish idiosyncratic reference systems. To the mother, "kooko" means "cookie" (semantically). To the child, "kooko" probably means something more closely related to perceptual qualities (shape, smell, location) and might also be applied to muffins, doughnuts, and baked apples. Pragmatic meaning, which is the primary thing the child has in mind, is still carried primarily by emphatic intonation. The child is not referring to an event, but is making a request. (If you don't believe that, try replying, "That's right, honey. It is a cookie.")

3. *Single-word stage.* Semantic and pragmatic meanings are carried precisely as in stage 2, but the child has now conventionalized the term ("cookie") so that anyone can understand it. It is no longer necessary to be the child's mother (and share that context) to respond meaningfully.

4. *Presyntactic stage.* The child begins to show understanding that pragmatic meanings previously carried by intonation can also be expressed by position of items. This insight is the birth of language structure. Syntax does not, of course, emerge fully developed. The first forms are nonstandard, resembling the nonstandard words of stage 2, but they work with a fairly wide variety of people. There is commonly still an emphatic intonation contour, but part of the pragmatic meaning moves to presyntax.

5. *Two-word stage.* Now the child says, "Mommy cookie!" The same semantic and pragmatic meanings are expressed, but both of them rely more on words. The pointing and intonation may persist, but they serve as redundancies. "Mommy cookie" combines two words in a way that shows that what the child has in mind is some kind of mommy-cookie synergy.

6. *Object-action stage.* The child is still limited to a two- or three-word utterance, but one of these words performs reference (semantics) and the other specifies function (pragmatics). That's an

oversimplification, but the child seems to have grasped the basic strength of the sentence—the ability to introduce a topic of conversation *and* to make a comment about it, with both items appearing primarily in the verbal channel. We suggest that this abstract insight is the most awesome aspect of how the child uses language to wrest a place of power in the world.

7. *Mature stage.* The child is able to use manners, a conventionalized question intonation, hypocrisy, reasoning, and many other sorts of speech acts to perform the intended pragmatic function.

The child does not move as a learning machine from one of these stages to the next. Rather, these are tactics the child uses again and again in tasks that vary in difficulty, until he or she develops a rich set of syntactic strategies. It's a perceptual-conceptual process in which the child makes sense out of experience. The general tactic is *giving form to two kinds of meaning,* semantic and pragmatic.

SUMMARY

Children's language is not meaningless. On the contrary, children use words and sentences to convey both semantic and pragmatic meaning. Semantic meaning reflects the relation between words and concepts of reality. Pragmatic meaning reflects the relation between words and their effects, or, perhaps more simply, between words and people. We know little about the stages in the development of pragmatic meaning. At this point we can only say that the child must learn what language can accomplish as well as what it can refer to. It may well be that the motivation for all language learning comes out of the child's increasing appreciation of words' effects on the environment.

When children speak, listeners must take into account what they mean as well as what they say. Given how little we know about semantics, this can be a difficult task.

SUGGESTED READINGS

Bruner, J. S. The ontogenesis of speech acts. *Journal of Child Language 2*, 1-20, 1975. This article may be hard reading for the beginner, but it is more than worth it. It is probably the best available discussion of where meanings come from.

Brown, R. *Words and Things.* New York: Free Press, 1958. Brown presents an easy-to-read and interesting account of what we mean by "meaning."

Carey, S. Semantic development: The state of the art. In E. Wanner and R. Gleitman (eds.). *Language Acquisition: The State of the Art.* New York: Cambridge University Press, 1982. This is an interesting, up-to-date account of the various theoretical perspectives on meaning.

Schiefelbusch, R., and L. Lloyd (eds.). *Language Perspectives: Acquisition, Retardation, and Intervention.* Baltimore: University Park Press, 1974. This book includes discussions of research based on semantic perspectives.

SUGGESTED PROJECTS

1. Find a child who is just beginning to use words (usually around 12 to 15 months old). Observe the child, and enlist the parents' help to discover (a) what the child's first words refer to and (b) examples of over- or undergeneralization.

2. Repeat the study of English kinship terms conducted by S. E. Haviland and E. V. Clark (This man's father is my father's son: A study of the acquisition of English kin terms, *Journal of Child Language 1*, 23-47, 1974), using a group of children aged 3 to 8 years. See whether you get the same results they got.

Chapter
7

Development of Syntax

*I*n Chapter 6 we discussed the origins of two kinds of meaning, semantic and pragmatic. Both of these kinds of meaning find expression in the child's early language. This chapter traces the process by which these meanings are linked to language form, or structure. It describes how the child who already knows how to make meaningful utterances begins to shape these meanings into sentence structures similar to those used by adults. Sentence structure, or *syntax,* has gained more recent attention from researchers than any other aspect of communication development.

ONE-WORD UTTERANCES

Researchers agree that children go through a stage during which most of their meaningful utterances are one word long. These one-word utterances do not always refer to the same kinds of concepts that adults think about. Also, these utterances do not always sound just like adult words. Outsiders may not believe that the child in this stage is "really" talking. But an adult who knows the child and shares background experience with the child knows that it really is speech.

The adult's decision that the child is making sense comes out of a mix of language and situational factors. The child uses some approximations of adult words—"kooka" for "cookie" or "icky" to describe a dirty diaper—in a situation making such speech appropriate. For instance, if a child says "kooka" while being given a cookie, and then later says "kooka" while pointing to the box in which the cookies are kept, the adult infers that the child has decided to call the object "cookie" by an approximation of the adult word. It is unlikely that the child has any-thing this linguistically precise in mind. The child probably knows little about words or objects. (In fact, only from adults' assuming that things go with words does the word-thing association begin to make sense.) Rather, the child is performing a response that is likely to accomplish something—in this case the reward is what grown-ups like to call a cookie. The ability to accomplish something through language is what matters at this point. The child calls the object "cookie" to get it.

So the child gestures and says "kooka." The adult thinks the child wants a cookie. The adult probably gets a cookie and hands it to the child saying "Yes, here's a cookie for you" or "OK, would you like a cookie?" Conventional wisdom has it that the adult is teaching language to the child by pairing this mature utterance with the child's immature one and a reward (the cookie). That's plausible, but there's little research evidence supporting this folk belief.

Next, the child begins to use "kooka" in multiple situations, because the utterance got a response in one situation. The word "kooka" might be used in conjunction with the appearance of a piece of cake, a peanut butter sandwich, a growling in the tummy, or lids from baby food jars. Adults often misunderstand this situation. The usual inference is that the child has made a mistake by thinking that all these objects are cook-ies. Adults chuckle and feel superior, then proceed to "educate" the child about reality and how just a few things are cookies. Hence the adult will by reflex and habit correct the child by saying "No, dear, not cookie. This is cake" or "No, those look like cookies, but they're not for eating. Those are jar lids. See, we put them on the jars like this." But regardless of the adult's intentions, what the child learns from any single interaction such as this depends on how much the child can understand, attend to, or even hear. The point is that adult responses to child utter-ances are sometimes based on some questionable assumptions.

What is the nature of these adult assumptions? Some grown-ups (and some researchers) assume that the child who says only single words is "really" saying little sentences. For instance, the child who points to the cookie box and says "kooka" is not simply labeling reality, but asking for a cookie. Researchers call these utterances *holophrases,* or little sen-tences, because they seem to indicate that if only the child knew enough about language or had a longer memory span, he or she would not say "kooka," but "I want a cookie." For some time a controversy has raged about how much children at the one-word stage really know about syn-tax. Believers in the holophrase theory argue that a child cannot use a one-word utterance to ask for a cookie without knowing something about the rules for combining words to make sentences. Others counter that you cannot talk about sentence structures in single words; therefore it is silly to argue that the child is saying sentences.

The holophrase dispute misses a major point. The child is clearly not saying differentiated sentences, but is, however, expressing differentiated semantic and pragmatic meanings, that is, the child knows how to use words to refer to concepts and, more importantly, knows how to use language to get things done. The adult who expands a child's utterances need not assume that the child knows something about grammar. Rather, the adult must assume that the child *means* something, has some intention. It is this intention (e.g., the request to receive a cookie) to which the adult responds.

The information provided to the child in these adult responses is quite complex: (1) It is information for the child about category boundaries ("That's not cookie. That's cake."). (2) It shows the child how to make pragmatic meaning linguistically explicit (How many times must a child hear "want X" in an adult expansion of the child utterance of pointing + X before figuring out the relevant two-word utterance?). (3) The adult's expansion does give the child a well-formed grammatical utterance (which may or may not be relevant to the child at this stage of development).

The holophrase argument over what the child at the one-word utterance stage knows about syntax masks a more revealing set of questions about what the child at this stage knows about the organization of reality and the use of language forms for communicating with other people. In fact, it appears that development of syntax begins rather later in childhood than we used to suppose. It now seems, for instance, that even two-word and some longer utterances represent stringing together of concepts more than sentence structures. To explain what we mean by this, we must review some research findings on the "syntax" of early multiword utterances.

EARLY MULTIWORD UTTERANCES

Researchers investigating children's early speech have typically asked, "What knowledge of sentence structure does a child's utterance show?" The usual answer to this question has been based on word order. Children do not simply combine words in groups, as the chimpanzees Washoe and Sarah seemed to. Rather, children's speech shows a definite preference for some word orders. Braine (1963) suggested that children at the two-word stage already use a simplified grammar that helps them choose certain word orders over others. Braine called this simple grammar a *pivot grammar* because it was a grammar with just two classes. One class was basically nouns and the other class (called the pivot class) was a mixed bag of everything else. These pivot words received their name from the observation that they rarely appear alone, but only in combination with nouns.

We won't describe pivot grammar in detail because the concept has been largely discredited. We mention it to note that researchers have assumed that children start with a simple grammar and develop more and more information about syntax until their grammar knowledge represents the mature language. By the time children are 4 years old, their notion of syntax is pretty advanced. To explain this part of development, researchers have increasingly relied on a theory called *generative transformational grammar.* We will discuss transformational grammar later in the chapter. For now, we note that transformational grammar assumes people use some rather abstract notions of sentence structure that are not closely tied to meaning—either semantic or pragmatic.

In short, researchers between 1965 and 1970 rarely asked questions about how children connect sentence structures to meanings. The focus of investigation was on the sentence structures themselves. This kind of thinking led to some elegant but essentially empty formal descriptions of the syntax of early speech. The descriptions are empty in the sense that you have to assume that children acquire some fantastic and abstract concepts by some divine or evolutionary miracle. The research didn't help to understand what processes were going on as children encountered communication situations.

In the early 1970s the focus of research began to change and take into account the way children hook words to meanings. In his magnificent book *A First Language* (1973), Roger Brown reports how he rechecked data from a decade of research describing what children were doing when they combined words. Were children primarily showing knowledge of sentence structure or primarily combining signs with meanings? As we mentioned in the previous chapter, Brown concluded that in the early stages of development children mainly show awareness of a small set of *semantic relations,* that is, they use language to reflect what they have learned about how objects, events, and people combine to make meanings. In other words, early speech shows primarily that children understand some things about semantic and pragmatic meanings. Early speech, even two- and three-word utterances, does not show that children have many definite ideas about syntax.

According to Brown's formulation, what children have learned when they begin to combine words is not grammatical concepts like subject and predicate, but *semantic roles.* From their experience with reality, they learn about "agents," people who perform actions or who make things happen, and about "patients," people or objects that receive action, change state, or move. Brown is not saying that children have labels like "agent" and "patient," but only that early word combinations reflect the ability to categorize the world in these terms.

This kind of linguistic analysis is called *case grammar.* Different researchers use different terminology, but a case grammar approach usually includes the following semantic roles. In the sentence "The carpenter hit the nail with a hammer," there are three noun phrases: the carpenter, the nail, and the hammer. Each noun phrase has a distinct relationship to the verb. The carpenter is the *agent,* that which causes the verb to happen. The nail is the *patient,* that which receives the force of the verb. The hammer is the *instrument,* that which is used by the agent to do the verb. Table 7.1 presents Brown's list of the semantic roles played by noun phrases in children's simple sentences. According to Brown's analysis of data gathered from children in the first stage of word combination, these are the kinds of semantic roles children seem to express.

One advantage of this analysis is that it takes into account something children make extensive use of at this stage of development: the nonlinguistic context. Without taking into account nonlinguistic context, it is impossible to say whether an utterance like "more juice" means that the child has drunk all the juice and wants more or whether mother has given the child one glass of juice and poured another for herself, prompting a comment from the child that additional juice has appeared. The disadvantage of this kind of analysis is, of course, that it involves much subjective interpretation on the part of the adult about what the child means. There is much to be said for an approach that does not necessitate assuming that a child knows adult syntactic categories such as "subject" or "direct object." However, as we pointed out in Chapter 6, there is some danger in substituting the assumption that a child in the early stages of making multiword utterances is able to use semantic categories consistent with adult interpretations.

A further question that must be addressed is "If children do not use

Table 7.1   CASE GRAMMAR CATEGORIES

Semantic Role	Definition	Example
Agent	Actor—person or object that performs an action	*The man* spoke. *The cold* pierced the thin jacket.
Patient	Receiver of some action or state	Tom hit *Ed*. *Harry* is old.
Experiencer	Someone having an inner or mental experience.	*Ed* saw the tree. *Bonnie* missed her friend.
Beneficiary	Someone gaining from an act, even though not its primary patient Possessor	Tom bought *Mary* a car. *Mary's* car.
Instrument	Object used by agent to perform an action	Tom hit the tree with *an ax*. *The letter* from Ed ended a period of waiting.
Location	Place of an action or process	He sat *behind his desk*. I am going *home*.
Complement	Object, event, or process that completes concept introduced by verb	I wrote *a letter*. Let's go *dancing*.

Source: Adapted from R. Brown, *A First Language: The Early Stages* (Cambridge, Mass.: Harvard University Press, 1973).

syntactic categories from the beginning, at what stage does it seem reasonable to posit the existence of such categories in later language behavior?" We have noted that children begin with perceptual categories, then move to primitive modes of expression that allow messages about both semantic and pragmatic meaning. About the time children begin to combine pairs of words (about 18 months), they begin to change from a primarily meaning-centered expression system to a primarily grammatical expression system. Another way to say this is that children begin to learn syntax.

Why do children learn syntax? This question is troublesome for two reasons. First, there seems to be no "reason" for children to use syntax, since they have been communicating quite effectively using a meaning-centered speech act system. Second, children learn syntax so incredibly fast that no current theory of learning comes close to explaining how it could possibly happen.

These difficulties have led linguists for the last decade to the assumption that the child does *not* learn syntax; rather, an innate set of language categories somehow springs forth at the time the child begins to use sentences. That notion may be true. But there are problems with this position, as we have mentioned elsewhere. Why, then, does syntax appear at all? The answer may be that syntax provides an efficient explanatory system for making sense out of perceptual-conceptual events. In other words, children start talking in sentences because doing so enables them increasingly to differentiate and make sense out of what they are perceiving and thinking about.

That's a pretty abstract formulation. Let's try a more concrete track. Recall our comments in Chapters 2 and 4 about the human perception system. Perception is categorical. Perception in humans works to isolate a figure against a background. The figure and the background make sense only in terms of each other. The beauty of syntax is that it provides an elegant system for presenting information about both figures and backgrounds. That structuring is called *predication.*

One universal thing about sentences is that they have subjects and predicates. The subject is what the sentence is about; the predicate (verb phrase) is what happens to the subject. The subject is background; the predicate is figure. The subject is the topic of conversation. It is often stated first and, after being stated, can be taken for granted. The predicate provides activity against the backdrop. For instance, in the sentence "John ran home," the subject (John) gives the background by telling what (in this case who) the sentence is about. The predicate gives the foreground by specifying what happened.

To summarize, children begin communication development by paying attention to and organizing the conceptual features of the world around them (developing semantic meanings) and by trying with increasing success to make things happen in that world (developing pragmatic meanings). The syntax of human language is a set of devices for focusing attention and giving power to that attention. Bruner (1975b, p. 4) discusses the attention-predication process this way:

> Attention is a feature-extracting routine in which there is a steady movement between selected features and wholes; a process of positing wholes (topics) to which parts or features or properties may be related from which new wholes may be constructed.
>
> The predication rules of natural language are surely a well-adapted vehicle for expressing the results of such attentional processing: topic-comment and subject-predicate structure permits an easy passage from feature to its context and back, while topicalization provides a ready means for regrouping new sets of features into hypothesized wholes to be used as topics on which to comment.

As we implied in discussing perception and conceptualization, the child constantly searches for more efficient ways to organize and pattern reality. Syntax organizes language to show explicitly what the child has been doing mentally. The child learns grammar so fast because syntax happens to fit neatly with the basic processes of perception and to make expressions possible that could not have even been contemplated before. This learning occurs not because the child has innate syntactic categories, but because syntax fits so beautifully into the attentional-perceptual-conceptual process that the child has used since birth to assimilate and accommodate to the environment. Language development continues processes begun in early infancy.

The question of when knowledge of syntax begins to be displayed in children's speech is difficult to answer. At some point in development the child clearly knows some rules governing word combinations that provide more than one way to say a given meaning. An utterance such as "Daddy go" and another such as "Daddy is going to work" may arise from the same organization of reality. The core meaning is the same, but the second utterance is generated by some set of rules beyond those used to generate the first. A child who says the second sentence is able to use the language code in a different way from the child who says the first sentence. This difference is accounted for by a knowledge of syntax. This knowledge, or at least the adult form of it, is described in the next section of this chapter.

ADULT SYNTAX

Each of us knows a great deal about sentence structure. You may protest, "I don't know a thing about sentence structure. I can't even diagram complex sentences!" Yet you demonstrate your knowledge of syntax continually. To show yourself how much you know, think about which of these sentences looks wrong to you:

1. The child aggravates her mother.
2. The aggravates child her mother.

Sentence 2 is obviously the wrong one. Because the words are out of order, it makes little sense. You noticed this right away, even though you may not be able to explain why. This is because you have *grammatical intuition,* which means that you know about the structure of sentences *even though you do not know what you know about it.* We can tell that you know the rules of syntax because you obey them every time you speak, you never say sentences such as 2, and you know such sentences are not grammatical in structure. Your grammatical intuition is so trustworthy that linguists' most common analysis procedure is to ask nonlinguists (you) to evaluate intuitively the structures of sentences. For example, you might be asked what you notice about these two sentences.

3. Americans love anarchy.
4. Anarchy is loved by Americans.

You probably notice two things. First, the two sentences say the same thing. Second, they are different in structure. If we gave you the sentence

5. Walruses swallow ice.

which has the same structure as 3, "Americans love anarchy," and asked you to produce the structural equivalent of 4, you would have little trouble supplying the answer:

6. Ice is swallowed by walruses.

which means that you understand intuitively the structural relationships between these sentences. You have that understanding even though you may never have heard of a *passive transformation,* which is the linguistic name for the operation you just performed.

The body of intuitive knowledge about grammar that each of us possesses is called *linguistic competence.* All speakers possess competence in their language, although they may not be able (or willing) to state the content of that competence explicitly or to demonstrate their competence. Suppose we asked you which of sentences 1 and 2 was wrong and you failed to answer. We could not say you did not know that part of grammar; we could only say you did not answer the question. Maybe your competence is deficient, but maybe you just did not answer for some other reason: You are angry at us for being boring writers, you forgot the question, you'd feel weird answering a question asked in a book. All these are problems of *linguistic performance.* The problem is not a lack of knowledge on your part, but simply the failure to show what you know.

This is an important issue in studying children, who can be very uncooperative about demonstrating their competence. In one study an experimenter asked a 2-year-old, "Which is right, 'two shoes' or 'two shoe'?" The child responded enthusiastically, "Pop goes the weasel!" (Brown and Bellugi, 1964). Every child language researcher has lived through hundreds of similarly exasperating moments. Can you say that the 2-year-old does not know correct plural form? Obviously not. Much of child language research consists of trying to trick children into showing what they know.

Which leads us to one of the central questions of syntax: What is it that we know when we know the structure of a sentence? Every sentence actually has two levels of structure, or syntax. The sentence you see or hear going from one word to the next is the *surface structure.* But sentences also have an underlying *deep structure.* When people (child or adult) know the structure of a sentence, they understand both levels.

To demonstrate that sentences have two levels of structure, examine these:

1. The elf swung the hammer.
2. The hammer was swung by the elf.

These two sentences look different (the words and word order are different)—they have different surface structures. Yet they also mean the same thing (both refer to the same organism performing the same action)—they have the same deep structure. Two sentences that are different from one another and still are the same must have two levels of structure.

Now examine this well-known sentence:

The shooting of the hunters was terrible.

Any particular sentence can have only one surface structure, but this sentence has at least two plausible meanings: (1) hunters were shooting inaccurately, (2) hunters were being shot (to the dismay of onlookers). Each of these meanings corresponds to a different underlying structure, so in this case there are two deep structures and one surface structure. In the case of the elf sentences there are two surface structures and one deep structure.

Any theoretical account of children's communication development must explain how they manage to acquire understanding of sentence syntax on both deep and surface structure levels. This is a problem because we do not know precisely what deep structure is like. We do know that one way to describe the structure of any single sentence is to divide it into its constituent parts—structure is by definition the relationship between parts.

If we asked you what would be the most natural way to divide this sentence:

The linguist described a sentence.

into two parts, you would probably divide it as follows:

The linguist   described a sentence.

These two parts are the main structural constituents of the sentence. The first part is a noun phrase (subject) and the second part is a verb phrase (predicate). To analyze the sentence further, we might divide the verb phrase:

described   a sentence

We could continue such subdividing until we ran out of words. You could intuitively tell where to divide each part of the sentence. These dividing places indicate aspects of its syntax.

This kind of analysis helps us to understand the structure of this one sentence. But to understand what the child is learning about sentence structure in general, we need to be able to describe much more than one sentence. We need to describe the entire set of possibilities in the language. We can attempt this more powerful description by making educated guesses (hypotheses) about the structures used in English sentences. Such hypotheses are the rules of syntax, or *phrase structure rules.*

It must be emphasized that these are not prescriptive rules. Unlike highway speed limits or rules for agreement of verb tense that you learned in elementary school English, linguistic rules do not tell us what we should do. Rather, like the "rule" that you rarely talk on elevators and that you face the person you are speaking to, they describe what is. Linguistic rules are not rules because authorities say they are, but because they provide an accurate description of the actual structures in human sentences.

Phrase structure rules divide sentences or phrases into two parts, as we did above. But phrase structure rules are more abstract. For example, instead of dividing the sentence as we did, we could write the following rule:

(a) SENTENCE → NOUN PHRASE + VERB PHRASE

The arrow → is much like an equals sign. It shows that the item on the left (sentence) can be rewritten as the two items on the right. In the case of our sample sentence, the noun phrase is "the linguist" and the verb phrase is "described a sentence."

We can continue to divide this sample sentence as we did before, using this rule:

(b) VERB PHRASE   →   VERB   +   NOUN PHRASE
                                (described)   (a sentence)

The two groups of words still to be analyzed in the sentence ("the linguist" and "a sentence") are both noun phrases identical in structure. We can describe these phrases as follows:

(c) NOUN PHRASE   →   ARTICLE   +   NOUN
                                (the, a)   (linguist, sentence)

At this point we have provided a set of rules that describes not only this sentence, but also many others of the same structure. For example, these same three rules apply to "The boy hit the ball," "The walrus suffered a stroke," and "A giraffe is an animal." By adding just a few more rules to this set, we could describe many of the most common sentences spoken in the English language.

We have gone through this exercise to illustrate that a small number of rules form the basis of what we know about syntax. To understand sentence structure, children have to know these rules. How children develop knowledge of the syntax rules is the subject of the rest of this chapter.

Before we get to that, however, we need to add one qualification. If we are describing sentences such as:

The elf swung the hammer.
The hammer was swung by the elf.

we want our description (that is, our rule to apply to any sentences of this form) to reflect both levels of structure, the deep structural similarity between the two sentences and also the information that either of the sentences can be converted into the other. Linguists accomplish this description with a second kind of rule, called a transformation.

The differences between the sentences are that the subject and object ("elf" and "hammer") have switched places with each other and the words "was" and "by" surround the verb ("swung"). All these operations can be shown in one rule, called a *passive transformation,* which can be condensed to look like this:

noun #1 + verb + noun #2 → noun #2 + are +
verb + by + noun #1

This may look complex when you first see it written in this form, but you did the operations easily earlier when we asked you to change the structure of the sentence "Walruses swallow ice."

Here is another example of how a transformation works. Deep structures are like a stack of propositions that express the sentence meanings. The deep structure of the phrase:

the big red dirty truck

contains these propositions:

1. The truck is big.
2. The truck is red.
3. The truck is dirty.

It is cumbersome to say all that. Instead, we use an *adjective transformation,* which deletes all the words that would have to be repeated and places the adjective in front of the noun it modifies.

There are many kinds of transformations. Most sentences employ several of them. They greatly aid the economy of spoken language.

Transformations are also the key to understanding the relationships between affirmative sentences ("I like you"), negative sentences ("I do not like you"), and questions ("Do I like you?"). Because asking questions and saying "no" are both important to children, how they learn these transformations is important.

To summarize, we can describe the structure of the English language using phrase structure rules and transformations. We can use these same rules to describe what children are learning when they learn syntax. We are now sufficiently armed with terms relating to a knowledge of syntax to face that problem—which is, after all, the purpose of this chapter.

CHILD SYNTAX

When children start to use syntax to generate or govern the structure of their utterances, they are not working with the full adult system. Their knowledge of syntax develops through identifiable stages. Brown (1973) has described these as follows.

Stage I. Semantic roles and grammatical relations. This is the stage during which the child begins to make overt his conceptualizations of reality. The early multiword utterances that appear in this stage are probably governed more by semantic than by syntactic rule systems, as we discussed earlier in this chapter.

Stage II. Grammatical morphemes and the modulation of meanings. During stage II the child begins to use word endings, such as those that signify the tense of verbs or plurality of nouns. Such function words as articles and prepositions also begin to appear. The order of acquisition of 14 grammatical morphemes identified by Brown is presented in Table 7.2. It is important to remember that the child only begins to use the forms at stage II. Their full acquisition may not be noted until well past this stage. The order of acquisition is probably controlled by a combination of semantic and syntactic complexity. The most astonishing aspect of the study of these 14 child constructions is that they generally appear in approximately the same sequence. This does not mean that a particular child should acquire a given morpheme by a specific age, but simply that most children will learn to use one grammatical morpheme, say present progressives, long before another, say contractible copulas.

Much of what we know about how children learn these language fragments is derived from analysis of mistakes they make in their speech. Mistakes are usually thought of as revealing what someone doesn't know, but let us show you how they can be used to learn what someone does know. When a child first learns to label body parts, the words "teeth" and "feet" may appear. Later parents may be surprised to hear the child saying "feets" or "tooths." What happened to the correct plural

Table 7.2   ORDER OF ACQUISITION OF 14 MORPHEMES

Grammatical Morphene	Example
1. Present progressive—"ing" ending on main verb. Children use this first without auxiliary verb	I playing.
2–3. Prepositions—"in," "on". These are the only prepositions used frequently by most children in early speech.	
4. Plural, regular and irregular forms	
5. Past irregular	got, went, came, fell, broke, sat.
6. Possessive—generally appears as " 's" endings	
7. Uncontractible copula—uncontracted form of "to be" verb used to connect subject and object.	What is this? I be bad.
8. Articles—"a," "the," appearing regularly before common nouns.	
9. Past regular—"d" endings on verbs	moved, pushed.
10. Third person regular—"s" endings on third person verbs	moves, pushes, thinks.
11. Third person irregular	is, has, does.
12. Uncontractible auxiliary verbs.	He is going home.
13. Contractible copula—contracted forms of "to be"	What's this? I'm bad.
14. Contractible auxiliary verbs	He's going home.

Source: Adapted from R. Brown, *A First Language: The Early Stages* (Cambridge, Mass.: Harvard University Press, 1973).

forms the child seemed to learn earlier? What happened was that the child learned a rule for making plurals. At first the child probably did not realize that "feet" was a plural for "foot." "Feet" was a word to refer to things you put your shoes on. "Foot" might have been a measure of size or a singular form for "feet," or it might not yet have been a word in the child's vocabulary. Later the child becomes aware of a formula for making plurals and generalizes this formula to new cases. The results: foots, feets, tooths, teeths, and the like. These "mistakes" are clues that the child is learning rules, not just imitating adult talk. The child may have heard only the word "shoe" before saying "shoes," and chances are that the child never has heard the word "feets" before saying it.

Stage III. Modalities of the simple sentence. In stage III the child begins to use the grammatical transformations described earlier in this chapter. Several kinds of questions, imperatives, and negatives all appear. There are several substages within this development.

Because mature sentence structure is made up of phrase structures plus transformations, it is theoretically appealing to say that phrase structures unfold early and transformations develop starting at stage III. There is some evidence to support this view. When transformations do develop, they unfold in a rather regular, rule-governed manner, much like the unfolding of some earlier structures. The transformations that have been most carefully studied are questions and negation. Both develop through three steps (Klima and Bellugi, 1966). In the first step the function is performed and the meaning gets across, but the structure is rudimentary. Questions are accomplished by rising intonation at the end of a sentence:

> Doggie gone?
> Taste it?

Negation is accomplished by simply putting the word "no" in front of the declarative sentence.

> No night night.
> No go outside.

During the second step children begin to put some of the verbal machinery into place, but they make many quaint "mistakes" in the use of pronouns and auxiliary verbs.

> Why me go?
> Who milk is dat?
> Do like grapefruit?
> That not red.
> I no want envelope.

In the third step most of the necessary auxiliary verbs and pronouns are present in adult form, although they sometimes disagree in number and appear out of adult order.

> Who took them all down?
> Did you drink your coffee?
> How can he be a doctor?
> I am not a doctor.
> This is not ice cream.
> You don't want some supper.

Surprisingly, all children who have been studied mastered these steps in the same order. This suggests that children must have some universal learning strategies that they bring to bear on mastering syntax. When we examine some of these learning strategies closely, we begin to see some of their linguistic "mistakes" in a new light.

Stage IV. Embedding of one sentence within another. Stage IV involves highly complex syntax. The child begins to use relative clauses ("The man *who came to sing* was funny"), embedded questions (*Whoever gets touched first* is the loser."), and similar constructions. It is a stage of development that has received relatively little attention in research, although Naremore and Dever (1975) point out that the use of such complex constructions may distinguish the language of normal children from that of mentally retarded children. The normal child's use of these constructions may begin at an early age, but, as with so many other aspects of language development, full control may not be apparent until the child is 10 or 11 years old.

Stage V. Coordination of simple sentences and propositional relations. During this stage the child who earlier combined sentences with "and" or "then" ("I hit him and he cried," "You have toast, then I have toast") learns to use more complex kinds of conjoining. Conjunctions such as "because," "so," and "but" are used to signal subordinate relations, and redundant sentence units may be deleted. The earlier sentence forms may be reconstructed to "He cried because I hit him" and "After you have toast, I'll have some." Again, this kind of language use is indicative of the presence of complex syntactic rules, and it is not fully developed until adolescence, although its beginnings can be seen in 3-year-olds.

OVERGENERALIZATION

In discussing stage II, we gave an example of overgeneralization errors in learning plurals. Such events are common throughout all stages and areas of syntax development. For example, one of Brian's first words was "bow-wow," referring to four-legged barking creatures. Shortly after he began to use this word, he started applying it to all four-legged furry creatures: horses, cats, everything. It was as if he had just discovered the class "four-legged creatures" and decided to call it "bow-wow." Adult response to his generalization was, of course, mixed, ranging from "That's right, that's a "bow-wow," to "No, that's a cow." Through this feedback process, Brian was forced to differentiate among varieties of animals, only one of which was "bow-wow." After three months of interesting variations on this theme, Brian could successfully name several classes of animals.

Brian's problem was that he had a good idea, but he overgeneralized its application. An overgeneralization sequence much like this one occurs in many aspects of language development and explains many child errors in speaking. Children use "strong verbs" (frequently occurring irregular verbs) correctly when they first learn to talk. But later, after they learn regular verbs, they overgeneralize the rules of past tense (for example, from the regular to irregular verbs, "I runned").

Slobin (1966) observed similar overgeneralization sequences in the language-learning strategies of Russian children:

> Overregularizations are rampant in the child's learning of Russian morphology. . . . For example, not only must the child learn an instrumental case ending for each masculine, feminine and neuter singular and plural noun and adjective, but within each of these subcategories there are several different phonologically conditioned suffixes. The child's solution is to seize upon one suffix at first—probably the most frequent and/or most clearly marked

acoustically—and use it for every instance of that particular grammatical category. (pp. 137-138)

Slobin uses the term *inflectional imperialism* to refer to this tendency for one affix to drive others temporarily out of usage. What is really happening is simple. The child formulates a rule, finds cases in which it works well, and immediately generalizes its use to many cases, in some of which it is inappropriate. This process is much like what social scientists do in the "implications" section of a research report. In overgeneralizing rules of grammar, the child is in error only in the same sense that 30-year-old journal articles sometimes seem naive. Still, modern theories spring directly from the insights of 30 years ago, and adult language springs from the overgeneralized hypotheses of children.

Overgeneralization, as discussed here, is the flip side of differentiation. It is only through rule-inducting overgeneralization that the child can produce grammatical categories sufficiently broad or inclusive enough to divide. Each differentiation creates new categories to be overgeneralized. Each of these concepts is meaningful only in terms of the other—like yin and yang, East and West. The cycle of overgeneralization-differentiation is natural and self-perpetuating. In development of grammar, each repetition of the cycle generates information that is more specific, detailed, reality-centered, and useful.

PROPOSITIONAL COMPLEXITY

Another way of viewing the increasing complexity of the child's language is to reconsider meaning. Not only is the child increasing the length and syntactic complexity of utterances; the semantic complexity is also increasing. In part, the syntactic complexity is made necessary by the increasing semantic complexity. Another way of saying this is that as the child becomes more mature as a language user, more and more concepts get crammed into each individual sentence. The earliest utterances by children are simple expressions of a single idea: "daddy go," "want juice." By the age of 4, however, children's language has changed a great deal, and we get utterances like "You can't have that balloon, because it's mine." We have talked about this increasing complexity in terms of syntax, but we can also talk about it in terms of meaning.

To do this, we need to think of sentences as "idea units" or *propositions*. Every sentence expresses at least one idea or proposition, consisting of a *predicate* and its associated *arguments*. A predicate can be thought of as the core of the proposition, an assertion about a state, action, or change of state. The argument of a predicate is the entity about which we are making the assertion. In the sentence "Susan sings," the predicate is the action word "sings." The singing is attributed to "Susan," which is the argument. In "Mother is tired," the predicate is the assertion of a state, "is tired." The argument of this predicate is "mother." *Every proposition has one predicate and one or more arguments associated with that predicate.* Our goal in identifying propositions is to determine how many idea units are contained in a sentence. Consider the following examples.

1. The money *is in* the box.
2. John *gave* the ring to Alice.
3. She *sang loudly.*
4. We *bought* a car *yesterday.*
5. *Wash your* face *before* you *go.*

In each example the predicates appear in italics. Since one predicate corresponds to one proposition or idea unit, we can say that sentences 1 and 2 each contain one proposition, sentences 3 and 4 each contain two propositions, and sentence 5 contains four propositions. How did we arrive at this analysis?

1. In this sentence the assertion has to do with a location (a state of being located). The predicate establishes the location, "is in," and the arguments tell what is located (the money) and what it is in (the box).
2. The verb *to give* is an interesting predicate because it is an assertion about three entities, that is, it can take three arguments: someone does the giving, something is given, and it is given to someone.
3. The basic idea unit in this sentence is expressed by the simple sentence "She sang." The second idea is "The singing was loud." Two assertions are being made, one of which is expressed by the action word "sang" and the other by the adverb "loudly," which captures the state of being loud.
4. The basic assertion in this sentence is captured by the verb "bought." The adverb "yesterday" tells us something about the buying; it asserts "The buying was yesterday."
5. This sentence is semantically quite complex. It is made up of four idea units. It packs all these simple sentences into one complex sentence:

   You *wash* face.
   The face is *yours.*
   You *go.*
   Washing is *before* going.

If you are beginning to get the idea that predicates are usually verbs, adverbs, adjectives, and possessives, you are right. Arguments are usually nouns and pronouns. Propositions correspond to single, simple ideas. Our language would sound quite unusual if we, as adults, went around uttering sentences consisting of one proposition each. It is a mark of our language maturity that we are able to construct multiproposition utterances. We can't do this, however, without a knowledge of the syntactic rules for combining clauses. Children who are just beginning to combine words usually speak in single-proposition utterances because they can deal cognitively with only one idea at a time, and because they don't know enough syntax to handle more than one idea per utterance. The syntactic rules necessary for constructing multiproposition utterances are learned in Brown's stages IV and V.

LATER SYNTAX DEVELOPMENT

By age 4 or 5 at the latest, the child has acquired most of the basic principles of syntax. Some researchers (C. Chomsky, 1969; Kessel, 1969) have demonstrated, however, that the child does not master some syntactic rules until as late as age 10 or 12. Syntax acquisition in later years is less rapid and dramatic than in early stages of development. Finishing the job of acquiring the grammar seems to be more like learning to read or to multiply than like early syntactic development. It appears to be more a process of individual learning. (This difference is discussed further in Chapter 9.)

From our speculations about overgeneralization learning strategies, we could predict the principles of syntax that are learned late. They are not rules of far-reaching application, but rather specific *exceptions* to such rules, which are important in only a few special instances. For example, sentences using the word *promise*

Bozo promises Donald to do a somersault.

are exceptional in syntax. Such sentences are an exception to a general rule called the *minimal distance principle,* which can be illustrated by this sentence:

Bozo tells Donald to do a somersault.

In this sentence the subject of the second verb ("do") is the noun closest to it ("Donald"); Donald is going to do the somersault. In the *promise* sentence it is Bozo who is going to tumble. Because the *promise* sentence is exceptional, children learn how to handle it later than the *tell*

COMPREHENSION AND PRODUCTION

There are basically two ways to find out what children know about grammar. You can tell them to do something, and if they do it, you know they understand what you said. They have demonstrated comprehension of language. Another way is to use production tasks, that is, to try to get children to use language spontaneously to show what they know. Both techniques are widely used, and data resulting from both techniques have been lumped together in this chapter. For instance, most data on pivot structures in development come from sentences children said spontaneously. The data on late development are mostly based on comprehension.

This distinction deserves mention because if you test the same children for both comprehension and production, they probably will understand more than they can say, just as when we read we understand words that we never say ourselves. This fact often makes it difficult to form conclusions about when specific rules are mastered. Additional research may correct this problem.

SUMMARY

Linguists distinguish between competence (abilities underlying language behavior) and performance (the actual observable act of speaking). The syntax of a language has two levels—surface structure and deep structure. The syntax of sentences is best described by rules. Phrase structure rules describe deep structure, and transformational rules describe the operations performed on deep structures to obtain surface structures.

Children begin speaking by uttering single words. Calling these words holophrases indicates the supposition that these words are implicitly sentences. The word and contextual cues add up to a full-sentence meaning. The most interesting information in one-word utterances is more about child meanings (concepts and organization of reality) than about sentences (knowledge of grammar).

With the start of multiword utterances development of syntax unfolds rapidly. Some theorists argue that such rapid development is possible only because children possess grammatical structures as part of their biological makeup. It is probably more accurate to say that human perceptual-conceptual processing is extremely well suited to developing a communication system that uses predication structures to indicate background and foreground information within each message. Syntax unfolds in children as a natural consequence of their perceptual-conceptual abilities.

Several key points about children's syntax development are:

1. Children's earliest word combinations are probably a reflection of their semantic structures rather than an indication that they know much about syntax.
2. The first indications of grammatical knowledge can be seen when children begin to apply morphological endings to words. The kinds of mistakes children make in this process indicate that they are learning to apply grammatical rules.
3. Later stages of language development reflect the child's increasing competence with syntax. When the child starts to manipulate

sentence forms by using transformations, embeddings, and combinations to contract multipropositional utterances, syntactic knowledge is apparent, and the child's movement toward adult syntax can be traced.

SUGGESTED READINGS

Brown, R. *A First Language.* Cambridge, Mass.: Harvard University Press, 1973. This book is the definitive statement on acquisition of language structure. It is written in an engaging style by the leading researcher in the area.

Chomsky, N. *Language and Mind.* New York: Harcourt Brace Jovanovich, 1968. This book, a printed version of three lectures on the history of linguistics, is Chomsky's most readable introduction to his theory of syntax.

de Villiers, Peter A. & Jill K. *Early Language.* Cambridge, Mass.: Harvard University Press, 1979. A brief and interesting account of children's development of language. It is easy to read and filled with relevant examples.

SUGGESTED PROJECTS

1. Choose an experimental study investigating the development of syntax in children and repeat it, using children the same age as those used in the original study. See if you get the same results. Two good possibilities for replication are J. Berko, The child's learning of English morphology, *Word 14,* 150-177, 1958, and J. G. de Villiers, H. Tager-Flusberg, K. Hakuta, and M. Cohen, Children's comprehension of relative clauses, *Journal of Psycholinguistic Research 8,* 499-518, 1979.

2. Tape record naturalistic interactions involving a 3-year-old and her or his parent and a 5-year-old and her or his parent. Transcribe the tapes, and calculate the mean length of utterance of the two children. Rules for doing this can be found in R. Brown. *A First Language* (Cambridge, Mass.: Harvard University Press, 1973), p. 54.

Chapter
8

Development of Pragmatics

"Not grammar, but the act of speech is the core and starting point of description of the place of language in human life."

W ith these words anthropologist Dell Hymes (1970) asks us to consider how we *use* language, quite apart from the structure or content of the language system itself. The last three chapters have described the development of the language system. This chapter describes the development of patterns of use, that is, the development of pragmatics.

Listening to child speech from this perspective requires us to ask these questions: What is the child doing with communication? How does the child use speaking? How do details of the child's linguistic and extralinguistic codes enter into actual speaking and listening situations? In short, we are investigating children's learning of the rules of social interaction within their community.

We may illustrate "rules of social interaction" with this example. Two American adult acquaintances meet on the street. We can predict that the things they say to each other will be brief, that both will speak, and that the likelihood of a word such as "hi" or "hello" is extremely high. The study of language (our focus in the last three chapters) can help us understand the grammar of the things people say, but linguistics cannot explain why we say "hello" at a given moment, instead of any other grammatical utterance.

The relationship between grammar and usage is like that between the rules of a game such as chess and the skills that allow you to be a good player. You can learn the rules of chess in just a few minutes: how each piece moves, what constitutes a checkmate, and so forth. But at this point you are a poor player; you know little about what to do in actual playing situations. Learning to be a good player takes longer to learn than the rules and usually requires a great deal of practical experience. Similarly, children learn most of the rules of grammar in a matter of months. But this does not mean that they are mature speakers. Learning to speak appropriately is like learning how to play chess well. There is no end to the task; it continues throughout life.

Although learning pragmatics is a lifelong task, children do show pragmatic skills at an early age. Even small children speak differently to friends than they speak to parents and still differently to a baby brother, a teddy bear, or an imaginary playmate. Children also speak in a different manner to the same people under different circumstances. How they speak to their mothers during a meal, for instance, is different from how they speak when they are playing together; and either of these manners of speaking can be varied still further in such situations as a toddler's need to use the bathroom or a kindergartner's stealing from the cookie jar.

If you listen to children's speech for signs of adjustment of speech to situations, you may still find use for the tools of linguistics discussed in Chapters 5 to 7. The difference is that now we are less concerned with details of linguistics and more with how these details are used within a particular situation. For example, an answer to a question can be grammatically perfect, yet still make little sense. Consider this exchange:

CHILD A: Why did you eat my cookie?
CHILD B: My mommy said that we are going to buy a house in the country.

Child B's answer is grammatical, but the answer makes no sense in terms of Child A's question. So it is possible to speak grammatical sentences without being an effective communicator. This also works the other way. You can communicate effectively without obeying grammar rules. Suppose that to A's question B responds, "Hungry." B is not speaking grammatically, but is providing a useful answer to A's question. These examples support a distinction between *demands of grammar*, or what grammatical forms are called for, and *demands of function*, or what verbal tasks must be performed in the situation (Hopper, 1971a).

Learning to talk is a dynamic interplay between learning bits of grammar and bits of appropriate usage (function). These two kinds of learning are not independent of each other. Children use grammar only when they figure out uses for it. Whether they "know" a bit of grammar is trivial to the parent or teacher of a child who is failing in school because of problems with language use. For these reasons, a strategy of providing a child-learner with situations requiring particular speech behavior may aid development of grammar and function. This idea underlies many educational innovations; we shall return to it in Chapter 11.

Development of pragmatics involves more than learning how to apply linguistic items (syntactic structures, morphemes, phonemes) effectively. The child also must discover a number of facts about life and how it works. The child has to learn both how the major components of communication situations interact with each other and how the functions of communication predict what is happening in a message. The grammatical models we've been describing explain a lot about children's speech, but we need a pragmatic perspective to study specifically what people are doing with speech, how speech acts function within settings of situation, family, school, and culture.

You may notice some similarity between "pragmatics" as discussed in this chapter (and shown as the top layer in the model in Chapter 3) and conversation, which is the term we use to describe the whole multilayered set of speaking-listening skills. In truth there is overlap between these notions. The whole of speaking does happen as conversation. Still, when sketching the parts of that whole (sounds, structures, meanings), one finds that certain parts (and not only the whole) have specifically pragmatic character. This chapter, then, explores that domain of the child's developing communicative competence that is specifically pragmatic. Many authors refer to this domain as speech acts.

SPEECH ACTS

Most writers trace the notion of *speech acts,* or pragmatic units of discourse, to J. L. Austin's classic work, *How to Do Things with Words* (1962). Austin wrote against a tradition that considered grammar and logic to be the only useful ways to study speech. He disagrees with the notion that any utterance is best analyzed by logical tests of the truth of its meaning. Austin notes that certain utterances cannot be described in terms of truth or falsity, but only in terms of use. He begins with examples he labels *performative utterances:*

I find the defendant guilty.
We christen this ship the Queen Elizabeth.

Austin labels these examples performative because they perform actions. They are not true or false; in fact their meaning is more or less irrelevant. What is relevant is that these utterances, when performed in the right circumstances, accomplish actions. These utterances change the state of the world in some way. They *do* something. Notice the phrase *in the right circumstances.* Austin's analysis is path-breaking because it addresses the notion of situation. For example, the sentence "I find the defendant guilty" must be spoken in the right circumstances to get its work done "happily" or appropriately:

- The speaker must be the right person, a judge or jury foreman for example.
- It must be spoken in the right setting, a courtroom.
- It must be spoken at the proper moment, at the end of a trial or hearing.
- It must be spoken according to the usual procedures of the speech community, not in a manner inappropriate to the setting (for example, "Sorry mate, you lose.").

In this chapter we refer to these aspects of situation as participants, setting, sequence, and cultural conventions.

At first, Austin's analysis of performatives seems to apply to only a few special cases of ceremonies and routines. But, as it turns out, you can describe any speech act in terms of the jobs it accomplishes, what Austin labels its *illocutionary force*. The illocutionary force of speech acts is the subject matter for the study of pragmatics. The study of the work accomplished in an utterance involves us in studying the relationships between speech and situation. Any utterance occurs in a local occasion, a place, a time, a set of participants and circumstances. As children learn to talk, they learn not only to speak, but to place each speech act appropriately (even artfully) within contexts. We can consider recent research about children's development of speech acts in relation to these aspects of situation.

Participants

It is obvious that the identities of the people who are present in any situation shape the situation and affect communication. If you hear a spicy joke and you are dying to tell it to someone, you have the sense to wait for an appropriate audience. You may not choose to tell it to your mother or to the checkout clerk at the grocery. A teacher who is furious with her principal will describe the circumstances differently with the principal than with a colleague. We make adjustments in our speaking behavior according to our audience hundreds of times a day. We often make such adjustments without even thinking about it. Children have to learn these skills. A 4-year-old may say to her father's boss, "My dad says you're an old tightwad." That is a pragmatic mistake, from the father's point of view, but it does not mean that the child is pragmatically undeveloped. That same 4-year-old already has developed skill in speaking to playmates, using jargon and sentence structures with them that parents and teachers rarely hear. (See the discussion on speech play later in this chapter.)

Research about child speech frequently overlooks the importance of participants as an aspect of situation. Thus children in nursery schools and kindergartens are often tested by adults the children don't know. Strangers can be frightening to children, which probably explains why they often speak so little in such contexts, even though they can be seen jabbering on the playground before and after. We should recall at such times that children often know things they do not say.

An even more unfortunate situation sometimes occurs with minority children. Imagine an 5-year-old urban black child who rarely interacts with a white adult. Suppose that a well-dressed Caucasian from a local university comes around to administer a "language advancement test." The child may say little in this novel situation. The researcher then holds the child back a grade or publishes a research report on delayed language in disadvantaged children.

Whenever you are analyzing a child's speech, ask yourself to whom the child is speaking. When a child responds to someone else's speech, who the speaker is may be as much the cause of the child's response as what is said. Dore (1979) observed that children on a class outing talked more, longer, and with more diversity when talking to another child than to a teacher. This should make us wonder about the failures of instruction. If you are in charge of a classroom, what you say and do affects the behavior of your students. Teachers who stress only authority and discipline may create entire classrooms of sullen, hostile, uncommunicative children. Teachers who encourage student participation and creativity may find students more responsive.

Another type of participant in speech situations is the overhearer. In many situations there are not only speakers and listeners, but also persons who are more-or-less listening. For instance, in radio call-in shows one hears telephone conversations between callers and a host. Much of what these participants say, however, is aimed at members of the overhearing audience of radio listeners. Similarly, some things that mothers and teachers say to one child are designed to be overheard by other children.

MOTHER: *[To child A.]* Tell your lazy brother to get the grass mowed.
CHILD B: Aw, mom, gimme a break!

Overhearers also function as audience to certain sorts of speech acts, such as teases:

FATHER: Son, do I have a good voice?
SON: You have a good voice, but you don't sing well.
MOTHER: Hah hah hah. He got you on that one!

In this instance the mother displays her hearing of the tease and her appreciation of its effectiveness. Teases happen more often when there are overhearers to act as audience than in two-party conversation.

In sum, the persons who are present in any interaction form a vital set of influences to which communicators must adapt. The child begins to master this adaptation at an early age, even before sophisticated grammatical conventions are acquired.

Setting

Just as participants are important to a communication situation, so is the physical setting in which speech occurs. Labov (1970a) suspected that black children were not performing well on language tasks because of the formality of the situation in which they were interviewed. So a field-worker dressed casually, sat on the floor with the children, and opened a bag of potato chips. In this setting the children spoke readily, and successful interviews were conducted.

Every child is more comfortable and talkative in certain settings than in others and may be apprehensive about new environments. A child may be quiet for the first hour in a strange house, for instance. Being quiet or behaving in an unusual way may be an adaptation to some unusual or threatening situation.

Young children rely upon details of setting in early attempts to communicate. Young children can indicate what they want by pointing and grunting, without saying a word. Even after children learn to talk, they still use objects in the setting—to show things, to point, and so forth.

Children also use what they can see to help them comprehend sentences. Try saying this sentence to a 3-year-old: "The elephant was kissed by the bear." If you ask who is doing the kissing, the child may be confused by this sentence structure (which is called a reversible passive). Usually the actor in a sentence is the first noun, so the child may guess the elephant. However, the child will know there is something queer about this sentence and will act unsure. If you present the same sentence and ask the same question while showing a picture of a bear kissing an elephant, the child can answer easily. To observe the 3-year-old's dependence on features of the setting, provide the same sentence, ask the same question, but show a misleading picture of an elephant kissing a bear. The child (up to age 7) will usually give a response agreeing with the picture.

For another example, hold a glass of water in front of a 3-year-old and ask, "What do you do with a spoon?" About half the time the response will be "You drink with it." Unusual or tricky alterations of visual context can fool even older children if the sentence's syntax is difficult. Carol Chomsky (1969) showed children a doll wearing a blindfold and asked, "Is this doll easy to see or hard to see?" Children of age 5 or 6 usually replied that the doll was hard to see; they were tricked by the difference between what they could see and what they saw.

These examples show how children use objects in the setting to help them interpret speech. Up to about age 7 children's dependence on visual surrounding is greater than that of adults.

Sequence

Sometimes we interpret an utterance "out of context." Suppose a movie critic writes, "Despite flashes of brilliant acting, this was a horribly dull film," and the next day's paper carries an ad for the movie attributing to the critic the phrase "brilliant acting." The critic could certainly claim that the quote was unfairly attributed and had been taken out of context.

What goes before an utterance can be just as important in conversation. Assume you are a teacher and your principal is Mr. Brown. Consider these two incidents:

1. Mr. Brown calls you into his office. His face is red, his eyes flashing. In his hand he holds your lesson plan for the month. "You can't use these books," he sputters. "The board of education would have my job. *What do you use for brains?*"
2. As you walk by Mr. Brown's office, he shouts, "Hey, your shoelace is untied!" You stop to look and he chortles, "April Fool!" You are mildly embarrassed as he says, "It's four o'clock in the afternoon, and you are still forgetting what day this is. *What do you use for brains?.*"

In both of these incidents the same person (participant) sits at the same desk (setting) and says the same thing. Yet your reaction is likely to be very different. This difference is due to other words immediately preceding the utterance.

Almost every utterance occurs within sequences or adjacency pairs (as we discussed in Chapter 3). For example, after one person says "hello" to another, if there is no response, the response is noticeably absent. This is true for any speech act that serves as the first part of an adjacency pair: a question, an order, a request, a compliment. This partial list begins to underscore a fact about speech acts. Most speech acts are named as if they were performed in a single utterance, but these actions are completed by a sequence, requiring interaction of two or more speakers. Frequently, these sequences are two turns long and consist of a first part and some reaction to it. One way you identify a request, for instance, is that the next turn grants or refuses it.

Once again, the study of pragmatics displays the complexity of what children must learn to do as members of a speech community. A child must learn not only the grammar of such constructions, but also what sort of second part goes with what sort of first part. We know little about how and when the child learns the importance of placing utterances into sequences and of hearing the sequential placement of others' speech. We do know that motherese constructions offer models of sequence to children.

Perhaps educators could focus on sequence in communication instruction. Workbooks could be developed in which paragraphs are missing one sentence, and the child could get a feel for conversational context by filling in the missing sentence. Perhaps tapes setting a situation could be played, and children could act out (and later discuss) "what happens next."

Conventions of a Culture

The sequences described above are, in some sense, built into the language, or the practices of a speech community. They are done somewhat differently in Japanese than in English. We still lack strong theories about what is the same (or universal) across languages. We are beginning to develop some data about the diversity of pragmatic practices in various cultures, thanks to a perspective that calls itself *ethnography of speaking.*

Dell Hymes, whose words began this chapter, is the scholar most responsible for the emergence of this new discipline. Ethnographers of speaking have taken their descriptive training (and their tape recorders) to various locations around the globe in order to study speaking practices (see, for example, the essays in Gumperz and Hymes, 1972).

Everything a child or adult says or understands represents some accomplishment within a web of customs of a speech community. Speech acts are accomplished according to traditions of "how things are done around here." These customs may vary a good deal from place to place and from language to language. For example, among the western Apache of the United States children who come home from boarding school are customarily silent for the first minutes after meeting their parents (Basso, 1970). An Apache child who failed to interact silently would be considered unusual or changed by contact with Caucasians. By contrast, a middle-class, white child who failed to speak upon returning home from boarding school would be considered to have a problem.

Children learn such community conventions. Eventually, they must also learn that in other communities things are done differently. Many children have latitude to speak at home, but their parents expect them to be quiet at church. School teachers expect children to respect situational limits on rights to speak, such as raising the hand and being recognized. There are many subcultural entities in a large, diverse speech community such as English speakers in the United States. Schools, extended families, minority groups, churches, and other groups identify each others' members largely by distinctive ways of speaking. Learning to adapt one's speech to multiple constraints is part of growing up.

To understand the impact of culture, try to look at your own culture as if you were a visitor from Mars. What do you see happening? How can you describe the speech practices of the people you observe?" This sort of discipline allows one to become to some degree a critic of culture. In recent years several aspects of American culture have come under attack on grounds of unfairness based on racism, sexism, and other biases. Usually, such critics hope that children can be spared such unfairness or bigotry. Cultures seem resistant to such changes, yet it's teachers' and parents' responsibility to consider them. We'll consider sexism as our example here. (Some issues from this section come up again in Chapter 12.)

It has been pointed out by a number of writers that speech and writing forms we use perpetuate certain unfortunate aspects of relationships between the sexes. Greatest attention has been paid to words, such as *chairman,* that seem to imply only men are being described. Critics recommend using *chairperson* or *chair* instead of *chairman, letter carrier* instead of *mailman,* and so forth. There has also been some attention to pronoun usage. The pronoun *he* has traditionally been used as a neutral or universal referent: "When a person goes to school, *he* must obey the rules." This usage represents the world only in male terms, it leaves females invisible, and critics recommend avoiding it.

One must also consider more subtle pragmatic displays of sexism in human communication. Consider this nursery school observation by Serbin and O'Leary (1975, p. 102):

> In one classroom, the children were making party baskets. When the time came to staple the paper handles in place, the teacher worked with each child individually. She showed the boys how to use the stapler by holding the handle in place while the child stapled it. On the girls' turns, however, if the child didn't spontaneously staple the handle herself, the teacher took the basket, stapled it, and handed it back.

In this example the teacher does not use different language for boys and girls, but does communicate to them different expectations of what they can do. Serbin and O'Leary found that, in addition to giving boys more opportunities to do almost everything, the fifteen teachers they observed spent more time talking with boys than girls. Boys were routinely rewarded for speaking up and active assertion of ideas. Girls were rewarded for keeping quiet. Boys were more likely to receive responses from teachers for either appropriate or inappropriate behavior. Although Serbin and O'Leary's findings may not be universally true, we suggest that teachers observe their own classroom behavior to detect whether they use different patterns of language and communication with boys and girls.

Do children recognize stereotyped ways of speaking for males and females? Edelsky (1977) presented to first graders sentences that contained stereotypical feminine forms (for example, "That's an adorable story.") and asked the children to identify the sex of the speaker. These sentences were consistently attributed to females, leading Edelsky to speculate that children become aware of stereotyped and sexist language patterns at an early age.

COMMUNICATIVE FUNCTIONS

We have illustrated some dimensions of situations that children learn to respond to: persons, setting, sequence, and culture. Children learn to navigate through speech events while adapting to these pragmatic dimensions. In addition, children accomplish a variety of communicative functions.

To examine function, listen to speech and ask, "What is the speaker getting accomplished? What is the speaker doing? What functions does each utterance serve?" When a parent says to a child, "Would you please take out the garbage?" it is important to realize that, in spite of the grammatical structure of the sentence, the parent is not asking a question, but is giving a directive. The child who does not respond to the directive has broken a pragmatic rule, or violated some expectation. (As with most pragmatic and linguistic rules, we notice the presence of a rule most when it is broken.)

Research has shown that listeners make subtle distinctions about what communication tasks are being set for them when they are asked various kinds of questions. Williams and Naremore (1969) studied the responses of fifth-grade children to three orders of questions:

1. Simple (requiring only a yes/no response): "Do you play baseball?"
2. Naming (requiring a single-word label): "What games do you play?"
3. Elaboration (requiring a sentence or more of description or elaboration): "How do you play baseball?"

They found that children consistently fulfilled the demands of these question situations. Further, they found that middle-class children tended to elaborate even in situations that did not specifically require it. These findings prompted them to speculate that some communication differences often found among different social classes may be primarily in pragmatics, not language.

To understand the pragmatics of child speech, consider what the child is trying to do? Suppose a child says, "Daddy shirt." She might be pointing to a shirt belonging to Daddy ("Daddy's shirt"). But suppose also that the child is holding a shirt of her own. Then she might be saying, "Daddy, here's my shirt." If she is not wearing a shirt, she might be saying, "Daddy, put on my shirt."

How do observers know all this? They make intuitive judgments about function, as they do about grammar. In early stages of language development children rely on pragmatic rules until their grammar grows. Form follows function; grammar follows pragmatics. You can tell what children are talking about because it is related to what they are doing. (See the discussion of rich interpretation in Chapter 6.)

This focus on what the child is doing can also help us avoid overemphasis on grammatical errors. Often adults correct a child's grammar even though the child can be understood. They stress form and ignore function. Take care to examine children's speech in terms of function, not just grammar or good manners.

The essence of pragmatics is that language is used functionally—to do actions. The most important questions about any messages concern what is being accomplished. Numerous researchers have recently examined functions of communication in child and adult speech (see Hymes, 1972; Bruner, 1975a, 1983). Some have proposed descriptive schemes of the functions people perform in everyday interaction (see Wells, 1981; Halliday and Hasan, 1976; Allen and Brown, 1976). In the discussions that follow we draw from these systems, but we are not trying to present a model of communicative functions; rather we are summarizing current research.

Communicative function is not really a distinct concept from that of the speech act. We use the term function to refer to types of speech acts—informing, persuading, speech play, and metacommunication. Up to this point we have been talking about the pragmatics of speech acts in general. Now we will focus on these types of speech acts.

Informing

If A informs B, the primary focus of the event is the transfer of descriptive material from one person to the other. Of course, two persons can inform each other simultaneously. Most textbooks are primarily informative. If a parent "names" some object in response to an 18-month-old child's asking "What is that?" the parent and child share an informative relationship.

The informative function is perhaps easiest of all functions to describe. Therefore, you might guess that informing is an early function to emerge in children. Actually, it seems to emerge quite late. Halliday's (1975) study of the speech of his son Nigel notes that informative utterances were late in appearing. Perhaps the informing function develops late because to give information to another person, you must tell that person something you know that he or she does not know. To be informative, the child must understand something about differences between self and others, something about how dialogue works, something about what she or he knows compared to what others know. This requires some role-taking skill (see Chapter 9).

Persuading

Aristotle wrote that the predominant function of human communication is persuasion. If A persuades B, the primary focus of the event is that A moves or motivates B in some direction. Arguing, convincing, nagging, correcting, requesting, and commanding can be identified as persuasive acts.

A number of researchers have examined children's acquisition of requests. Garvey (1975) studied requests and responses to them among nursery school children aged 3 to 6. Children of this age sometimes address requestlike utterances to self or to a toy. When children addressed their requests to other persons, more than three-quarters achieved their goal, and 3-year-olds were successful as often as 6-year-olds, indicating that even young children have functional command of requesting. The main difference between younger and older children in Garvey's study was that older children used more indirect requests. Indirect requests are those that inquire into the other's willingness to do something ("Can you take the doll?).

There is controversy in current speech act theory about whether such requests are really "indirect" or just conventional ways of doing requesting in the adult world. In this view the older child has simply learned adult customs, although the younger child's performance of requests is functionally adequate. A third position is that adult forms of requests (and other speech acts) seem indirect because they are sequential preliminaries to more blatant forms. If the milder form does not get the desired response, a less subtle form follows. Whatever the explanation for the difference between adult and child requests, all acts of child persuasion are blunter than the adult acts.

Of course, some initial requests, orders, and other acts of persuasion are met by resistance, and arguments ensue. Consider this example from Wilkinson and Rembold (1982, p. 169) in which a first-grade child makes an initial request which is denied:

> JAKE: Read in your mind.
> MITCH: I don't have to.
> JAKE: *[Grabs Mitch.]* Yes, you do.
> MITCH: No, I don't.
> JAKE: Yes, you do.
> MITCH: No, I don't.

The request is repeated as a demand, but this insistence is met by further refusals. Just as children learn to address and respond to requests, they also learn to resist persuasion and to "argue" when requests are not fulfilled.

Some of the most fascinating research of recent years has examined children's modes of arguing with each other. Children's arguments are characterized by bluntness. Note that Mitch and Jake do not change their stances during the confrontation, nor does either child give backing for his position. Rather, each repeats the original contention, and arguments are settled by force or persistence. Brenneis and Lein (1977, p. 57) give this example:

> ROSE: That's my ball.
> LINDA: That's my ball.
> ROSE: That's mine.
> LINDA: That's mine.

The blunt repetitiveness of these child arguments is quite uncharacteristic of adult arguments. Children use these forms not only in resolving disputes, but even in beginning them. Goodwin (1983, p. 663) notes that children pick arguments with each other by what he calls "aggravated correction":

> A: Get your four guys.
> B: You get *three* guys.

or

> A: And that happened *last* year.
> B: That happened *this* year.

In both instances the second speakers pursue disagreement, going out of their way to disagree with a side issue. Goodwin notes that, in contrast, adult arguments are begun and worked through by means of "mitigated" forms, rather than aggravated forms, and forms that allow the other a chance to correct self, rather than be corrected by another. A mitigated version of the last example might be:

> A: And that happened *last* year.
> B: I'm not sure, but I think it was *this* year.

B begins with a disclaimer ("I'm not sure but") and then qualifies the counter-claim still further by adding "I think." These mitigating devices seem to save the other embarrassment or offense.

Another less blunt move typical of adult arguments is to initiate repair (see Chapter 3) with a question-repeat, but allow the original speaker to make any actual corrections.

> A: And that happened *last* year.
> B: *Last* year?
> A: This *year.*

These descriptions of children's arguments show consistency across studies and across research methods. Preschoolers and first-graders use the strongest forms, but older children's disputes (up to third or fourth grade at least) retain this blunt character. How are adult forms for arguing developed in later childhood? This seems a priority topic for future research.

Children do learn to collaborate as well as to compete. Cooper (1975) documents increases in children's problem-solving skills in peer interaction between the ages of 3 and 5. Older children are able to make their turns more informative, both nonverbally and verbally. So at the very time that children often by-pass opportunities to avoid verbal battles, they are increasing collaborative skills as well.

Speech Play

Many arguments emerge in the course of children's play activities. Observers of children's play have noticed that play is frequently competitive and that much of this competition is carried on verbally during the course of play. Consider this example from a girls' jump rope game (Goodwin, 1985, p. 321):

> PRISCILLA: *[Cajolingly to Pam.]* Wanna play some rope?
> PAM: Okay. First!
> PRISCILLA/MICHELLE: *[Speaking in unison.]* Second. Second to highest!
> PRISCILLA: All around the gooseberry bush. I called it.

Pam earns the right to jump first by calling first. Two other girls vie to earn second slot, but in two tries they speak in unison, so neither wins this right. Priscilla finally breaks the tie by saying "all around the gooseberry bush," then claiming her right, "I called it." Examples such as this show us that the verbal practices of play are very much like those in other aspects of children's speech (see Garvey, 1977). Goodwin (1985, p.316) notes, for instance, that

> Differences of opinion concerning the rules of the game of jump rope can develop throughout its course. Such differences can result in disputes that momentarily halt the ongoing activity of the moment (jumping rope) to initiate talk about it, thus having the character of "remedial exchanges."

Thus, it seems that children learn some things about framing, competition, dispute management, and much else—all "on the fly" during play.

In addition to talking during play, children engage in fantastic "playful" speech. Children maintain a stable culture of play talk that endures from generation to generation, surprisingly unchanged (Iwamura, 1980). Riddles and rhymes make up a large part of children's play culture. We hear children saying them, and most of us recall saying them when we were children.

CHILD 1: Knock knock.
CHILD 2: Who's there?
CHILD 1: Olive.
CHILD 2: Olive who?
CHILD 1: Olive *[I love]* you.

A barefoot boy with shoes on
Stood sitting in a tree
And when I put my glasses on
I heard this melody.

JAY: Why do rhinoceri have flat feet?
MOM: Why?
JAY: From stamping out forest fires.

Glory glory halleluiah
Teacher hit me with a ruler
Conked her on the bean with a rotten tangerine
And her teeth came marching out.

Sometimes when adults hear these rhymes and riddles, they say, "Now, isn't that just like a kid? Isn't that cute?" They commonly regard child play forms as silly and not worthy of notice, except when they employ bad language. Bauman (1976) argues that to understand play the observer must surmount a "triviality barrier." Reading the examples of play talk, you know it is play, but could you state what features make it typical of child's play or what stage of development such play represents? These questions involve information discussed in nearly every chapter of this book. For example, Bauman describes a developmental sequence in the knock-knock joke. (To the charge that knock-knock jokes are trivial, Bauman replies, "Don't knock knock-knocks.")

A knock-knock joke is a highly ritualized humor game that is usually based upon punning. Children at age 4 recognize the words "knock knock" as a summons to a ritualized playlet, even though their understanding of the play may be limited:

CHRISTINE (age 4): Knock knock.
BRIAN (age 7): Who's there?
CHRISTINE: Christine Hopper.
BRIAN: Oh, you baby.

The 7-year-old sibling knows knock-knock rules and ridicules his sister because she understands only that there is play based upon greeting. Christine at age 4 displays a primitive stage of knock-knock development. Bauman reports a second stage in which the child (about age 5) can do the steps in the whole knock-knock routine, but shows no awareness of the necessity for a pun.

CHRISTINE: Knock knock.
BRIAN: Who's there?
CHRISTINE: Play.
BRIAN: Play who?
CHRISTINE: Play with my record player.

Finally, perhaps at age 6, the mature form emerges, though there are still many flawed performances—to both the consternation and delight of older children:

As with riddles, the first attempts are flawed, as in "Knock-knock." "Who's there?" "Rita." "Rita who?" "Rita I need another kiss. " This brings together in a garbled way elements from two traditional knock-knocks: "Rita (= read a) good book lately," and "Anita (= I need a)nother kiss, baby." (Bauman, 1976, p. 11)

One thing to note about this developmental sequence in knock-knocks is the similarity between the learning of these pragmatic routines and some other parts of communicative development, such as questions and intonation patterns. Even young children care about doing these forms "correctly."

The concern begins with a desire to interact, but grows into a concern for doing the whole routine correctly. In later stages of development, as children learn more sophisticated knock-knocks and develop their own, the concern moves to using language as an object of manipulation and examination. Most mature knock-knocks are a form of language play, not only in the sense that language is used to play, but in the sense that language is the toy with which the child plays.

Now look back again at the examples of child talk. They seem simple, but the effectiveness of each one turns on a different aspect of the language system. The knock-knock joke is primarily phonological; it is based on sound punning. The "barefoot boy" rhyme and the rhinoceros riddle are semantic. A set of combined antitheses creates contrived anomaly. Given results of experiments in anomaly (McNeill, 1966), one might guess that the speakers of these two examples are 8 or older. The "glory glory" rhyme is primarily pragmatic. Its content and vocabulary focus on violating and enforcing social rules, which are recurrent themes in the speech of adolescents. Perhaps a developmental sequence exists in children's verbal play that emphasizes sounds at ages 5 to 7, then incorporates grammar and semantics at ages 8 to 10, and finally adds pragmatics in adolescent years (Sanches and Kirshenblatt-Gimblett, 1975).

In sum, both in uses of talk while playing and in children's language play, one can observe developmental processes at work. Observe children's games to ask what values they celebrate. Sacks (1980) argues that the game "Button, button, who's got the button?" serves as a training ground for deception skills. In this game children stand or sit in a row while the "it" participant pretends to pass each of them a small, flat object. One of the children actually receives this object, but both the passer and the recipient try to hide the exchange. This game is "a training ground for liars and deceivers. But it is equally well a game which is directed to the detection of liars and deceivers" (p. 323). Children at play learn serious life skills and lessons, such as the fact that others cannot detect their thoughts, only their actions, especially speech actions.

Metacommunication

As there is a relationship between persuasion and play, there is a relationship between play and *metacommunication*, or communication about communication. Bateson (1972) is generally credited with articulating the contemporary notion of metacommunication in descriptions of the play of zoo animals. Bateson noted that monkeys and otters at play undertake sequences of activity that are closely modeled on combat. For instance, a monkey will jump toward a playmate and nip its neck. As the nip is not a bite (it doesn't draw blood), the entire sequence is not combat, but play. Perhaps all mammal species engage in such sequences of mock combat. In order to accomplish such sequences, Bateson writes, these animals must be able to exchange certain messages that bracket a whole string of other messages (the sequence of acts); the bracketing or *framing* message says, "This is play." Metacommunicative messages are like picture frames, which tell the viewer not to apply the same communication rules in examining a picture as they use in examining the wall behind it.

Garvey (1977) describes the child's development of social play between the ages of 3 and 6. She notes that at this age the play frame is marked explicitly by wording ("Pretend to call me on the phone.") or by role assignment ("I'll be the teacher.").

Martlew, Connolly, and McCloud (1978) observed a 5-year-old's play alone, with a peer, and with the child's mother. In these three contexts the child displayed different play styles. In the solo setting play consisted of dramatic dialogue with few stage directions or explanations. In the peer setting the play style consisted of interaction and mutual acceptance. Sometimes the peer interactions became arguments. With the mother talk had a more teacher-pupil quality and arguments were rarer.

Another aspect of metacommunicative framing involves the use of quotes. Bates (1967) traces the development of children's abilities to use and understand quotation. A precursor to quoting appears in the answer to the common question of the form "What does the cat say?" The child first learns to respond "meow" and then a few months later to say,"The cat goes 'Meow.'" During this time the child also begins to distinguish things an animal won't say; for example, the child learns that a particular animal doesn't go "bow wow," but goes "meow."

Perhaps the most studied aspect of children's metacommunication is *metalinguistic speech,* or speech that calls attention to the forms of language. Examples of metalinguistic talk include commenting on a pun or rhyme, offering corrections, and saying something about words as words, such as "The word *cat* has three letters." The development of metalinguistic speech shows the child's ability to decenter, that is, to regard speech an an object. (For this development in Piagetian terms, see Chapter 9.) This is an ability that many preschool children do not have. They are too tied up in content to focus on word form. For example, a 4-year-old who is asked whether sentences are "good" or "silly" may make the following responses:

ADULT: "The chair ate the car."
CHILD: That's silly. Chairs don't eat.
ADULT: "John and Bill is a brother."
CHILD: That's OK.
ADULT: "The boy kissed the girl."
CHILD: That's silly. Boys wouldn't kiss anybody.

Notice that the child focuses only on the content of the sentences and completely disregards the bizarre syntax in the second sentence. This is typical of children even into the early grades of elementary school. Young children have a great deal of trouble talking about language, as anyone who ever asked a group of 4- and 5-year-olds what a "word" is will testify. Their difficulties are more than a matter of vocabulary. For young children language *is* meaning, and the speech stream they hear is not segmented into separate sounds and words. Awareness of this segmentation, for many children, comes only with their introduction to writing.

Multiple Functions

We have described four functions that children learn to perform when they speak and listen: informing, persuading, play, and metacommunication. These categories are not mutually exclusive. The performance of one function may depend on or include other functions. In fact, both children and adults perform more than just one function in many turns at talk. This richness in speech aids humans in many ways, but it makes researchers' and teachers' tasks difficult and confusing. For instance, many researchers have attempted to "code" each child utterance as performing a single function. This simplification may make it easier to formulate hypotheses, but it creates only a superficial description of children's speech.

Consider this example. A child comes in from riding her bicycle with the knees of her pants torn. She says, "Momma, I fell off my bike and hurt my knees." Chances are that the child will also be crying and moving rapidly about or holding her hand over the injured area. These messages from the child function as information; she tells her mother some previously unknown facts. At the same time she tries to persuade her mother that the injury is severe enough to demand parental attention, but not severe enough for medical attention. The child may also be persuading her mother not to punish her for ruining the pants. In addition, she may be expressing frustration and anger that the accident has taken place and may be asking the mother to respond with support and sympathy.

Perhaps you had hoped that our function list would allow you to sort utterances neatly into function bins. Human interaction does not work that way. Many utterances perform multiple functions; many single utterances may be examined as information, as play, as persuasion, and as metacommunication. All communication is information. It has been argued that all communication serves persuasive functions. Surely much of interaction is aimed at getting our way. Speech play is a vital training ground not only for speech skills, but perhaps also for all other functions of speaking. Almost every message can be described in terms of its components of metacommunication. Each of the function labels represents important generalizations that every child must understand in order to become an effective communicator.

These functions were discussed largely from the standpoint of speakers, but listeners also employ the same functions. Just as you impart information, you seek information through listening. Just as you control others, you are controlled by others. Just as you know something about the line between what's real and playful, you recognize that line in the messages of others. Also, these functions are expressed nonverbally as well as verbally.

You may ask, "If utterances perform several functions simultaneously and the functions are so intertwined, what is the purpose of the function system?" In short, the message is one that has been repeated frequently throughout this book. We can learn by dividing and classifying aspects of children's speech, but to understand what is really happening, we must observe the whole complex system in action without attending too closely to any single unit.

UNDERSTANDING THE CHILD'S PRAGMATIC WORLD

Through play, the child learns that language is not only a tool for communication, but also something that can itself be regarded as a perceptual-conceptual object. Not only may you communicate, but you may communicate about communicating. We suggest that this important insight is a major difference between human communication and animal communication. This awareness also allows intervention toward more profitable communication patterns. A major point of the study of the pragmatics of children's speech is that children are not just little adults. Let us begin by understanding the pragmatic world of the child, not by trying to "improve" the child into a proper adult.

SUMMARY

Language is a tool for getting things done. It is learned through use, for use. The study of language form (grammar, phonology) is incomplete without a focus on how these forms are used in communicating. Children seem to have this view of language from the beginning.

The study of speech acts, or what we do with language, involves the study of relationships between language and situation. Language use is affected by the participants (who is in the situation), the setting (where the situation is), the sequence (what was said before in the situation), and the conventions of the culture (the speech community in which the situation exists).

In addition to learning how to use language situationally, children learning language also learn about communicative functions (informing, persuading, speech play, and metacommunication). As the child's abilities develop, multifunctional utterances become the rule rather than the exception.

It appears that by examining aspects of context and function in children's speech, parents and teachers can most effectively interact with children as children achieve mastery of appropriate modes of speaking. The final chapters of this book, which suggest ways parents, teachers, and clinicians can aid development of children's speech, concentrate on pragmatics. Pragmatics is the area in which adults can most aid the development of children's speech.

SUGGESTED READINGS

Baugh, J., and J. Sherzer. *Language and Use.* Englewood Cliffs, N. J.: Prentice-Hall, 1986. This book does not focus on children's speech, but it contains some of the best recent essays in pragmatics and the closely related area of sociolinguistics.

Ervin-Tripp, S., and C. Mitchell-Kernan (eds.). *Child Discourse.* New York: Academic Press, 1977. This book contains a number of highly readable studies of children's development of pragmatic skills: arguments, play, story telling, and much more.

Goodwin, M. H. The serious side of jump-rope. Conversational practices and social organization in the frame of play. *Journal of American Folklore 98,*

315-330, 1985. This readable article describes play and metacommunication among a group of black preadolescent girls. There are many rich examples of play, framing, and some interesting contrasts between boys' and girls' play styles.

Halliday, M. A. K. *Learning How to Mean. Explorations in the Development of Language.* New York: Arnold, 1975. This review of studies of the earliest stages of pragmatic development contains a nice mix of detailed case study reports and other forms of investigation.

SUGGESTED PROJECTS

1. Select a study of metalinguistic awareness in children and repeat it, using a group of children the same ages as those in the original study. Write up your results. (Hint: Possible starting places are E. Bialystock, Children's concept of word, *Journal of Psycholinguistic Research 15,* 13-32, 1986; L. Wilkinson, A. Wilkinson, F. Spinelli, and C. Chiang, Metalinguistic knowledge of pragmatic rules in school-age children, *Child Development 55,* 2130-2140, 1984.)

2. Interview several people from cultures other than mainstream Unites States to find out how their pragmatic rule systems differ from the mainstream. Areas to investigate might include: Is status (age, profession, etc.) a factor in communication? How is status established? Who can begin and who can end an interaction? Are different communication behaviors expected of males and females? What are the differences? How do children learn these rules? What communication roles are expected for children?

PART Three

LANGUAGE IN THE LARGER WORLD

Having taken the language system apart in Part Two we are now ready to put it back together, but, more importantly, we will put it together in a context. We will begin, in Chapter 9, with the cognitive context of language use. Chapter 10 puts the child and the language system together as we consider how language learning occurs in normal children. Chapter 11 examines individual and cultural differences in language learning. In Chapter 12 we move into the classroom to examine teaching communication skills to children, and in Chapter 13 we consider the clinical setting in which children's communication abilities are assessed. Finally, Chapter 14 looks at relationships among spoken language, reading, and writing.

As you read this part of the book, remember that children approach the task of learning language as intelligent beings. In this task they are influenced by their individual personalities as well as by the language environment in which the learning occurs. As we consider how teaching, in the classroom or in the clinic, might be most effective, we must keep in mind the child's natural learning.

Chapter
9

Language and Cognition

*W*e have strongly implied throughout this book that language has roots in cognitive development and that the child's early communication behavior reflects overall cognitive structure and perception. Our position is that child language molds cognitive processes (or thinking) much less than cognition structures communication development. This statement reflects what we know about the child from the earliest stages of behavior.

It is probably clear to you as an adult language user that there are kinds of thinking for which language is essential. For example, if you try to add 1,246 and 18,452, you need to "talk to yourself" in order to get through the intermediate stages of the problem. Similarly, complex problem solving such as that required in social science theories would not be possible without language processes.

Even more than language shapes thought, however, our cognitive development underlies language and its use. The truth of this statement is best illustrated by the work of the giant of child psychology, Jean Piaget. This chapter reviews some of Piaget's ideas about cognitive development and discusses some ways in which language and cognition interact.

DEVELOPMENT OF COGNITION

In order to discuss relationships between language and cognition, we must examine how cognition develops in children. We owe most of what we know about child cognition to the research of Piaget. According to

Piaget, human cognition develops in a series of identifiable stages. Children at birth are totally centered on themselves and dependent on their sensations. Piaget labels the stage from birth to around age 2 *sensorimotor.* Between 2 and 7 years children are in the *preoperational* stage. The third stage, called *concrete operational,* lasts from 7 to 11, and around age 11 children enter the last stage, called *formal operational.*

Before we begin to discuss these developmental stages, some words of caution are in order. In Piagetian theory the most important thing is the *order* in which developmental stages occur. Piaget says that children do not enter a given stage until they have gone through all prior stages, and they do not skip stages, because every stage builds on what came before it. However, children's rates of development differ, so the ages given for certain behaviors are not rigid. We have generally used the ages Piaget himself uses, but anyone who observes many children will tell you that age is not always a good predictor of cognitive skills. Also, these stages of development are not like boxes, where you must be completely in or completely out. The transitions between stages, particularly the substages of the sensorimotor period, are often blurred, and it may be impossible to find an individual child whose *every* behavior matches the description for a particular stage.

Sensorimotor Development

It is during the sensorimotor stage that the cognitive foundations for language development are laid. At the beginning of this stage a newborn infant is capable of only the most primitive reflex actions. The newborn has no concept of self, no ideas of cause and effect, and no knowledge of what Piaget calls *object permanence,* the concept that things and people exist in the world even when we cannot directly perceive them.

We are so used to our ideas about reality that it may be difficult to imagine what this stage of life is like. However, we can see evidence of it in the infant's behavior. For example, 3-month-old Josh is watching his mother push a toy car around on his high chair tray. His eyes follow the car as his mother pushes it from one side of the tray to the other. His mother picks up an empty cup and puts it over the car in the center of the tray. Josh continues to look across the tray, in the direction the car would have gone had it not disappeared. He does not attempt to remove the cup or search in any other way for the car, even though he saw his mother put the cup over it. For Josh it is as though the car ceases to exist when he can no longer see it.

Infants in the early stages of sensorimotor development can sense objects through sight, hearing, touch, smell, and taste. They react to objects when they are in contact with them. When the objects are absent, however, the child cannot react to them. Josh does not search for the car, because he has no way to store an image of the car in his mind when it is not there. Sometimes, an infant will cry or complain when a favored object (or the mother herself) is removed from sight or touch. This crying does not occur because the baby remembers and misses the absent toy or person, but rather because the sensations caused by the presence of the toy or person have ceased. At this stage the world for the infant consists entirely of his or her own internal sensations and reactions.

Another example of the infant's dependence on internal sensations and motor reactions can be seen in the behavior of 4-month-old Carolyn as she watches her father swinging a teddy bear above her bed. She kicks and waves her hands, obviously enjoying the activity. When her father stops swinging the bear, she stops kicking briefly and then immediately begins to kick and wave her arms again while she watches the bear. It is as though she believes that the bear's movement is somehow connected with her own motor reactions. She is not able to distinguish between her own actions and those of another person, nor is she capable of imagining what could have caused the bear to move in the first place.

Infants gradually develop more elaborate ways of acting on the environment. They learn that their actions and sensations do not create reality. As Sinclair and Coulthard (1975, p. 236) say, "It is only gradually, by performing the same action on a number of different objects (e.g., shaking rattles, spoons, dolls, etc.) and different actions on the same object (e.g., shaking, licking, and throwing a rattle) that action and object become differentiated." This gradual differentiation of object from action and of the self from objects and others is accompanied by an increasing ability to conceive of an absent object or event by means of a mental representation of it.

The development of representational ability can be seen most clearly in the child's capacity to imitate actions of other people. According to Piaget, until about age 4 months, infants are able to imitate only actions they can see or hear themselves perform. Even then, the actions must be ones the child is already capable of, and the imitation must occur immediately following the model. For example, 3-month-old Chris is lying in his bed, opening and closing his fist. His mother begins to imitate the gesture. He watches her and immediately repeats the action. Around 8 months Chris will be able to imitate actions he cannot see himself doing (such as making faces), and still later (around 12 months) he will be able to imitate new actions he has not previously performed (such as making nonsense syllables like "beeb" or "nani").

Some time after this, around 18 months, Chris will be able to engage in what Piaget calls *deferred imitation,* or imitation of a behavior the child can no longer see. An example of deferred imitation can be seen in the behavior of 16-month-old Angela. Angela and her older sister watch some house painters at work on the family house. Angela observes closely for some time. That night when taking her bath, Angela uses her sponge to "paint" the bathroom wall, imitating the gestures she had seen the painters make with their brushes. The progression toward deferred imitation shows the child's increasing ability to make mental representations of objects or events in the world. The child is becoming less and less dependent on immediate sensory input.

A further development during the sensorimotor period with implications for language learning is the child's discovery of means-ends behaviors, sometimes called "instrumental" or "problem solving" behaviors. Over the course of the sensorimotor stage the child's means-ends behaviors become more varied and more complex. Early in the stage children have no sense of the separation of actions and objects; if they want some object or want to make something happen, they have no sense of how to achieve this goal. By the end of the first year, however, children are becoming active experimenters and can often go through a whole range of behaviors to try to make something happen. For example, Marie at age 10 months was given a partially opened matchbox with a small plastic doll inside it. She could see the doll, but did not know how to open the box. She tried shaking it and hitting the top. She stuck her fingers into the opening and tried to pull the doll out. In the process she quite accidentally enlarged the opening and succeeded, at which point she threw the box aside to concentrate on the new toy. At age $11\frac{1}{2}$ months, given the same problem to solve, she again tried several strategies. When none of them worked, she held the box up and began to cry. Her mother opened it for her. At age 14 months, Marie was again given the matchbox problem, with the box completely closed. She shook the box and perceived that there was something inside. Immediately, she looked at her mother, handed her the box, and vocalized. When her mother did not open the box at once, Marie took her mother's hand, put it on the box, said "Mama," and watched her mother's face. Marie had learned that other people can make things happen and that communication is one means to achieve her goals. She could not have done this six months earlier, before her sense of the separation between object and action was complete.

In summary, the child's development during the sensorimotor period establishes the foundation for language use. The development of object permanence and representational ability make the symbolic function of language possible. The interwined development of cause-effect reasoning and means-ends behaviors lead to the communicative function of language, in which the child uses language as a tool to get things done.

Preoperational Thought

Around age 2 children have begun to make clear distinctions between themselves as individuals and the rest of the world, and they set out to explore their autonomy. Harried mothers call this period the "terrible 2s" because of the child's uncooperativeness. Piaget would call it the beginning of the period of *preoperational thought.*

Preoperational children know they are individuals, they know language is used for communication, and they know thinking can solve problems. What they do not know is how they are different, how they can communicate using language, how they can figure out proper solutions to problems. One major reason for this lack of communicating and problem-solving strategies is simple inexperience. Children see people reaching conclusions, but know little about the reasoning behind the conclusions. Thus they "reach conclusions" themselves without going through any real reasoning process. A little later they realize that there must be reasons for conclusions, but almost any "pseudo-reason" will do:

ADULT: I'm going to spank you.
CHILD: Don't spank me because I have Kleenex in my pocket.
ADULT: Why is this called a handkerchief?
CHILD: Because my mommy ties it around my head when the wind blows.
ADULT: Why did the balloon break?
CHILD: Because it couldn't hold its breath.

Another reason for the lack of communicating and problem-solving strategies is the preoperational child's inability to conceive of a point of view other than his or her own. The child knows that other people exist, but assumes they see things just as he or she does. Consider this conversation between Brian (age $3\frac{1}{2}$) and his mother:

MOTHER: What is Kenny's mommy's name?
BRIAN: Mrs. Myers.
MOTHER: What is Adam's mommy's name?
BRIAN: Mrs. Black.
MOTHER: What is your mommy's name?
BRIAN: Mommy!
MOTHER: What do other children call me?
BRIAN: Mommy.
MOTHER: No, other children call me Mrs. . . .
BRIAN: Mommy.
MOTHER: What is my last name?
BRIAN: Hopper.
MOTHER: Then children call me Mrs. . . .
BRIAN: Mommy.

Brian knows the formula for calling a mother "Mrs. —," but cannot apply this to his own mother. He cannot see his own mother from the point of view of another child.

Children are just as tightly tied to their visual point of view. If you ask a 4-year-old to show you a picture, she will often show it to herself, on the assumption that you will also be able to see. Preoperational children lack role-taking ability; they cannot put themselves in another's shoes. As a result, the children's thinking and talking are largely based on what they can see. For example, 4-year-olds usually believe nickels are more valuable than dimes because they are bigger.

A third aspect of preoperational thought is the use of oversimplified concepts. Children are able to think about only one aspect of a situation at a time, so some of their concepts are different from those of adults. You can demonstrate this by trying one of Piaget's famous *conservation* experiments. The ability to conserve is the ability to comprehend that the amount of a substance remains the same, even when arranged differently or placed in different size containers, unless some substance is added or taken away. In one experiment two identical containers are filled with water:

A   B

A 4- or 5-year-old will say that there is the same amount of water in both containers. Children at this age typically make this judgment by observing the height of the water in the containers. If the experimenter pours the water from one of these containers into a taller, thinner container and asks the child, "Do we still have the same amount of water in each glass, or does one glass have more?" the child almost always replies that the tall, thin glass has more.

A   C

If the experimenter pours the water from the tall, thin container back into the original one, the child will again assert that the quantities are equal. One child, on being asked how it could be that the quantities could change when no water was added or taken away, answered tranquilly, "It's magic."

Children in this stage seem to pay attention to only one aspect of the situation, container height, and to ignore width, which is also a factor. They seem to be operating according to a perceptual rule: The higher one has more.

A similar experiment uses two rows of objects (say, checkers or pennies), each containing the same number of objects but with the objects in one row placed close together and in the other spread far apart:

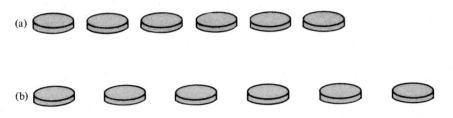

The row with the objects spread apart will be judged by 3- and 4-year-olds to contain more items; 5- and 6-year-olds, who can count well, usually do not fall for this one.

These conservation experiments have been popular with researchers studying 4- to 7-year-olds for several years. Mehler and Bever (1967) tried a conservation task with 2-year-olds and made a startling discovery. They used two rows of clay lumps, one row having six members and the other having four:

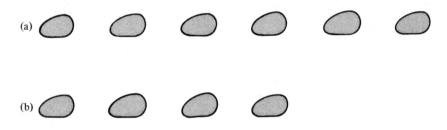

Ordinarily, all children can tell that row a has more. But if you push the lumps in row a closer together, 4- and 5-year-olds will say row b has more:

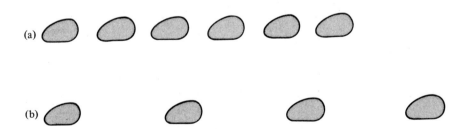

They follow the rule "Bigger means more" and are fooled. Mehler and Bever's remarkable finding was that 2-year-olds were not fooled! They correctly chose row a as having more. This means that the younger, less preoperational children had not yet learned the "bigger means more"

rule. In everyday life the older preoperational child makes pretty good judgments using this rule, but in conservation experiments the child is fooled. It is not until about age 5 or 6, when counting is learned, that the child stops misjudging in this experiment. This suggests that "inability to conserve" is not a general part of immaturity (because in some instances very young children do conserve), but rather it is part of the preoperational thought stage.

THINKING AND TALKING

Now we are ready to consider how speaking abilities and cognitive abilities are related in communication development. Because we are concerned in this book with the earliest stages of language use, we will limit our discussion of cognitive development to its earliest stages and so will not consider Piaget's third and fourth stages.

Language Shapes Thought

It has been argued that language is not merely a means of expression, but also a kind of mold, which shapes the mind of the speaker. The words and sentence structures you use affect how you see your world (Whorf, 1956). In this view differences among languages represent differences in how speakers of those languages see the world. For example, Eskimos have many terms that would translate into English as "snow." Some refer to soft, slushy snow; others to little, cold flakes; still others to hardened snow in a glacier. Because we do not have names for these different kinds of snow, we cannot perceive them as clearly as Eskimos do. For another example, there are some languages that use only one word to represent the colors blue and green (just as we use *blue* to cover shades from aqua to navy). Speakers from such a culture would have a hard time distinguishing differences among shades of blue and green because their native language would not have provided practice in this distinction.

Whorf's view is supported by the fact that languages use different words, but it cannot account for the ways in which languages are alike (see Chapter 2). In short, although one's culture affects one's outlook, there is little evidence that the development of language per se is important to development of thought.

However, there is a related sense in which children's speech affects their thinking. Children often seem to guide their actions and thoughts with speech. A child often seems to "describe" what she is doing: "Now I'll draw a pig . . . and here's a place for him to live." This use of speech (sometimes called "private speech" or "mediating language") has no communicative function. The child is not talking to anyone; she is simply guiding her actions with speech. Similarly, children can add two numbers together only by saying them out loud. We all use speech at some time or other to help us guide our thinking. A child or adult "in concentration" often moves his lips as he tries to solve a difficult problem. Also, both adults and children often ask themselves questions to solve cognitive problems.

If any of these uses of speech aids thought development, then we ought to be able to teach concepts to children through training in speaking. Sinclair-de-Zwart (1969) examined children's performance on conservation tasks (like those described above) and tried to train children to do better on these tasks by asking questions about them. She found that there were no basic differences in overall linguistic ability between "conservers" and "nonconservers," although conservers used more comparative terms (e.g., "more" or "less") to describe the situations and nonconservers used absolute terms (e.g., "a lot" or "a little"). Sinclair-de-Zwart then taught the use of comparative terms to the nonconservers. She experienced no difficulty in teaching the forms to the children, but afterward the children did no better on the conservation tasks than they had in the first place. The conclusion is that knowing the linguistic forms used with advanced thinking does not make children more capable of doing the advanced thinking. Language is not the source of logic, but, on the contrary, seems structured by logic.

Thought Shapes Speech

Piaget felt that language is part of a much larger complex of process thinking. His earliest research (in the 1920s) concentrated on language, but his later work examined more generalized cognitive processing. This emphasis is based on the assumption that how children think is a dominant influence upon how they talk. Through his work and that of other researchers, it is becoming evident that this assumption is accurate.

It is even becoming clear that the stages of cognitive development discussed in this chapter are associated with three kinds of strategies for sentence processing (Bever, 1970). During the sensorimotor phase handling of sentences is intuitive, during the preoperational stage it is closely tied to perceptions, and only with the beginning of adultlike thought patterns is mature sentence processing possible.

Children do not begin speaking until near the end of the sensorimotor phase of cognitive development, but they listen with comprehension well before being able to talk. Handling of sentences during this period is intuitive, that is, there is no awareness of rules and structure, yet children can understand most sentences they hear. At this stage they seem to understand the basic relationships between parts of a sentence in underlying structure (for example, that the noun phrase at the start of a sentence is "doing" the verb).

In the preoperational stage children's handling of sentences, like their handling of conservation tasks, is closely tied to perception. This "perceptual strategy" enables preoperational children to assign meanings to many sentences that would be meaningless to younger children, even though some of the meanings assigned would make adults wince. What happens is that children use semantics or context to help them understand sentences with difficult structures. For example, if you said, "The ice cream is eaten by the police officer," a 5-year-old might not understand the structure of the sentence any better than a 3-year-old. But the 5-year-old will be able to figure out that something is eating and something is being eaten and that this sentence has only one candidate for each of these actions. Thus the 5-year-old may be able to "guess" the correct meaning of this sentence. The same 5-year-old, however, would have trouble with "The elephant was kissed by the bear." because this sentence is "reversible"—the elephant or the bear can be either kisser or kissed. The words in the sentence contain no semantic cues about which does the kissing. In this situation the 5-year-old's performance is little better than the 3-year-old's.

Five-year-olds also get cues from context. If you show a 5-year-old a picture of a bear kissing an elephant and say, "The elephant was kissed by the bear," the child will be able to tell who did the kissing. You can tell the child is depending on context because if you show a picture of the elephant doing the kissing and say the same sentence, the interpretation changes to agree with the picture. This kind of sentence processing is tied to what children perceive in the same way as are their interpretations of conservation tasks. It is not until about age 8 that children can decipher difficult sentences without being totally dependent on the context in which the sentence is uttered.

IN CONCLUSION

The decade of the 1970s saw a great surge of research on the relations between cognitive development and language. This research has continued into the 1980s, but the questions have changed somewhat. In the beginning many researchers proceeded on the assumption that much of what we know about the progress of language development in children could be explained by looking at cognitive development. Language was seen as being in some sense an aspect of cognitive development. After many studies, involving both normal and language-disordered children, the picture now seems to be more complex. It is true that the study of cognition has given us a much better idea about the child's intellectual development prior to the appearance of spoken language. We know that the child demonstrates a range of cognitive abilities (such as mental representation) that seem logically to precede the appearance of language. We also know that the child has a range of ideas about the nature of the world that serve as the meanings to be expressed in early language. What we cannot say is whether there are specific cognitive prerequisites for the acquisition of any specific aspect of language (such as past tense endings on verbs). We also know little about how language and cognition interact once the child has acquired language. Finally, even if we knew the answers to these questions, we still would not know how the child manages to learn, in so short a time, that system of rules and forms we call language. While it is important to study cognitive development, and while our understanding of children's cognitive abilities has enriched our understanding of early language use, we still lack the answers to many of the most pressing questions.

SUMMARY

The child's developing cognition underlies his or her developing skills with language. Most of what we know about cognitive development in young children comes from the work of Jean Piaget. Piaget describes in great detail the child's cognitive development during the sensorimotor period, a period that establishes the foundation for language use.

The next stage of cognitive development Piaget labels preoperational. Children in this stage are narrowly limited to their individual views of the world and their own oversimplified concepts of reality. This egocentric and limited view of the world is reflected in the child's language use.

SUGGESTED READINGS

Donaldson, M. *Children's Minds*. London: Fontana, 1978. This text focuses on cognitive development and language in preschool and school-age children. It is short, readable, and full of interesting examples.

Flavell, J. *Communication and the Development of Role-Taking Skills in Children*. New York: Wiley, 1968. Flavell explains well the development of the ability in preoperational children to see things as others might see them.

Furth, H. G. *Piaget and Knowledge*. Englewood Cliffs, N.J.: Prentice-Hall, 1969. All of Piaget's theorizing is collated in this book. Chapter 3, on language, is particularly good.

Furth, H. G. *Piaget for Teachers*. Englewood Cliffs, N.J.: Prentice-Hall, 1972. A more readable and applied treatment of the same material covered in Furth's *Piaget and Knowledge*.

Piaget, J. *The Child's Conception of the World*. Trans. M. Wordon. New York: Harcourt Brace Jovanovich, 1928. This book presents Piaget's ideas about how children structure their world. It contains many excellent examples of children's speech to illustrate points.

Pulaski, M. A. S. *Understanding Piaget*. New York: Harper & Row, 1971. Pulaski provides a simplified and highly readable summary of Piaget's ideas, with a focus on cognitive development rather than language per se. Many examples of children's speech are included.

SUGGESTED PROJECTS

1. Repeat some of Piaget's conservation experiments with children aged 3, 4, 5, and 6. Watch how their behavior changes and also how the language they use to talk about the tasks changes.

2. Review the research on private speech or mediating language. Try to devise an experiment to discover whether and how language plays a role in nonverbal problem solving. (Hint: Laura Berk presents a readable summary of some of this work in *Psychology Today*, May 1986.)

Chapter
10

How Children Learn to Communicate

*I*n previous chapters we looked at what the child has to know as a language learner. It was necessary to discuss each area in detail because each has its own terminology and because some phases of development take place in only one or a few of these areas. But communicative development grows as an organic whole. This chapter brings together some communication acquisition processes that occur in several of the specialized areas discussed in Part Two. The question we are asking is "How do children learn to talk?" In essence, we are looking for explanations— for variables that bring about changes from babbling through child speech to adult language use.

BIOLOGY AND COMPETENCE

First, we restate the importance of the fact that human babies are members of a species of speaking animals. There is a strong biological predisposition toward developing implicit knowledge of linguistic (syntactic, phonological, semantic) relationships. This is just another way of saying that people are able to learn a language because they are human. They are also able to learn to *speak* a language, that is, to learn the usage patterns of their community. We agree with Piaget that all this is a result of general processes of cognitive development: People learn to talk because that is part of learning to think as humans do.

This developmental emphasis highlights the ways in which all people are alike. Linguists like to say that each of us has a linguistic competence consisting of what we know about language. We would expand that concept to say that people possess *communicative competence,* covering knowledge of the entire range and scope of communication. This humanistic conception of communication encourages us to think that all people are related to each other.

But as we look around the world, we see that some are more closely related than others. We also see that even though we all have human intelligence, some are smarter than others. Even though we all have communicative competence, some communicate more effectively than others. All people are different as well as alike. A biological perspective on communication development explains how all people are alike, but not how each is different from the other.

In the process of acquiring language, children share a common human birthright, but each child must face that process as an individual. Our theory of communicative development must take into account the dynamics of how children encounter communication events and how they learn.

Some early studies of grammar failed to do this. They built theories strictly on the basis of the internal workings of grammar. Researchers assumed that children would learn the "simplest" rules of grammar first and more complex varieties later. But when Bates (1967) predicted order of acquisition of some syntactic rules on the basis of complexity of the rules, results were directly the opposite of predictions. She concluded that children's progress in language acquisition is more a result of their learning strategies than of the rules of grammar. We share this view, and the present chapter focuses largely on children's learning procedures.

Looking at learning strategies is especially important to educators, clinicians, and parents because these people are all concerned with why some children communicate more effectively than others. Before we examine the kinds of learning strategies children might use in acquiring communication skill, we will briefly survey the attempts to explain language acquisition by theorists over the past few decades.

ACQUISITION THEORY

Behaviorist Approaches

For many years language learning was viewed as a fairly simple process. It was believed that children learned to talk by imitating what they heard and that parents or other adults shaped children's language by correcting their mistakes. This kind of description received scientific respectability in the work of B. F. Skinner and other behaviorists. These theorists hold that learning occurs when a child's behavior results in some behavior from the environment or some reaction within the child that is reinforcing. Reinforcement of a behavior increases the probability that that behavior will occur again in similar circumstances. For example, if a child wants a cookie and says "cookie," and the mother gives the child a cookie, receiving the cookie reinforces saying "cookie," and it becomes more likely that the next time the child wants a cookie, he will say "cookie."

One problem with this approach, of course, lies in what is to be regarded as reinforcement. It is difficult to find any clear explanation of what kinds of behavior by parents or others in the environment can be reinforcement for the child's learning of adult grammatical patterns. In addition, since a child's behavior cannot be reinforced until it has occurred, the question of how the child ever comes to make grammatical sentences for parents to reinforce remains unanswered.

In essence, this behaviorist approach suggests that the language-learning child is a passive participant in the learning process, highly dependent on the actions of others in the environment for her learning. In addition, the approach views what is being learned (language) as largely irrelevant, that is, language learning is viewed as no different from learning to ride a bicycle or work a puzzle. The process remains the same.

The Structural Revolution

It took a revolution in linguistic theory to cause us to look at the child as an active participant in the learning process. Noam Chomsky's theory of transformational grammar shifted the focus from the process of language acquisition to the product of that learning. Chomsky argues that language is a rule-governed system and that an infinite number of sentences can be accounted for by a finite set of grammatical rules. Integral to his theory is the idea that users of language "know" these grammatical rules and use them to interpret or construct sentences. This knowledge is referred to as "linguistic competence," and the child's task is to acquire this competence. In other words, the child learning language is not simply imitating sentences he hears, but rather is learning rules that are used to generate those sentences. The evidence in favor of rule induction and against imitation as an explanation of how the child learns language has mounted sufficiently to leave little doubt that the view of the child as an active hypothesis tester is the more reasonable one.

In addition to providing us with a different outlook on the process of language learning, Chomsky's theory has also caused us to take a new look at the child's output. Language researchers, looking with new eyes at the utterances of young children, are asking not "How many words does the child use?" but "What rule does the child know which would account for this utterance?" The realization that children's utterances are as systematic and rule governed as adult utterances has led to attempts to identify stages of language development.

The fruitfulness of this approach to normal language development can be seen in the variety of language assessment instruments devised over the past decade. Some of these are systems for analyzing a child's spontaneous speech, such as Lee's developmental sentence scoring (1975) and Tyack and Gottsleben's (1974) analysis scheme. Others are structured tests that attempt to elicit a particular linguistic form from a child or to have a child demonstrate comprehension of the form. All these assessment instruments depend on the data concerning the stages that normal children go through as they learn language, and they are designed to allow the tester to analyze an individual child's progress through these stages.

Semantics and Cognition Hypothesis

While the acquisition of grammar is obviously a part of the child's language acquisition, it is not the only part, as acquisition theorists have pointed out. In particular, Bloom's (1971) discovery that children may often use a single grammatical structure ("mommy sock") to represent quite different meanings ("This is mommy's sock" or "Mommy put my sock on me") caused researchers to begin to look beyond linguistic forms to the meanings children express with these forms.

This emphasis on meaning, or semantics, coincides with a return in cognitive psychology to the work of Jean Piaget. Language researchers ask what meaning the young child might be able to express in language, and Piagetian psychologists provide a set of possible answers drawn from their research into early cognitive development. Generally stated, this approach to language acquisition leads to ideas such as that expressed by Bloom, Lighttown, and Hood (1975) that children learn grammar as a means to represent what they already know about events in the world. Numerous studies (Bowerman, 1976; Clark, 1973; Cromer, 1974) have attempted to show the relationships between the child's development of sensorimotor intelligence (see Chapter 9) and the child's early language.

Miller, Chapman, Branston, and Reichle (1980), in a study of language comprehension among children at sensorimotor stages V and VI, point out that it is exceptionally difficult to find clear-cut causal relationships between cognitive level and comprehension of sentence meaning. They suggest instead that we retreat to a correlational version of the cognitive hypothesis. In other words, the research to date makes it possible to say only that certain cognitive levels and certain language behaviors seem to occur around the same time as children mature. It is also worth noting that research has been limited to children in the sensorimotor stage of development, and we know almost nothing about the relationship between later cognitive levels and later language development.

Even though the work investigating cognition and language is only in its early stages, it has served to remind us that language is not only a system of rules governing combinations of linguistic forms. It also involves meaning and the relationships between form and meaning. As we examine a child's use of various linguistic forms, we must be aware of the meanings represented by those forms and of the child's cognitive ability to handle those meanings. However, we must remember that there is no simple relationship between cognition and language, and knowing how a child responds on a language test will not tell us how the child would perform on a test of cognitive development. The relationships are more complex.

As Rees (1980) points out, there are in fact two types of cognitive ability related to language learning. One type involves the development of a set of concepts that are precursors to meaning. It is this set that has been investigated in the research cited above. Another set of cognitive abilities is related to the development of linguistic forms. This set, called "operating principles" by Slobin (1973), encompasses those strategies children use to work out the structure of the language. These operating strategies can be used to predict the forms children will find easiest to learn. For example, one operating principle is "Avoid exceptions." The assumption that children will follow this principle would lead us to predict that children would have an easier time learning regular past tense forms (such as "walked" and "played") than irregular forms (such as "hid" and "saw"). In fact, this is the case, and many children go through a stage of overgeneralizing the regular past tense endings ("hided" and "seed") in an attempt to avoid exceptions to the past tense rule.

As this discussion suggests, it would be a mistake for us to assume that we could predict much about language behavior based on knowing about a particular cognitive ability. Clearly, we will be better served at this point if we think of language development as a part of the child's overall intellectual development. Language is acquired during the same period as certain concepts and certain cognitive strategies. While it is clear that a child will not use a language form for which the child has no meaning, it should be equally clear that the child's meaning for the form may not match the adult's meaning for it, and that the presence of the linguistic form cannot be taken as evidence of the development of a concept, especially if the presence of the concept is then to be used to predict the development of the linguistic form! Much work remains to be done on the cognition hypothesis.

Functionalist Theory

Although functionalist views of language acquisition are a recent development, the call for such an approach is not new. The key to this approach is the notion that grammatical structure cannot be understood outside the context in which language is used. The functionalist approach to language holds that grammar is a secondary or derived system, related to the constraints of the communication task. As Bates and MacWhinney (1982, p. 168) express it, "the child's acquisition of grammar is guided, not by abstract categories, but by the pragmatic and semantic structure of communications interacting with the performance constraint of the speech channel."

In this view of language the child's task becomes one of mapping a diverse set of semantic and pragmatic functions onto a finite set of grammatical forms. Children discover the structure of grammar through their experience with its use in a variety of communication contexts. A functionalist approach forces us to concentrate first on what we can do with language. We may then regard individual differences in language as different mappings of language form onto language actions. Clark (1983, p. 2) says that researchers who follow the functionalist approach "seek not only to characterize the processes of speaking and listening by themselves, but also to describe how these processes are influenced, changed, or disrupted by the activities in which they are embedded."

Applying this approach to the study of language learning, we arrive at a position that appears to us to combine the best of all the available theoretical approaches. It might be summarized by saying that children do not learn language in isolation. Language is a tool that is learned in the context of its use. To understand how it is learned requires knowing the characteristics of the learner (Chapters 2 and 9), the characteristics of what is being learned (Chapters 5 through 8), and the context in which learning occurs (Chapters 3, 11, 12, 13). A close look at this total picture convinces us that Wells (1986, p. 44) is right when he says:

> ... children progressively construct a representation of the language of their community. And they do so on the basis of the evidence provided for them in conversation with more mature members of that community. Furthermore, because human beings are similarly endowed as language learners, the sequence in which they construct their internal representations is very similar from one learner to another, and so are the underlying principles in terms of which their representation of the language system is ultimately organized.

LEARNING STRATEGIES

In discussions of the strategies children employ in learning to talk, the dispute between those who emphasize the effects of the environment and those who emphasize the child's innate abilities or knowledge often generates more heat than light. Of course, both are important for language learning. Let us consider several learning strategies that the child might use.

Reinforcement

The behaviorists argue that the kind of learning most important to the child's communicative development is operant conditioning. As we have said, operant conditioning occurs when a child's behavior results in some behavior from the environment or some reaction within the child that is reinforcing. Reinforcement increases the probability that the child's behavior will occur again. The critical part of any operant conditioning situation is the reinforcement, but in a given situation it may be difficult to determine what was reinforcing and what was learned. For example, the behaviorists maintain that children learn to make grammatical sentences through a complex and delicately balanced combination of discriminative reinforcement in which certain of the child's language behaviors are reinforced and certain others are extinguished (because they are not reinforced). However, it is difficult to find any clear explanation of what kinds of behavior on the part of parents or others are reinforcement for the child's learning adult grammatical patterns.

One possible (and obvious) reinforcement is praise for correct grammatical patterns and correction of incorrect patterns. However, there is some question as to how much correcting of grammar the average parent does and what the child learns from it. For example, Brown and Hanlon (1970) argue that parents do not correct children on the basis of grammar. They found that when a child says a sentence that is true but ungrammatical, such as "Mama isn't boy, he a girl,"the parents are likely to say, "That's right!" (which is reinforcement and should make children speak ungrammatically). But if the Walt Disney show is broadcast on Sunday, and the child says, "Walt Disney comes on Tuesday," the parents are likely to say, "No, it comes on Sunday." According to Brown and Hanlon, parents of young children reinforce sentences that are true and ungrammatical (but understandable) more often than sentences that are grammatical but wrong.

Syntax cannot be learned by this kind of reinforcement alone and must be learned in some other way. This view makes sense when you consider how complex grammar is, yet how quickly children pick it up. Even if it could be established that reinforcement plays a major role in children's learning of grammar, the question of how the child picks out grammatical sentences to say would remain. Because children cannot be reinforced in an operant conditioning situation until they emit some behavior, the question of how they come to make their first grammatical sentences is important.

But syntax is not all that children must learn in order to communicate. The evidence that parents do reinforce sentence truth value indicates that operant conditioning may be an important learning strategy for acquiring knowledge about how sentences function within speech situations (pragmatics). A great deal about when to speak in what manner to whom is learned according to what modes of speech are reinforced. You learn not to swear around your grandmother from her reaction. You learn to compliment her dinner the same way. This may offer a hint to parents and teachers: You may be able to improve the things a child says by giving praising when you are pleased, but years of teaching grammar by correction in the public schools should indicate that you are unlikely to improve a child's grammar solely by praising good constructions or reacting negatively to syntactic aberrations.

Imitation

One of the first characteristics of child speech everyone notices is that children imitate adult utterances. This imitation typically assumes the form of *telegraphic speech,* leaving out functions (inflections, auxiliary verbs, articles, prepositions, and conjunctions) and including high content words (nouns, verbs, and adjectives). The resulting speech is interpretable but condensed. If a parent says, "There's a red truck," the child is likely to say, "Red truck." Brown and Bellugi (1964) called this "imitation with reduction" and theorized that it was important to grammar learning. Even more important, they found that parents often "imitate" child utterances, expanding them by restoring the very words children are likely to leave out. This "imitation with expansion" seems an efficient teaching device because it pairs the child's immature sentence with the adult representation. Consequently, the parent's expansions could be regarded as a potent form of reinforcement.

But even though children and parents do imitate each other, it has never been proved that this imitating helps children learn to talk. In fact, Cazden (1965) presents limited evidence that brief language training using imitation with expansion produced little improvement in performance. Perhaps imitation, though a common event, is simply not an efficient enough learning strategy to explain much about communication development. Consider the following example from McNeill (1966):

> CHILD: Nobody don't like me.
> MOTHER: No, say "Nobody likes me."
> CHILD: Nobody don't like me.
> *[Eight repetitions of this dialogue.]*
> MOTHER: No, now listen carefully. Say "Nobody likes me."
> CHILD: Oh! Nobody don't likes me.

The child finally *partially* corrected his utterance, so it is possible to teach through imitation. But for this case, at least, the process seems quite inefficient.

The major importance of imitation to communicative development might be in learning the individual sounds and words of a language. Children often play with sounds; they imitate with little regard for what a sentence means. Perhaps this play is important in learning about the sounds and words of a language. It is difficult to conceive of how children could learn to use the proper word for any object in their environment except by imitating others.

Modeling

When Cazden (1965) tried to teach language to children using imitation with expansion, she also employed (with a different group of children in the same experiment) a technique she called "modeling." Teachers who used this technique tried not to repeat or expand child utterances; rather, they attempted to comment on what the child said—to answer questions, offer contributions on related topics, and so forth. In this way they offered a model of mature speech for children to emulate, without imitating.

Cazden found that the modeling training improved performance, whereas expansion did not. This might lead to the hypothesis that children may learn some aspects of communication simply by "absorbing" and emulating sentences of adults they hear speaking. However, Cazden worked with a small number of children and her subjects were black and classified as economically deprived, so this isolated finding should not cause us to overestimate the importance of modeling.

Perhaps a more important reservation about the modeling hypothesis is this: If we say modeling is important, we have described a situation in which learning takes place, but we have said little about the nature of the learning strategies themselves. We do not know by what processes children learn in this situation or even how they select models. We may find that models matter, but we must search for children's major learning strategies in the acts they perform.

Self-Motivated Practice

The child seems to practice a lot while learning to communicate. This is similar in some ways to such later behavior as "practicing the piano." There is repetition of simple forms (similar to scales or elementary tunes), and there is concatenating of these forms into larger patterns. Such practice is different from piano practice in that no adult needs to force the child to practice. It is entirely self-motivated; the child seems simply to enjoy the experience of play with words.

Constant practice of musical patterns is, of course, the key to learning to play the piano. Is practice a major aspect of learning to communicate? It would strain credulity to argue that young children practice talking because they hope to be famous speakers in the sense that some children practice piano because they hope to be musicians when they grow up. Yet the practice itself could help communication whether the child knows it or not. One might even guess that children's esthetic joy in making noise is nature's way of making them learn to talk.

Again, however, we must not assume that practice, just because it happens, represents an important learning strategy. There is evidence that learning can take place without it at some stages of development. As we discussed in Chapter 2, a baby whose throat operation prevented babbling for several months performed appropriately for his age on the day after his throat was repaired. The entire act of babbling, once thought important to sound development, is now considered to be less important. Children make sounds while babbling that they are unable to use in meaningful speech until many years later. Finally, there is the fact that children first learn to use irregular verbs correctly ("ran"), but later regularize them ("runned"), in spite of having practiced the correct forms. In this case practice seems unimportant; learning apparently results from inducing and generalizing rules.

Rule Induction

Brown and Bellugi (1964) speak of a syntax acquisition process they call *induction of latent structure.* A child hears a number of sentences that use similar syntactic constructions and through her ability to generalize comes to realize what rules are being followed. Our understanding of this induction process is incomplete. Some researchers have suggested that such induction is simply stimulus-generalization learning cued by the order of words in sentences. This explanation is incomplete because word order by itself does not provide enough cues to deep structure. Yet the induction process certainly involves the child's making generalizations from limited sets of stimuli. Communication development, in fact, is characterized by generalizations based on extremely limited evidence. That is why language structure develops so fast. If children waited for enough evidence to justify the generalizations they make, they would never learn to talk.

Oversimplified and inaccurate generalizations are called *overgeneralizations.* In Chapter 4 several examples of overgeneralization were discussed. Regular tense endings on irregular verbs and regularized plural endings on irregular nouns are among the many instances that could be cited. This evidence suggests the following rule-induction sequence:

1. The child discovers some meaning, concept, or task that has communicative implications.
2. Closely related to this, the child discovers in the environment a new piece of the code that speakers in the child's language community use in apparent conjunction with this speech function.
3. The child overgeneralizes the function of the discovered piece of code and applies it to a larger class of events. Given that there are fewer pieces in the child's code than kinds of speech events, many utterances that employ these overgeneralized rules will appear (to adults) to be "quaint errors."
4. The child receives mixed reinforcement about the overgeneralized usage.
5. The child sorts out some events in which using the rule has unhappy consequences, forms these into a new class or classes, and searches the linguistic environment for a new general rule to cover these exceptional cases.
6. Discovering such a rule, the child again overgeneralizes it to some events for which it is inappropriate.

It should be repeated that overgeneralization is the flip side of differentiation. Global categories are grist for differentiation and vice versa.

(Readers familiar with Piaget's thought will note similarities with the concepts of assimilation and accommodation.)

The concept of rule induction raises as many questions as it resolves. We know little about what particular events in the environment best facilitate rule induction. But some tactics are *not* likely to help much:

1. Teaching rules or principles explicitly in the absence of appropriate application to meaningful communication
2. Imitating children exactly or forcing them to imitate
3. Correcting children's improper grammar without understanding and paying attention to what the child is communicating

We shall elaborate on tactics that might help in the next chapter. Basically, we need to give children a chance to operate in circumstances in which communication can help them. Probably nothing is more helpful than a chance to operate within the most natural of all communication settings—conversation.

HUMPTY DUMPTY REASSEMBLED

Table 10.1 is an attempt to bring all of this together. In it are listed the learning strategies and the major aspects of development discussed in this chapter. An X indicates that a strategy is important to a phase of communication development. A question mark indicates that we are not certain at the present time if a strategy is important to a particular phase. Two things are immediately evident: (1) There are many question marks (because the research field is young and children are complex). (2) Most of the Xs are for the rule-induction learning process (which is, of course, the process about which we know least). Beyond this, we can make the following educated guesses.

Table 10.1 LEARNING STRATEGIES IN COMMUNICATION DEVELOPMENT

	Aspects of Development				
Learning Strategies	Early Syntax	Later Syntax (transformations and exceptions)	Sounds	Meaning	Pragmatics (usage)
Operant conditioning	?	X	?	?	X
Imitation	?	?	X	X	
Modeling	?	?	?	?	X
Practice	?	?	?	?	X
Rule induction (overgeneralization)	X	?	X	X	X

X, important strategy in aspect of development; ?, uncertainty about importance.

Early syntax, which children are strongly biologically predisposed to acquire, is learned almost solely through rule-governed overgeneralization. This does not deny the fact that environment is important. Children must generalize on the basis of the language they hear. If that language is not correct standard American English, they obviously will not learn correct standard American English. Beyond this, it is possible that syntax can be taught in some cases through modeling.

Later syntax (exceptions to general rules and complex transformations) is learned differently from early syntax. The process is much slower. Either the older child is less of a linguistic genius than the young child (probable), or the problems are more complex. As mentioned in Chapter 4, we know that certain rules are acquired late, but we know little about how these rules are learned. Because of the slowness of learning, the sort of powerful rule induction responsible for early syntax is unlikely. The best candidates for important places are imitation and modeling, in the context of operant conditioning.

The acquisition of sounds is also shrouded in mystery. Children certainly practice sounds a great deal, but there is only limited evidence that this is important to learning. Imitation occurs and is probably important in working out some sound patterns. Obviously, a child must hear the sounds of a language to learn it, so in that broad sense imitation is vital. But most important seems to be induction of rules from perceived speech. The ability to distinguish between sounds and to follow difficult rules about what sounds go where is about as remarkable and rapid as acquisition of syntax.

Even less is known about the acquisition of meaning. Clearly, much of what the child learns in this area is learned through imitation (using a particular label to refer to a particular thing). However, imitation alone cannot account for the child's ability to operate within the system of semantic markers and selection restrictions discussed in Chapter 5. Some rule-induction strategies may affect this learning; a kind of overgeneralization appears to take place in children's concept learning, and certainly environmental shaping plays a role.

In the area of pragmatics there is little evidence. We guess that learning in this area is about a half-and-half mix of environmental shaping (learning resulting from how people react to your communication) and rule induction. The rule induction can be seen to operate in the fact that we often know what is appropriate in a particular situation without ever having encountered a similar situation. There is a sense in which patterns of usage, like rules of syntax, allow the speaker infinite numbers of alternatives out of which to create messages.

This model of how children learn to talk is like an egg shell reassembled—very fragile, with many cracks. It does represent the state of our knowledge. But we feel that the perspective provided by this chapter can serve as a basis for some recommendations about how we can make things better. The rest of this book offers such advice.

SUGGESTED READINGS

Brown, R., and U. Bellugi. Three processes in the child's acquisition of syntax. *Harvard Educational Review 34,* 133-151, l964. Also in E. Lenneberg (ed.), *New Directions in the Study of Language.* Cambridge, Mass.: MIT Press, 1964; in R. Brown, *Psycholinguistics.* New York: Free Press, 1970. This extremely well-written article was one of the first attempts to give a theoretically based account of the learning of grammar.

Ervin, S. M. Imitation and structural change in children's language. In E. Lenneberg (ed.), *New Directions in the Study of Language.* Cambridge, Mass.: MIT Press, 1965. Ervin discusses learning strategies and gives a large number of examples of overgeneralization in child speech.

Wells, G. *Learning Through Interaction.* Cambridge: Cambridge University Press, 1981. This is a superb presentation of language learning from a functionalist perspective. We recommend it both for its presentation of the facts of language development and for its theoretical perspective.

SUGGESTED PROJECTS

1. Choose three of Slobin's (1971) operating principles and under each principle list a set of "facts" about language development which would cause you to believe that children are using this principle to learn language. The operating principles are found in D. I. Slobin, Cognitive prerequisites for the acquisition of grammar, in C. A. Ferguson and D. I. Slobin (eds.), Studies of Child Language Development (New York: Holt, Rinehart and Winston, 1973).

2. Prepare a paper on the role of imitation in language learning. Besides the references in the chapter, you might want to consult J. Berko-Gleason and S. Weintraub, The acquisition of routines in child language, *Language in Society 5,* 129-136, 1976; L. Bloom, P. Hood, and P. Lightbown, Imitation in language development: If, when, and why, *Cognitive Psychology 6,* 380-420, 1974.

Chapter
11

Language Diversity

We have stated throughout this book that children go through an identifiable series of stages in the process of acquiring language and that this similarity among children is probably due to a common biological heritage. In saying this, of course, we are not implying that all children are identical. Individuality is maintained and reflected in many ways during the language-learning years. The language samples below, from two children similar in age and level of syntactic development, will show something of what we mean. Chris is 25 months, and Angela is 24 months.

MOTHER: Look, Chris. I'm rolling out the cookie dough. See, it's getting flat.

CHRIS: Flat. Flat. Roller dough.

MOTHER: Right. I'm rolling the dough to make it flat. Next we'll cut out the cookies.

CHRIS: Cut out cookies.

MOTHER: Right. With the cookie cutters.

CHRIS: Cookie cutters.

MOTHER: Yes. Where did you put them?

CHRIS: Huh?

MOTHER: Where did you put the cookie cutters? Are they in the bowl?

CHRIS: Inna bowl. Cookie cutters.

MOTHER: Can you find the star for me? Hand me the star cookie cutter.

CHRIS: Star. Star cookies.

ANGELA: What dat?

MOTHER: That's the pizza dough, for the crust.

ANGELA: Where pizza?

MOTHER: We haven't made the pizza yet. First we have to make the crust. Then we put all the stuff on it.

ANGELA: Put sausage.

MOTHER: Yes, we'll put on sausage and cheese and tomato sauce.

ANGELA: Me cheese.

MOTHER: Yes, you can sprinkle on the cheese when we're ready.

ANGELA: Spink cheese.

MOTHER: Right, you sprinkle cheese.

Several differences between these children are immediately apparent. Chris is an imitator; Angela is not. Chris seems to be passive in regard to controlling conversational topics; Angela gives the impression of being an initiator. Although it is not clearly indicated in the transcript, Chris has much better control of phonology than Angela has. These are only a few of the possible differences one might expect to find between two children learning language. Although research into differences in language learning is fairly new, there is an increasing body of literature in the area, and the findings are intriguing.

INDIVIDUAL DIFFERENCES IN LANGUAGE DEVELOPMENT

There is some evidence that personality and general cognitive style affect the process of language learning. Some children seem to be risk takers. They will try a new word or form even though they may not be certain about its meaning or use. Other children seem more cautious, unwilling to make mistakes or to forge ahead in the face of uncertainty. These differences have been observed in the learning of phonology (Branigan, 1979; Ferguson and Farwell, 1975) and syntax (Peters, 1977). Nelson (1981) observed differences in vocabulary development between children she labeled "expressive" versus "referential." Expressive children seem to focus on personal relations and feelings, while referential children focus more on objects. Other researchers have noticed that some children seem to prefer nouns to refer to people and things, while others prefer pronouns (Horgan, 1981). It is not always entirely clear what lies behind these kinds of differences.

Children also differ in perseverance, curiosity, sociability, independence, and other characteristics. All these influence the child's individual approach to the language-learning task. They also influence the ways other people interact with the child and so affect the amount and kind of conversation the child is exposed to (Wells, 1986). Imagine the difference between an interaction with a highly active, stubborn, independent child and an interaction with a quiet, passive, tractable child. The two children are likely to hear different vocabularies and to encounter different language functions in their experiences with the world. Working from different sorts of input, they are quite likely to come up with different sorts of language behaviors.

Many people believe that gender is a factor affecting language learning and that girls are faster language learners than boys. Research in the late 1950s and early 1960s tended to confirm this belief. More recently, however, researchers studying children's spontaneous language use in ordinary situations have failed to find any language advantage associated with being female.

This is not to say that gender differences do not exist. In spite of the efforts of even the most well-meaning parents, girls and boys are socialized differently in ways that have implications for language learning. Wells (1986), after conducting a nine-year study of children's language learning in Bristol, England, reported that parents give boys and girls different toys and engage boys and girls in different conversational situations. Boys tend to be talked with and to talk while they play with toys. Conversations with girls occur more often in the context of helping with household tasks. Other differences related to gender are summarized by Cherry and Lewis (1976). While none of these environmental differences is likely to affect the rate of language development, it may certainly affect the range of semantic and pragmatic meanings made available to the child.

SOCIAL CLASS DIFFERENCES IN LANGUAGE DEVELOPMENT

The issue of social class and language is a difficult one. It is not always easy to tell what people mean when they talk about social class. Most of the generally accepted definitions consist of some rating of family income, education level, and housing. This is not a problem if the person being classified is a single mother who dropped out of high school and lives in a tenement on welfare. It becomes somewhat more difficult to classify a family in which the father has a Ph.D. but is driving a taxi while he looks for a teaching job, the mother is a high school graduate working as a computer programmer, and they are living with her parents. The main problem with classifying families into social class levels is the assumption that everyone at a particular level will be the same. This is, of course, not at all the case. There will be as many differences within a particular social class grouping as there are between classes.

This brings up the obvious questions of why anyone would expect social class to affect a child's language learning and what differences it could make. The answers involve a complex mix of societal expectations, public school demands, and preschool language experiences. Public school education in the United States is based on what we generally think of as a middle-class model. Many expectations for language use arise out of kinds of experiences children who are not middle class are unlikely to have.

Consider, for example, the use of language in "civilized" conflict resolution. All young children get into disagreements. They argue over turf and toys and identities. Sometimes these conflicts end in physical violence or name calling or tears. Many middle-class (and other) parents try to teach their children to use language to avoid and settle conflicts. Mothers will say, "Why don't you ask Susie if you can have the toy when she's done with it. She's playing with it now, but after her turn, you can have a turn." Or, "No hitting, Jonathan. If you are angry with Daniel, you can tell him. You can say 'Daniel, you make me so mad. I won't play with you anymore.' But you must not hit." These little teaching scenes and others like them are designed not only to keep children from hurting each other. They also are leading children to believe that the world is organized in a particular way (everybody can have a turn if she asks nicely) and that there is something powerful about words (you will feel better if you scream "I'm angry at you."). These are assumptions that any middle-class elementary school teacher would agree with. Imagine what happens, then, when such teachers (or a group of children who have been socialized into this middle-class view of the world) encounter a child who has not been led to have these expectations about language and the world. A child who has learned or been told that if you want something someone else has, you take it and run, or that if someone hits you, you hit back, will not fit the middle-class model. This kind of socialization gap is often reflected in class differences in language development and use.

This analysis is admittedly oversimplified, but it can lead us to thinking about kinds of experience that might serve to differentiate, say, an inner-city, street-smart 6-year-old from a protected, suburban, school-focused 6-year-old. If the schools were run by the street-smart child's social group, the suburbanite would be in trouble. But since the schools are run by the other group, the street-smart kid is in trouble. And the trouble is real; it is not a matter of surface smoothing. Schooling and the larger world that follows it demand a set of meanings, a set of speech acts, and a level of proficiency with language form which can come out of only particular kinds of language learning experiences. To the extent that a child lacks those experiences, that child will be truly disadvantaged.

Wells (1986) examined social class effects in his Bristol study. The 128 children in the study were carefully chosen to be representative of four social class levels, from lower to upper. Their preschool language development was closely studied, and then a representative subset of the group was followed as they went through the early grades of school. Wells found that the most advanced and skilled language users in the study had better educated, professional parents and the least advanced children had minimally educated, unskilled parents, but except for these two extremes (representing 10 percent of the children in the study), there was no clear-cut relationship between family background and level of language development when language ability was measured in terms of spontaneous conversation in the home. When language ability was measured in terms of school achievement (using formal tests), the children from the lower end of the social scale fared less well, however. Wells ascribes this finding to a single factor in the children's family backgrounds. He says:

> If some lower-class children did suffer from linguistic disadvantage, therefore, it was not in relation to their command or experience of oral language, but in the relatively low value placed on literacy by their parents, as shown by their own very limited use of these skills, by the absence of books—either children's or parent's—in the home, and by the infrequency with which they read to their children, if they ever did so at all." (1986, p. 144)

This finding clearly emphasizes the importance of language in all of its forms in the environment of the language-learning child and highlights book reading and stories as a critical part of that environment for all children.

NONSTANDARD DIALECTS

This brief account has pointed out some individual and group factors that might lead to differences in language development. It suggests that variations among children and in environments provide many avenues to language and that, while some of these avenues may be easier to travel than others, they have a common end point. There are, however, some avenues that lead to different places. In particular, ethnic differences in society may be reflected in forms of language and ways of language use that do not fit the mainstream pattern.

Children from ethnic minority groups usually speak what are called *nonstandard dialects* of English. This means that there is some consistent and recognizable way in which their speech is different from the speech of middle-class whites. Many educators feel that this difference in speech accounts for the fact that minority-group children often do poorly in school. Questions about relationships between school performance and speech patterns for these children have not been satisfactorily answered. This is a complex issue. What should the policy of teachers and parents be toward nonstandard speech? To give any useful answers, we need some background on what nonstandard speech is like.

The use of the term nonstandard obviously implies the existence of a standard. Before we can talk about nonstandard dialects, it makes sense to ask about the standard dialect. In this country the use of the term *standard English* has generally been confined to English teachers and their friends. It is used to mean "proper" or "correct" English. Standard English is the form of speech described in old-fashioned grammar books. As such, it is actually spoken by few people. However, it is a form of speech usually expected from well-educated people. Fortunately or unfortunately, it has come to be identified as the speech of educated, white, middle-class Americans.

It is important to remember that even when educated, white, middle-class Americans talk, they often make grammatical errors. The difference between the everyday mistakes speakers are likely to make and a dialect variation is that ordinary errors are likely to be individual, random, and inconsistent, whereas a dialect is comprised of consistent and predictable variations from standard English. An individual might sometimes say, "These boys was playing." Such a departure from the rules of standard English cannot be predicted. In a dialect, however, the specific variations from the standard form are quite recognizable and predictable. That is why writers and actors can sound like hillbillies or Jewish mothers. They can identify the consistent differences between the speech of these groups and the speech of the typical middle-class, white American. When they imitate the major characteristics of the speech of a particular group, their audience recognizes them as a member of the group with which that dialect is associated.

This leads to another characteristics of a dialect. It is usually associated with a particular group of people who have in common something besides the way they talk. Dialects are most often associated with geographical areas. We have a southern dialect, shared by people who live in the southeastern parts of the country. It cuts across political boundaries and to a certain extent across social class boundaries. White, rural laborers and the country club set in any southern town will sound alike in many respects. Dialects are also associated with second-language learning. People who are not native English speakers will tend to sound different from native speakers when they learn English. The Puerto Ricans in New York City and the Mexican-Americans in the southwest are typical of groups that speak foreign-language influenced dialects.

People who talk about the problem of nonstandard dialects in the schools are most likely to be talking about the speech of the black child or the child who speaks a Spanish-influenced form of English in the inner-city schools of our large northern cities. It is perhaps cynical, but in many ways true, to say that the predominantly white, middle-class educational establishment in these cities has, in the past twenty-five years or so, been confronted with large numbers of children who do not sound like white, middle-class children. Some people see this as a problem. The questions are whose problem is it and what is to be done about it. The greatest attention to date has been given to how these questions relate to the speech of black children.

BLACK ENGLISH

Early researchers believed that black children's speech represented a disorganized and poorly articulated version of white speech. They took the position, known as the *deficit* theory of American dialects, that non-standard speakers were deficient in grammar. Most preschool intervention programs in the 1960s were based upon the deficit theory. Educators felt that if minority children could be taught standard English, their school achievement problems would vanish. This was an attractive theory because it attributed a host of failure problems to one observable cause—inferior language.

Later research demonstrated that nonstandard varieties of English are as highly structured and rule-governed as standard English. It is now more fashionable in scholarly circles to say that dialects are simply different from each other. According to this *difference* theory of American dialects, no dialect is inferior to others. Educational problems result not because minority children know no grammar, but because the schools offer instruction only in an alien grammar. The solution of difference theorists is *bidialectal instruction*—teaching children grammar of both their native dialect and standard English in the early grades. In theory, children will be fluent in both dialects and able to use each when it is most appropriate.

The difference approach seems preferable to the deficit approach, but in actual practice the differences between the two approaches may be slight. In bidialectal instruction minority children are still required to learn society's dominant dialect—a dialect spoken by people with whom they are rarely allowed to associate. Teachers still feel that the dominant dialect is standard and that instruction in nonstandard dialects is to be tolerated only to promote learning the standard. Because there is still little "good literature" written in nonstandard dialects, the older student has only standard English books to read. So children are, in effect, asked to enter a new speech community in which they are second-class citizens.

The inadequacies of programs based on difference theory lead us to ask, "Are the grammar differences between standard English and black English important and pervasive enough to cause such difficulty?" The answer seems to be no. If we examine the two dialects, we find that black English differs from standard English only in a few grammatical rules and some pronunciation features. The few differences in syntax occur mostly in surface structure; differences in deep structure seem small indeed (Labov, 1970b). The major differences between black English and standard English are summarized below.

Syntactic Features

   1. Possession. Standard: "Joe's pencil"; black: "Joe pencil."
   2. Negation. Standard: "I don't have a pencil"; black: "I ain't got no pencil" (use of double negative and word *ain't*).

3. Subject-verb agreement. Standard: "We were there," "They are here"; black: "We was there," "They is here."
4. Third person singular verbs. Standard: "He sings"; black: "He sing" (omission of *s*).
5. Present tense constructions. Standard: "I am going," "He is here"; black: "I going," "He here" (omission of auxiliary *to be*).
6. "If" constructions. Standard: "I'll ask Mary if she wants to go"; black: "I'll ask Mary do she want to go."
7. Regular past tense. Standard: "He walked"; black: "He walk" (*-ed* may be omitted). Note: Irregular past tense is not different; "sang" and "went" remain "sang" and "went".
8. Future tense. Standard: "I will go," "He is going to go"; black: "I'm 'a go," "He 'gon go."
9. Expression of habitual action. Standard: "He's always sick"; black: "He be sick" (as opposed to "He sick" meaning "He's sick right now").
10. Pronominal apposition. Standard: "John is funny," "Mary says to come in"(no pronominal apposition); black: "John he funny," "Mary she say to come."

Phonological Features

1. "R" may be omitted before consonants or if it is a final sound in a word. Standard:"guard," "carrot," "four"; black: "god," "cat," "foe."
2. "L" may be omitted before consonants or if it is a final sound. Standard:"help," "bowl"; black: "hep," "bow."
3. Consonant clusters at the end of words are shortened. Standard: "first," "told," "let's"; black: "firs," "tol," "les."
4. Final consonants are weaker. Standard:"want"; black: "wan."

Several things should be pointed out about this list of characteristics. First, all of these features may not appear in any individual black child's speech. The list is a general description of features in the speech of a large group, and individuals will vary. Just as all speakers of standard English do not sound alike, so all speakers of a nonstandard dialect do not sound alike. Additionally, the use of the dialect may vary according to the degree of formality in the situation, with fewer dialect features in very formal situations and more in informal situations.

The second thing to remember is that even if one found a child whose speech contained every feature listed, there is no reason to assume that that child's speech would be unintelligible to a listener. There is no sacrifice of semantic information in the dialect when speech is taken in context. The claim of many teachers that they cannot understand what the inner-city, black child is saying may be due to something other than the child's speech. And there is certainly no evidence to suggest that a child who speaks black English cannot understand standard English.

Some people have suggested, in line with the deficit theory, that black children brought up in a poverty-stricken environment do not receive sufficient language stimulation in the home and therefore start school with inadequately developed language skills. These people like to say that such children need language enrichment programs. Let us examine this view carefully. First, as we have pointed out several times, we do not know how much or what kind of language a child has to hear to learn how to talk. All we know is that the child must be exposed to some language. So it is difficult to determine what constitutes "inadequate" language stimulation. Second, we have no evidence that inner-city, black children fail to develop language. Indeed, the evidence is all to the contrary. On the playground or in the street they are just as talkative as any other children. This may not be true in the classroom, but that can (and should) be explained in other ways. The truth of the matter is that children learn to speak the language of their environment. If their parents and friends speak French, they learn French. And if their parents and friends speak a nonstandard dialect, they learn the dialect. They do not learn standard English. This is not the same thing as saying that their language development is inadequate.

SPANISH-INFLUENCED ENGLISH

The English spoken by children of Spanish-speaking backgrounds is in many ways more difficult to describe than the black English vernacular. The form of the English spoken results from the influences of a second language, Spanish. There have been a number of attempts to classify the "interference points" for the Spanish speaker learning English. These interference points are areas where the two languages differ in their representation of a given form. Interference affects not only the English vocabulary, where Spanish words may be substituted for English, but also English phonology and syntax, where Spanish sounds and constructions may appear.

The nature of the interference will depend on the variety of Spanish spoken and on the variety of English being learned. For example, Puerto Rican Spanish differs from Mexican Spanish, and a New York City Puerto Rican speaker is exposed to different English than a Texas Mexican speaker. The nature of the interference also depends on the extent of the child's bilingualism. Some children enter school as monolingual Spanish speakers and must learn English as a second language in school. Others enter school as monolingual English speakers, with perhaps only some Spanish vocabulary or some phonological interference. Many others come to school with knowledge of both Spanish and English, usually more of one than the other.

Some interference points are summarized below. Since the nature of the interference is affected by so many conditions, the summary can be only very general. The important fact for a teacher to remember is that these features do not signal ignorance. They make perfect sense in terms of Spanish.

Grammatical Interference Points

1. Morphological endings on words vary. The -*s* is often omitted in plurals, possessives, and third person singular verbs, because Spanish rarely pronounces such an ending. Also, past tense endings may appear to be absent ("They play yesterday"). Similarly, comparative endings on adjectives are not used, because Spanish employs added words rather than suffixes to show comparatives ("His shirt is more pretty" instead of "His shirt is prettier").
2. Negative commands may be expressed by "no" instead of "don't" ("No go there" instead of "Don't go there").
3. Articles may be absent, because Spanish uses articles quite differently from English ("She is teacher").
4. *To be* may be used incorrectly, because Spanish employs *to have* in many idioms in which English uses *to be* ("I have hunger," "He has 6 years," which are literal translations from Spanish).
5. "Do" may be absent from questions, because the corresponding Spanish construction needs no such verb ("You like ice cream?" instead of "Do you like ice cream?").
6. Word order differences are common ("Marie no is here," "George can go?").

Phonological Interference Points

1. Initial voiceless plosives are not aspirated in Spanish, so the pronunciation of "coat" may sound like "goat." All final plosives are voiceless in Spanish, so "pig" will sound like "pick."
2. Spanish has neither voiced nor voiceless /th/, so /d/ may be substituted for voiced /th/ ("dis" instead of "this") and /s/ may be substituted for voiceless /th/ ("sing" instead of "thing").
3. Spanish makes no distinction between /b/ and /v/ ("berry" instead of "very").
4. Spanish has the /s/ sound, but it does not have the /z/, /zh/ (as in "treasure"), and /sh/ (as in "shop") sounds of English. Spanish has the /ch/ (as in "chair"), but it does not have the /j/ (as in "jump").
5. The Spanish articulation of /r/ and /l/ differs from the English articulation and may be substituted for it.
6. The vowel sounds that occur in the English words "pig," "fat," and "sun" do not occur in Spanish, so "pig" may become "peeg," "fat" may become "fet" (rhyming with "set"), and "sun" may sound as though it rhymed with "John."

The phonological and grammatical interference points described here reflect only some of the problems facing the native Spanish speaker who learns English as a second language. For example, both languages use several means of indicating the grammatical functions of words and sentences—whether a word is subject versus object, modifier versus modified, singular versus plural; the tense and mood of verbs; and whether a sentence is a question, command, or statement. These things are conveyed through word order, word endings, and functional words. In the English sentence "The boys jumped on the trampoline," we know by word order that the sentence is a statement, "boys" is the subject, and "trampoline" is the object of the preposition "on." We know by the -*ed* ending of the verb that the action occurred in the past and by the -*s* ending of the subject that more than one boy jumped. A functional word, the preposition "on," tells us the location of the jumping. Spanish also uses the grammatical devices of word order, word endings, and function words, but they are not the same as those used in English.

The degree to which Spanish characteristics appear in the English language use of any individual child depends, of course, on such factors as the length of time the child has been speaking English, the extent of English language use in the child's home, and the regional and social variants of English and Spanish being used. Between the two extremes of a child from a family that emigrated from Guatemala six months ago in which no one speaks English and a child from a family that has lived in the United States for two generations in which Spanish is only rarely used there are many variations, and each child must be treated as an individual case.

Technically, Spanish-influenced English reflects language overlap and should not be called a dialect. In this chapter, however, we are using the term dialect to mean a language form characterized by systematic variations from standard English and associated with a particular group of people. In that sense Spanish-influenced English is a dialect of English, not a separate language. It should be remembered, however, that this dialect, like others, may vary considerably from speaker to speaker and situation to situation. The interference points described here can thus be taken only as a broad outline.

FUNCTIONAL ASPECTS OF NONSTANDARD DIALECTS

If there are so few significant deep-structure syntactic or phonological differences between the nonstandard dialects of minority-group children and the standard English of the white teacher, where is the problem? It does appear that the economically handicapped minority child is at a true disadvantage in our schools. But perhaps the problem is not a linguistic one, resulting from the child's grammar, as much as a communicative one, resulting from attitudes about uses of language.

As mentioned in Chapter 8, children acquiring language are learning more than the rules of a grammar. They are also learning appropriate ways of using language in communication situations. One way in which cultures may be expected to differ from one another is in the kinds of communication situations they admit and in the rules for appropriate usage within these situations. Given that the typical disadvantaged child and the typical middle-class child are growing up and learning language in different cultures, it seems reasonable to expect that these two groups of children would be different in the ways they use language to communicate.

The differences in language usage between these two groups can perhaps best be seen by looking at an example of language use by a lower-status black child. The example given here (Loman, 1967, pp. 155-158) is part of a conversation between a 10-year-old girl (G) and an older woman (W). Both are black residents of Washington, D.C. G is describing a movie she saw.

w: *Our Man Flint.* Tell me about it. What was it about?

G: It was zis strong. I' was about dis strong man. An' he was cu.

w: An' he was what?

G: An' he was cu'.

w: Uh huh.

G: An' he dived off o' dat big thing, an' dived into de water.

w: Dived off what big thing?

G: I' was bou', i' was dese mount'ns.

w: Okay. Go ahead. About the big man an' what?

G: He see, he puts, he say, an' he puts some o'dese girls in dese cans an' trow 'em.

w: In cans?

G: Uh huh. An' put 'em in ne water.

w: What for?

G: For, for he c'n, for dey c'n go to de boa' an' be safe. For da thing.

w: Well, was he a good man or a bad man?

G: He was a goo' man.

w: Wha' was his name?

G: Flin'.

w: Oh, that's right. Okay, so go ahead, an' what happens?

G: An', an' he ain', an' no more water wasn' comin' down. So he dived off o' dat big mount'n an' dived into de water an' star' swimmin' over to da boa'.

w: An' then what happened to the girls in . . .

G: An' den', an', an', girls in ne can. Dey were, dey, de, de cans. Made 'em go to de boa', an' den ney take de girls out de can, an' put 'em in ne boa', 'n give 'em a towel an' wrap aroun' em.

w: An' so then what happened?

G: An' nen na' was de e'.

w: So then the girls were saved?

G: Uh huh.

w: So the whole movie was about Flint's saving these girls?

G: Uh uh.

w: Well, den what?

G: I' was abou' our man Flin', an' nere was dis telephone, say boom, boom, boom, boom.

w: Telephone, what did the telephone have to do with i'?

G: I' was dis man.

w: Uh huh.

G: An' he had some o' dese suggetures for Flin', some o' dese tricks for Flin', an' Flin' say he didn' need i'.

w: Bu' wha' was zis man gonna do for Flin'?

G: Nofin. See dis, dis worl' wan'ed, destroy. Da' worl'. De other worl'.

The first thing to notice about this interchange is the difficulty W has in getting G to tell what the movie was about. W is asking for an overall summary statement, such as "It was about a plot to take over the world by people from outer space, and Flint has to stop them by blowing up their space ship." G keeps giving descriptions of isolated incidents in the movie instead of telling what the movie was about. This tendency on the part of disadvantaged children has been noted in their discussions of television programs as well (Williams, 1970). The point is not that there is anything wrong about describing particular incidents, but that in the absence of information about what the movie is about, that is, in the absence of a context, the descriptions become very difficult to understand, as can be seen by W's questions. G seems to assume that W knows everything about the movie that she knows, so that remarks like "an' he dived off o' dat big thing" will be perfectly clear. W, of course, does not share the context. She has not seen the movie, so she has to ask "What big thing?" This assumption of shared context where there is, in fact, no sharing, is a major characteristic of the speech of disadvantaged children.

One explanation for this is that the disadvantaged minority group child is brought up in an environment where shared context is the usual thing. The child seldom has to speak with "outsiders," who have had different experiences and different points of view. The middle-class child, however, has encountered a broader range of communicative situations. Because such children have more individual experiences that do not include everyone they know, they are accustomed to having to explain things to people who were not present when things happened. Because of environmental differences, the disadvantaged child is accustomed to using language differently from the middle-class child.

This difference becomes particularly striking when disadvantaged children begin school and encounter that important outsider, the teacher, who does not share their experiences and their point of view. This probably marks the onset of such children's educational disadvantage.

A second characteristic of the speech of the typical disadvantaged child is a lack of *elaboration.* An elaborated sentence is one that puts two or three ideas (each of which could be a simple sentence) into one sentence, such as the sentence you are now reading. That last sentence puts all these simple sentence ideas together:

1. Elaborated sentences combine ideas.
2. Each idea could be a simple sentence.
3. This sentence is elaborated.

Elaborated sentences use large numbers of adjectives, dependent noun phrases and clauses, and complex embedded structures.

Middle-class, white children learn to use elaborated sentences. This is a mixed blessing. Elaborated sentences can aid precision in some situations, but in other situations they can get in the way of communication and clog up interaction. As any political press conference will show, educated standard English speakers can often use many words to say little. This is a problem if the speaker's intention is to be clear and concise.

Even this often cited difference between lower-class and middle-class speakers may not be as widespread as it appears to be. Williams and Naremore (1969), analyzing interactions of middle-class and lower-class children with adults, discovered that lower-class children are capable of using elaborated speech when called on to do so. The difference between the two groups of children seems to be that middle-class children use elaborated speech even when they don't have to.

If you want to see how this works, ask a 4- or 5-year-old middle-class child, "What games did you play today?" The response may be something like "I played baseball with Jimmy and Karen and . . . um . . . we played in the street, and . . . um . . . we played until Eddie got hurt, . . . um . . . he fell down, . . . um . . . and then I had to go home for dinner." At each of these pauses the child will struggle to find something else to say and use the vocalized pause to "keep the floor" because he or she isn't finished elaborating. This child, having always been encouraged to talk a lot, has come to love elaboration for its own sake. A lower-class child, asked the same question, may answer in a word or two. The answer is more precise, but to a teacher looking for elaboration, such a child may appear sullen or hostile or lacking in language skills.

So far our discussion has suggested that lower-status children do not develop the same communication patterns as middle-class children. As we have indicated before, this is not to say that they have no speaking skills. The street culture of the urban ghetto, for example, is a highly verbal world, and children must become adept with words if they are to function within that culture. After a detailed study of complex verbal patterns used among gangs of adolescent boys in New York City, Labov and his colleagues (1968, p. 1) conclude:

Our main finding is that there are a wide variety of verbal skills developed in the Negro Non-Standard English community, which have little connection with the school environment, and which are completely unknown to teachers. Furthermore, many of these skills would be defined as irrelevant to success in the NNE community.

The point is that nonstandard usage causes harsh reactions from standard speakers. Within speech communities some usage patterns have high status value whereas others mark the speaker as inferior. We are all sure that our own usage is correct. The term standard English itself suggests that one usage is better than others. In reality it is only better in some times and places.

Our solutions, which we shall discuss only in the most general terms, are in the sphere of usage instruction. If teachers begin to listen closely to the speech of minority-group students, they will learn their usage patterns and discover that their speech is quite intelligible. Because it is intelligible, we need not be so anxious to change it. That does not mean that we need to speak nonstandard to them. They can learn to understand standard usage patterns as easily as we can learn nonstandard. The mix of speech styles in the class will provide ample opportunities to learn about different usage patterns and situations in which each is appropriate. If the classroom contains an ethnic mix of students, there will be ample models to aid learning many kinds of usage patterns, and little special instruction will be needed. As long as we persist in preventing this ethnic mix, we never will change nonstandard speech patterns, no matter how hard we "teach."

In the past generation educators in the United States have expended tremendous resources toward the goal of trying to make all children speak like radio announcers. That kind of uniformity is not only impossible to achieve but also undesirable. The method typically used has been instruction in grammar, which is just as unhelpful for remedial purposes as for usual instruction. We suggest the alternative of openly encouraging cultural diversity and working to help each child become comfortable with several usage styles. The major changes must come in the attitudes of those who teach the children. These attitude changes are more important than changing the speech of children.

Did you ever stop to consider that mastery of two or three dialects or languages creates a big social advantage for a child? Have you ever talked with a car mechanic or store clerk whose dialect you had trouble adjusting to? If you and the mechanic could both speak several different dialects, such a situation might present less of a problem. This is one reason for teachers to emphasize opportunities available to linguistically different children. A teacher should under no circumstances try to wipe out a language or dialect in favor of standard speech.

The differences between standard and nonstandard dialects are not extensive linguistically, but they seem important because we have become used to attaching social importance to them. Thus nonstandard speech leads some job interviewers to label its speakers as bad risks. But if all Americans started speaking flawless English tomorrow, it is unlikely that job discrimination would vanish. The real issue is that many white Americans do not like to be around dark-skinned people, regardless of how they speak. Again, what needs changing is our social attitude. Until we change our attitudes toward nonstandard speech and people who are different from us, we will continue to move toward separate and unequal social coalitions.

SUMMARY

Our focus on what is univeral in children's learning language sometimes causes us to lose sight of the fact that children are individuals. Each child approaches language learning at an individual rate, with an individual learning style (influenced by personality and gender), and sometimes with a different end product in view.

Social class is a powerful determinant of language use. This is not surprising since language learning is such a large part of socialization into a culture. Class differences in society are reflected in approaches to both speaking and writing.

Dialects, whether social, ethnic, or geographical also reflect consistent and recognizable differences in language use. The varieties of English spoken by many black children and by Hispanic children from Spanish-speaking homes have been a target for much research and rhetoric over the past years. Understanding that children who speak these dialects have learned the language of their environments, as all children do, may help us to maintain our perspectives about the role of language in culture and the consequences of sounding different from the mainstream.

SUGGESTED READINGS

Burling, R. *English in Black and White.* New York: Holt, Rinehart and Winston, 1973. This book provides a readable introduction to American dialects in general and black English in particular.

Fillmore, C., D. Kempler, and S.-Y. Wang (eds.). *Individual Differences in Language Ability and Language Behavior.* New York: Academic Press, 1979. This is a fascinating exploration of some of the factors leading to differences in children's language.

Labov, W. *The Study of Nonstandard English.* Urbana, Ill.: National Council of Teachers of English, 1970. This study is a good introduction to the language patterns of nonstandard dialects and to the social attitudes that surround nonstandard usage.

Williams, F., R. Hopper, and D. Natalicio. *The Sounds of Children.* Englewood Cliffs, N.J.: Prentice-Hall, 1977. This book contains chapters on dialects, black English, Spanish-influenced English, and language attitudes and is accompanied by sound recordings.

SUGGESTED PROJECTS

1. Prepare a paper summarizing gender differences in language learning. Evaluate the possible effects of various factors, and discuss the possibility for a "gender neutral" learning. Begin your search of the literature with L. Cherry and M. Lewis, Mothers and two-year-olds: A study of sex differentiated aspects of verbal interaction, *Developmental Psychology 12,* 278-282, 1976.

2. Watch television for a week, and note examples of ways language is used to reinforce ethnic, social class, or gender stereotypes.

Chapter
12

Teaching Communication to Children

*T*his chapter discusses problems in communication instruction and proposes strategies for improving speech skills. First, we consider some issues involved in teaching grammar to children, both in traditional and "new grammar" formats, and we suggest that a teaching strategy based on functions of speaking is the most practical approach to communication instruction.

Second, we present some procedures that can be used in the classroom. We suggest only a few and describe them only in general terms because we have found that exercises and lessons borrowed from a book are usually less effective than those springing from the teacher's personality and a set of goals.

TEACHING GRAMMAR

Some educators and writers argue that advances in psycholinguistics make it possible to teach children prescriptive grammar. There are some benefits for teachers in knowing about developmental psycholinguistics, but the argument has some dangerous consequences.

Research in developmental psycholinguistics has brought many ideas to the fore that can be useful to elementary instruction. Applied psycholinguists have urged teachers to be more concerned with children's knowledge and less concerned with surface aspects of behavior. Teachers who follow this advice usually place less stress on articulation errors, spelling, and the number of words in a child's vocabulary than do teachers unfamiliar with psycholinguistics.

However, the application of such principles suggests three interrelated problems:

1. Developmental psycholinguistics as a research field is still fairly new. Teachers must exercise great care in attempting classroom applications of not totally tested theories.
2. Although research to date has given us some tools with which to evaluate children's grammatical development, we know little about trying to teach them grammar. Classroom attempts to teach grammar explicitly to young children (no matter how well intentioned) will probably fail. Further, these attempts may have dangerous side effects on the children and the general classroom atmosphere.
3. Even if we could explicitly teach grammar to children, there is no evidence that it would significantly improve their communication skills. Because a major task of education is to improve communication abilities (speaking, reading, writing, listening), this reservation becomes important.

As these three problems indicate, teaching grammar rules to children does not necessarily help them communicate effectively. When children come to school, they already know most of the grammar, even if their knowldege is *implicit*, that is, they use grammatical forms but do not know that they are following rules. If you try to teach children rules of grammar, you are not necessarily increasing what they know. You are only increasing their *explicit* knowledge, that is, what they know that they know. This does not necessarily improve spoken performance.

Give an 8-year-old child a bicycle and two hours to play with it. At the end of that time the child will probably be riding with confidence and enthusiasm. At this point, begin teaching the child techniques of bicycle riding: "Be sure to move your legs with fluid motion in an easy, natural arc. Grip the handlebars tightly, but hold your arms in a state of relaxed readiness. Head up! Eyes straight ahead." Ten minutes of such talk would probably suffice to make the child unable to ride, destroy his or her enthusiasm for it, or both. Perhaps some kinds of knowledge are best left implicit in the initial stages of learning.

This analogy may apply to explicit grammar instruction for children. Teaching grammar, particularly in secondary-school English class, has a long tradition, even though there has never been much evidence that students' speech or writing is greatly improved by such instruction. Some educational theorists apparently believe that recent developments in linguistic theory now make teaching grammar practical. Linguists themselves do not argue this position. Rather, the idea that "new linguistics" is more effectively teachable than "old linguistics"seems to be wishful thinking on the part of frustrated teachers—"If I teach them 'new grammar,' they will finally learn to diagram sentences, and tell the difference between *like* and *as.*" This vision is not only misleading, but dangerous.

In the first place, it is dangerous because "new grammar" stands firmly against declaring one kind of usage to be "proper" and another to be "incorrect" if that other has come to be used frequently ("Winston tastes good *like* a cigarette should."). New grammar is only descriptive, and according to new grammar, "like" is as grammatical as "as" because speakers use and understand it.

In the second place, explicit grammar teaching to small children can have unfortunate effects on the classroom atmosphere. If children come to see prescribed structures as schoolroom games, important only in class, they will not only not use the "learned" structures in everyday speech, but may also lose respect for education. If the teacher is particularly forceful or authoritarian in teaching grammar (even new grammar), the entire classroom atmosphere may suffer. High-powered, high-content teaching in instances where failure is likely makes learning unlikely, a fact pointed out forcefully by John Holt in *How Children Learn* (1967) and Charles Silberman in *Crisis in the Classroom* (1970).

In the third place, linguistics deals with no units larger than the sentence. Knowing grammar is of little help in putting complex ideas together, constructing rhetorical strategies, or even reading an entire page.

All these problems make teaching grammar difficult. But we are still left with the issue: Given that we want children to communicate effectively, what kind of teaching strategies can we apply toward that end? The answer, we suggest, is to utilize teaching strategies based upon pragmatic aspects of language development (that aspect of development discussed in Chapter 8). The following sections will show the benefits of such an approach and sketch some sample teaching strategies.

If it is unwise to teach grammar directly, how can educators aid grammar learning? To answer this question, it is necessary to consider why the child, who knows most of the grammar before school, goes about acquiring a new grammatical rule. McNeill (1966, p. 64) states that children ordinarily learn a new distinction of adult grammar not because they are taught it by some adult, but because they discover a new "meaning for which they must find some means of differentiation and expression." In this view children are innately structured so that the acquisition of grammatical principles is an easy task, provided they have some uses for them.

As we discussed in Chapter 8, what seems to happen is this. First, children learn some new function language can perform—to get the milk passed from the other end of the table or to get parents to allow them to stay up late. Next, they search the language behavior in their environment until they locate the grammar rule or rules needed to express this new distinction in meaning. Mastery of that rule and incorporation of the rule into usage follow quickly. It is not the mastery of the new grammar rules themselves that holds the key to the development of new structures, but rather the connecting of these rules with real-life speech situations. If this is so, then the best way to teach grammar is to teach pragmatics. As medieval explorers discovered, it is sometimes easiest to get east by sailing west. If we base our communication teaching upon functions of speaking, children will learn grammar.

This does not imply that function can be taught with no reference to the state of the child's grammatical development. There are some grammatical distinctions that no child learns until age 8 or 9, and trying to teach the accompanying functions is likely to be futile. Educators need to study in detail each pupil's performance in grammar and function and to design appropriate teaching strategies on the basis of that information.

Further, form and function in speaking are interdependent. On any given occasion a teacher may have to assist either of these aspects of development. We are not suggesting that elementary instruction focus exclusively on function. There are occasions on which a child needs help with grammar, and the teacher certainly should provide it.

Teaching function, in sum, develops grammar, but this is not the most important reason for a pragmatic focus on appropriate usage in varieties of speech situations. Inappropriate grammar may cause people to call you uneducated; losing the ability to keep straight the rules of usage, flying into a rage for no reason, or laughing uncontrollably in church may get you into serious trouble. A thorough knowledge of verbal behaviors appropriate in varied situations is essential to survival in a complex world.

Finally, whether teachers are teaching grammar or function, they *should not teach rules explicitly,* apart from situations in which they are appropriate. The specialized terminology used in this book and in research need not be used in the elementary classroom. Teachers should keep in mind the aspects of situation discussed in Chapter 8, but should not present them as abstract principles for children to memorize. Rather, teachers should formulate classroom activities that will help the children develop practical knowledge about how speech varies according to context. It may, on occasion, be helpful for a child to be able to verbalize a principle, but the child cannot necessarily use a rule just because he or she has memorized it.

TEACHING PRAGMATICS: SITUATIONS

Now we list some alternatives you should consider when planning units of instruction. Because our recommendations center on functions of communication, detailed suggestions focus on this area. Following this are some suggestions about other areas of instruction and about the classroom environment as a whole.

In Chapter 8 (pragmatics) we discussed in some detail four aspects of situation that have important effects on communication: participants, setting, sequence, and cultural conventions. We lump our suggestions here into those same categories. In real life these variables all interact with each other. We list exercises under individual categories so that you can gain a balanced approach by giving some emphasis to each area.

Throughout all these suggestions, a dominant theme is that a teacher's strongest teaching lever is *modeling,* that is, being the kind of communicator that you want students to become. A good model provides an example of how the teacher wants the student to act. This means that teachers must constantly monitor the classroom situation and adjust their behavior to changing communication climates. Too often we may be intent upon "getting the message across" and "covering the material," yet adjust poorly to the situation.

A. *Participants*—how communication is affected by the people who are interacting.
   1. *Audience analysis.* Present children with topics of interest and concern to them. Don't ask a first grader to argue international politics, but to talk about issues of neighborhood concern, the lives of television characters, and the like. Give the students the assignment of saying the "same" message to two different audiences. Alternatively, students could prepare persuasive campaigns for the different audiences. This works best when the message can actually be presented by children. Follow such exercises with discussions of tactics employed, effectiveness, and possible side effects.
   2. *Communications with a variety of people.* Place children in real-life encounters that necessitate wide shifts in communication behavior. This can be accomplished by encouraging children to talk to people encountered in field trips such as guides, police officers, children enrolled in schools for the blind or deaf, local business people and store owners, local officials. Little instruction is needed. Activities that point out how language behavior varies according to the people present can be fruitful—not to point out "principles," but to facilitate future adaptations.
   3. *Role playing.* Children know that certain people are addressed in a certain way and can quite spontaneously demonstrate or talk about what they would do or say under certain circumstances. This can also be done through role play. Examples: What would you say to the principal if you were the only ones sitting at a lunch table together? What would you say to your friend's dog if you met the dog on the street? What would you say to a baby if it was crying because it just scraped its knee? After children get used to this exercise, it could be expanded into longer role plays.

4. *Dramatics.* Extended role plays can be structured with story lines or be improvised. Begin the activity by assigning each child a role to play. Stop the interaction periodically to allow characters to enter and exit in order to have the children show how behavior varies according to participants. With younger children, many of the same functions can be accomplished through the use of puppets. Pantomime may also be effective. Children should also perform memorized plays as often as possible.

5. *Telephoning.* Divide children into teams of two and have them talk to each other by telephone. It is best if actual telephones (in different rooms) can be used. Then instruct one of the team to be a "parent" and talk to the other. Then switch. Then have both be parents. Other possibilities are storekeepers, business people, teachers, preachers, the president.

6. *Teacher as model.* Keep tuned to how the composition of classes or discussion groups varies with absences or new faces. Such changes can also be the subject for discussion. After the principal visits and sits in the back of the room for a half hour, start a discussion of how you and the children behaved differently.

B. *Setting*—how communication is affected by the place in which it occurs and visual cues to sentence meanings.

1. *Context-conflict games.* Several possibilities stem from the experimental finding that confusion is caused by asking a question about one item, while holding up a picture of a different item. If not tied to failure or fear, a game in which pictures are used to trip up answerers can be fun. It can be used to provide evidence that visual communication cues do not always agree with linguistic cues and that conflict between context and meaning is possible.

2. *Context as aid.* This is the more positive side of context cues. Use of pictures, dolls, and even little role plays can aid children in understanding structures that are difficult for them (for example, determining the agent in a sentence such as "The elephant is kissed by the bear."). After practice with context items has made children more aware of the linguistic structures, they may be able to interpret the structures better. Note that we should not ask what Piaget calls "the American question," "Can we make them do it *younger?*" Techniques such as these may be helpful if children are ready to learn a distinction. If they are not ready, the techniques will make little difference.

3. *Role plays with varied settings.* Have children construct stories or act out plays based on being in familiar and unfamiliar settings. Follow the plays with discussion about the impor-

tance of place to communication. Some sample places: country store, department store, gas station, home alone, church, haunted house, old castle, crowded modern skyscraper, barnyard.

C. *Sequence*—how communication is affected by what is said before and by what is likely to be said next.

1. *Out-of-sequence game.* Expose students to one message (oral or written), then a short summary or quotes from the message. Discuss ways the summary or quote is accurate or inaccurate in terms of the first passage. Does it convey the whole meaning of the first passage or only part? If one person wrote the first passage and somebody else "summarized" it, how might the person who wrote the passage feel about the summary— happy, angry, amused, sad? Why?

2. *Passages with gaps.* This works much like the out-of-sequence game. Present students with stories, descriptions, or other passages in which the beginning, middle, or end is omitted and ask them to compose the missing section. Differences among the student versions form the basis for discussion.

3. *Incomplete dramas or puppet shows.* Give children partial stories or plays. Let them act out their own endings. A variation is to give the initial situation and a required ending and let students construct the show that gets to that ending. Groups of students (three to five in a group) could discuss in advance how to do the shows. Amount of planning could be varied from much to none. Either groups or the entire class could discuss the success of attempts afterward.

4. *Ritual sequences.* Have students enact ritual moments from life, for example, those surrounding greetings. You could begin with a role play of meeting an acquaintance, asking students to say "what everyone always says." Emphasize the usefulness of these rituals; don't make fun of them. Or, tell a group of children to imagine two acquaintances meeting, and ask volunteers to supply in sequence, one turn at a time, what will be said until the participants get to the first unritualized topic (for example, Hello. Hello; How are you? Fine; How are you? Fine). This combines well with telephone games. Other ritual moments might be a service encounter in which a customer decides to buy something, the clerk takes the money, then counts out change; a leave taking; and an introduction of one person to another.

5. *Adjacency pairs.* Supply children with half of an adjacency pair and ask them to supply the other half. Begin with supplying first parts and asking children to give second parts. Then move to supplying second parts with children reconstructing the first parts. Finally, ask children to practice some "diffi-

cult" second parts. For instance, ask them to refuse requests without actually saying no ("May I borrow your ball?" "Well, I have to use it.").

6. *Teacher as model.* When students make remarks that are clearly inappropriate to what was said before and the general drift of discussion, the teacher might inform them (without humiliating them) of the inappropriateness. When the teacher wants to change discussion topics but the class wants to continue, the teacher can shift topics by steering conversation gently. The teacher should make remarks appropriate to what has been said, and connect what has been said to what is to be discussed discuss next.

D. *Cultural conventions*—how communication is affected by the cultural beliefs, practices, and group memberships of all participants.

1. *Mythical culture role play.* In this role play each character does something "odd" because he or she is a member of a mythical culture, for example, stands very close or very far away from others when talking to them, does not face others or make eye contact when talking to them. The point is to get children to observe these differences without too much disruption to communication.

2. *Blue eyes and brown eyes.* This is to be done with care and understanding and plenty of discussion afterward. Choose some characteristic to sort the class into groups: blue/brown eyes, light/dark hair, right/left handedness, light/dark shirts. Devise some ways to make one group the "underdogs" for perhaps an hour or a day, for example, needing permission from a member of the "advantaged" group to say something; being allowed to use only certain water fountains; having to sit in back of class or in specially assigned seats. Be sure to turn the experience around after a time, so that the advantaged children become underdogs. Afterward ask children to talk about the experience and what happened: "How did you feel when . . . ?" "What was the biggest disadvantage of being an underdog?" "What was the biggest benefit?" It may be appropriate to discuss racial prejudice, discrimination against women, or similar topics following this experience. After left-handers are underdogs, discuss the experience of being in a small disadvantaged group, as opposed to one that consists of half of the class.

3. *Mars.* This could work as a role play or as something that children do in their imaginations, say with lights lowered and heads on desks. Ask the children to imagine that they are from Mars, and they speak no Earth language. One day they wake up to find they are in an Earth classroom. As Martians, they don't even realize this is a classroom, since on Mars there are

no classrooms. How can they begin to communicate? What is the first problem to be faced? Imagine the rest of the story. The stories can be told, written, or drawn in pictures.

4. *New place.* Assign groups of children to find out about communication practices and customs in some distant area of the world, such as China, India, Egypt, Tanzania, or Peru. Culminate the activity with displaying art, dressing up, playing recordings of music, and so forth. The goal here is to foster appreciation for cultural differences and lay groundwork for the children's developing into adults who are interested in, not threatened by, cultural differences. Alternatively, children could report on a place some of their own ancestors came from.

5. *Dialect imitation.* Find tapes or records of as many dialects of English as you can. Possibilities: Cajun, black, New England, Texan, southern, Jamaican, Spanish accent, Appalachian. Ask each child to listen repeatedly to a short segment and to practice speaking along with the recording, sounding as much like the speaker as possible. This could culminate in a set of performances in which children demonstrate the dialects. Discussion should emphasize the benefits of diversity. Goal: children who are willing to listen to any English speaker.

6. *Action on local problems.* Within the school, neighborhood, and city there are dozens of problems that are of concern to certain groups and capture the students' interest: disrepair in the school building, petty theft, abuse of a vacant lot, pollution from a nearby plant. Students should be encouraged (mainly in groups) to take action on these problems—plot persuasive strategies, attempt fund raising, and generally try to make things better. The fact that they helped get new linoleum in the cafeteria may be a great source of pride and a demonstration of the power of communication. And consider the gold mine of communication practice in writing leaflets, business letters, and letters of outrage and in telephoning local residents, officials, and media personnel. Not only might these projects help members of various cultural groups, but also children will begin to experience "group culture" by working and collaborating closely with classmates. Discuss the growth of group culture and group norms with students.

7. *Teacher as model.* By their own actions, teachers should show appreciation for diversity. They must allow themselves their own interests and identity, of course, but they can be genuinely open and probing as they try to help students to communicate about their growing identities, individual characteristics, and group memberships. Teachers and other responsible adults can work to provide models of understanding, tolerance, and intergroup appreciation.

TEACHING PRAGMATICS: FUNCTION

The preceding teaching suggestions are aimed primarily at helping children take the situational variables into account as they interact with others. The following strategies are related to the categories of communication function that were introduced in Chapter 8: informing, persuading, speech play, and metacommunication. It is worth repeating that all these communication functions present themselves in interaction nearly all the time. Our recommended exercises focus to some degree on individual functions so that you can be certain to give each area some emphasis, and so evaluation can center on each function. In actual classroom interaction children could be expected to use verbal resources from all functional categories, even during exercises designed to tap primarily one kind of response.

A. *Informing*—passing new information from one communicator to another. We noted in Chapter 8 that this function develops late in children. Teaching informing skills is and should be a major focus of communication teaching.

1. *Demonstrations.* Some teachers use "show and tell" as an activity to involve children in delivering public presentations to classroom-sized groups of peers. The merits of this practice are often criticized, but with some planning it can be modified to aid the teaching of informing skills. Consider using a form of show and tell in which the child whose turn it is takes a position at the front of the class, but may speak only in response to questions from the audience. For example, a child may bring from home a toy, photo, or drawing. The child simply holds the object up for others to see, and the others ask questions. This allows for a dialogue performance format and also gets some children past the stage fright associated with speaking in front of groups. It also relieves the child of the need to prepare an exact formal message. But more important than any of these benefits is the practice that *audience* members get in asking questions so as to gain maximum information and make sense out of the situation. Show and tell can also follow a demonstration format. Children can bring objects from home or pick items from a box supplied by the teacher and explain to a group (perhaps a small one) how the object is used.

2. *Serial communication.* This experience involves a chain of communicators. The first person gets an informational message, say, a picture or written sentence, and whispers the sentence or a description of the picture to another party, who whispers it to another, and so on down the line. The last receiver says aloud the message as he or she understands it. The

first person reads or repeats the original message. There is usually considerable distortion, which causes amusement and learning. The telephone can be used. Have one child tell a story over the phone to someone else, then bring in a third party who did not hear the first conversation. The point to be stressed, especially with young children, is that misunderstandings are not necessarily someone's "fault"; they are just something that happens in human communication. We can try to be as clear as possible, but we should still expect to be misunderstood sometimes. This could lead to discussion of *dialogue*—how accurate communication is normally achieved by two parties reacting to each other and each alternating short turns, not just by saying something "clearly."

3. *Outline games.* Some ways of arranging the parts of a message are more informative than others. Children can be given scrambled message outlines adjusted to almost any learning level and asked to put the parts in the best order. Young children can be told to put pictures in the order in which they probably happened in a story. Older children can be told to arrange parts of a message written on scraps of paper in the most sensible and probably effective order.

4. *Question activities.* The question is the most important information-gathering tool. Any successful player of the game 20 questions knows that some questions produce more information than others. Variants of 20 questions provide opportunities for children to discover this. For example, a child could bring something to school in a bag and allow other children to ask questions to figure out what it is. If a resource person is to visit the class (a librarian, police officer), children can be told to write down questions to ask the person. Topics might be assigned for the questions. Children can be given the task of writing a question, asking it, and recording the answer. Later the child can report to a group about the question and its answer.

   Children naturally ask questions. Teachers should help them develop their questioning ability into a sensitive probing instrument. Without ever using such words as "scientific method," children can be taught how to ask questions of data and to obtain their own answers. All these procedures can be undertaken by students in pairs and small groups, with the teacher consulting those having problems. If this results in a classroom atmosphere that is loud and chaotic, do not be shocked; children can work very well in such an atmosphere with supervision and some inviting learning tasks.

5. *Pantomime.* One effective way to teach informing others of feelings is pantomime, partly because so many feelings find

expression largely through nonverbal communication. With young children, a teacher can work with a group of five or six by whispering a word for a feeling (angry, sad, jealous, delighted) in a child's ear. The child then makes his or her face look like the feeling, and other members of the group try to guess the feeling being expressed. With preschool and first-grade children, describing a situation will probably work better than using a feeling word. For example, "Make your face look like you just got a puppy for your birthday and that's exactly what you wanted." Or, "Make your face look like you were just sent to your room for punishment." Older children can be given words describing feeling written on slips of paper. They may take turns with another child in facial expression of a feeling until the other guesses it. Students can also make some written record about how what facial cues let the receiver "read" emotion. Charades are pantomimes of explicitly informative character and should be performed frequently.

6. *Empathy repetition exercises.* Just as it is important to be able to give information, it is important to be able to receive and interpret others' messages. One way to practice this skill is to have the class divide into groups of two to five each. Each group should be told to discuss some topic of local interest. Each child is allowed to speak only after he or she paraphrases what the previous speaker said to that speaker's satisfaction. This exercise was designed by psychologist Carl Rogers for use in developing empathy in adults, but it can be used with children. Children (as well as adults) will be surprised how difficult it is to paraphrase what somebody else said to that person's satisfaction.

B. *Persuading*—sending and receiving messages to change others' attitudes or behavior. Observations of classrooms suggest that children get plenty of practice in control functions. In fact, there may be a preponderance of controlling communication to the exclusion of other types. Most attempts to subject children to discipline fall into this category. The following experiences are aimed less at getting children to understand basic principles of controlling and being controlled (which is scarcely avoidable) than at teaching children effective and moral means for controlling others.

1. *Scarce resources.* One cause of arguments is that competing parties want things that are scarce—money, prestige, the new magazine that came today. It seems worthwhile to give children practice in directing or controlling their own behavior and that of others through making suggestions and striking bargains (instead of each other). Divide a class into groups of five children and instruct each group to construct a work of

art, such as a collage. Give each group some materials that are in short supply, say, one scissors, one tube of paste, two crayons. After the children naturally exercise control over each other in this setting, the methods they use can be discussed.

2. *Me too.* How can a child who has not been included in some activity in which he or she wants to participate use communication behavior to get included in the group? Teachers can create fictionalized situations and allow children to role play, or they can hold discussions to help children learn what might be effective to accomplish that goal.

3. *Refusing.* An important kind of controlling behavior, in which many adults lack skill, is saying no politely but firmly. Children can practice this skill in role-playing situations in which someone asks to borrow something or asks them to do something. The class could make a list of all the ways there are to say no: indirectness, rudeness, irony, apology, excuses, and so on.

4. *Persuasion.* Traditionally, high school and college students have practiced controlling behavior by delivering prepared messages to a class audience. Young children can undertake similar tasks of supporting assertions with reasoning, for example, by identifying a toy as their favorite and trying to justify the choice to others. Children might also design art, slogans, or jingles to advertise some real or imagined product.

C. *Speech play*—the speech of children during play activities and all the imaginative and humorous uses of language that are typical of children's speech. Joking, make believe, and any simulation or role-playing activity require some use of speech play. Speech play is among the most useful techniques for communication skills training. Our suggestions here are sketchy, for one thing about play is that it is hard to plan. Our general advice is to provide a safe environment conducive to speech play and frequent recreational recess.

1. *Restaurant.* Pretend you are a family going out to eat in a restaurant. Have children take the roles of waiters, cooks, and family members, and let them decide how to order, how to take an order, how to address service persons, how to address customers, how to talk to coworkers, who should pay the check, and so on.

2. *Picture story.* Story telling is an important form of imagining behavior. Primary school children are often ill at ease about telling stories in front of adults, but on some occasions it can be managed and can provide good practice. One technique is to ask children to draw a picture that tells some story. After they have finished their pictures, the children may tell their stories within a small group.

3. *Jokes, riddles, and rhymes.* Sometimes children who will not speak in other contexts will share jokes, riddles, and rhymes with others. Trying to add these activities by making them official parts of the classroom schedule may defeat their purpose by eliminating their spontaneous and unthreatening nature, but certain times (such as right after lunch) might be made available for speech play.

4. *Rhythm and rhyme games.* A favorite nursery school game is to give children a pair of long sticks, which they beat together in time to music. This might have some applications in elementary school with more complex rhythms (for example, reggae) and rhythms of poetry and chant. The rhythms of a ballad, for example, could provide interesting vocal rhythm games. Allow children to make up rhythms of their own and then invite them to set the rhythms to words. Rhyming can be an equally rich source for games. For example, say words and ask children to give rhymes for them, have each child around a circle give a rhyme for a word, and have a pair of children take turns saying words and rhyming words said by the partner.

5. *Teacher as model.* The main function of the teacher as model for speech play is to exhibit enthusiasm about language use— a sense of joy about the way the parts of the code fit together and provide almost endless play opportunities. It is only when children see language used as a dry academic activity that games such as those described will seem silly to them.

D. *Metacommunication*—giving information about messages that are being conveyed, or communication about communication. Like play, metacommunication is tricky to encourage. Most all encouragement is in itself metacommunicative. Most all the "discussion" suggestions at the end of exercise material above are metacommunicative. Further, to encourage too much examination of message may lead children to self-consciousness. Remember that it is possible to talk about talk too much.

1. *Framing cues.* Ask children to describe framing cues for various kinds of events. How can you tell when:

Your parents are: angry/amused/proud.

Your brother: doesn't want to play/wants to ask a favor/might be telling you a fib.

Your friends are: kidding/serious/worried.

A baseball player is about: to throw to first base/to throw to home plate/not to throw.

Children might disagree on their perceptions about these things and come up with some outlandish theories. Promote discussion and alternative theories.

2. *Metalinguistic games.* Encourage any kinds of games that promote word play, such as rhyming games, games in which children try to list names of objects or animals that begin with a certain letter, games in which the teacher makes jokes that confuse the word and the thing ("Does a cat have three letters? Does the word *cat* purr?").

3. *Grammar games.* Play games in which children are put in verbal situations that require responses using specific grammatical structures. For young children, this can be quite simple; for example, a question starting with "why" requires an answer with a clause using "because." Another idea is to have one child say a simple sentence and have others expand the sentence by "playing" with complex embedding structures (see Moffett, 1968).

GENERAL RECOMMENDATIONS

Aside from these particular suggestions for a function-based communication curriculum, we have some general advice for teachers of communications skills.

Begin with simple ideas and later move to complex ones. Worry less about not moving too fast than about maintaining contact with students. Let children generate their own enthusiasm and pace.

With young children emphasize manipulation of objects, rhythm play, and overcoming stage fright, shyness, and fear of failure. Using puppets and having children talk through them may help. Also break the class into groups of three or four, so each speaker has only a few listeners and a greater number of chances to speak.

As children grow up, they still manipulate things, but the nature of the manipulation changes from physical (hitting sticks together) to cognitive (persuading parents to help raise funds for a field trip). Continued opportunities to make such manipulations, see the results, and compare results with predictions provide valuable training.

Effective communication education rarely can grow from just a set of preplanned textbooks or prewritten lesson plans. Each teacher must adapt the communication curriculum on the basis of where the students are and what they need to learn.

Classroom organization need not be totally preplanned, but can be spontaneous and exciting, even if occasionally chaotic. The students should be accustomed to working individually, in small or large groups, and as an entire class. Much of the teacher's work should be consulting with individuals about problems and helping students to learn from each other. The teacher can then be more a decision maker and less an information machine.

We advocate a communication atmosphere very different from what exists in some authority-centered elementary classrooms. We despair at too much quiet in elementary schools. Jean Piaget frequently observed that children need to accompany actions and thinking with talking. Such private speech is natural and aids learning (see Chapter 9). Just talking is an important aid to thinking; open-ended discussions provide opportunities for students to test and sharpen their ideas and perceptions against those of other children. Encourage children to criticize others' ideas and to give reasons for their reactions. These experiences exercise a child's thinking and provide dialogue practice.

Every class should contain as heterogeneous a mix of students as possible. The class with a variety of speakers provides the best laboratory for increasing speech and comprehension. Classes should be integrated not only in terms of sex, ethnicity, and social class according to the full spirit of the law, but also in terms of levels of intelligence. Even age segregation is in some ways detrimental to learning. Children should have ample communication opportunities with people of all ages, especially with elderly citizens. This variety teaches that there are many kinds of communication strategies, each appropriate in some kinds of communication situations. In a heterogeneous classroom the student sees these communication strategies at work and may choose varying models for varying situations. A heterogeneous classroom provides practice in audience analysis. The child will learn that it is unproductive to speak the same way all the time.

Finally, development of communication skill comes not through memorizing principles of a theory of communication, but through exercising the communicating "muscles" in encounters with real problems. Set goals for the class in cooperation with students and let the students attain them through discussion. Remember that it is possible to have discussions without teaching a set of rules first. We argue against teaching principles of grammar, rhetoric, usage, extralinguistic expression, or reading. If you are worried that if you don't teach rules, you won't know what to test, then de-emphasize testing.

Children learn to communicate by communicating. Only after a child has effective communication skills will the statement of principles be useful. To foster such learning, children must speak more often than they do in some of today's classrooms. Emphasis on order and quiet must be replaced by emphasis on expression and discussion. Communicating should be an everyday educational staple, the hub of curriculum, not just added enrichment.

SUMMARY

In the ordinary course of events children are not taught how to talk. They learn through their interaction with a talking environment. Probably for this reason attempts to teach children grammar as a way of improving their ability to communicate almost never succeed. Children learn communication skills by communicating, and this is as true inside the classroom as it is outside. As a substitute for frustrating and unsuccessful attempts to teach usage through rules, we have proposed in this chapter a variety of teaching strategies based on pragmatic aspects of language. Our approach is based on the assumption that if a child finds a use for a particular language form, that form will become a part of the child's repertoire.

SUGGESTED READINGS

Allen, R., K. Brown, and J. Yatvin. *Learning Language Through Communication*, Belmont, Calif.: Wadsworth, 1986. This text for language arts teachers stresses the speech component as the basis of all the language arts during preschool and the primary grades. The authors provide up-to-date reviews of theoretical material and exercises based on a functional approach to communication.

Lindfors, J. W. *Children's Language and Learning*. Englewood Cliffs, N.J.: Prentice-Hall, 1987. This text in language acquisition is targeted to teachers. It contains a trove of exercise material that they will find useful in implementing the functional approach to teaching and in introducing grammar instruction usefully.

May, F. *To Help Children Communicate*. Columbus, Ohio: Merrill, 1980. This coherent and readable book covers the teaching of communication to children. It suggests what communication skills must be taught and some ways to teach them. The author's writing skill and personal commitment to children add to the book's value.

Moffett, J. *Teaching the Universe of Discourse*. Boston: Houghton Mifflin, 1982. Moffett outlines a comprehensive theory for teaching children to communicate using writing, speaking, reading, and drama. He presents a good case against teaching grammar, and his student-centered approach to almost everything is healthy and inventive.

SUGGESTED PROJECTS

This chapter is filled with activities. We urge you to try them out with some willing children and form your own conclusions. You may even want to come up with your own activities for specific goals.

Chapter
13

When Language Development Goes Awry

*T*he process of normal development has certain implications for those involved in intervention for children with abnormal speech or language. Trying to make an abnormal child more "normal" without knowing about normal children is like trying to glue together a shattered piece of pottery without knowing what it looked like before it was broken or what it should look like after it is fixed. This chapter discusses how considering the basics of development can aid the clinician in diagnosing and treating language and speech problems.

DIAGNOSIS: EVALUATING SPEECH AND LANGUAGE DEVELOPMENT

A child may be referred to a speech clinician by a school for "language problems" or by a parent because "she doesn't sound right" or "his sister was much further along at his age." The first task the clinician has is to evaluate the child's language development. Without discussing particular means for conducting this evaluation, we can discuss some of the issues involved.

Problems with the Test Situation

First, the use of the term *evaluate* implies that some comparison will be made between a child's language performance and some ideal performance. What is the standard to which clinicians compare a child's language development? How do they decide whether development is within normal limits? For many clinicians the answer to these questions lies in the use of standardized tests. A standardized test is one for which performance norms have been calculated; that is, the test has been given to a large cross-section of children of different ages, and the performance score of, say, the "average" 3-year-old has been obtained by averaging the scores of all the 3-year-olds who took the test. (The statistical operations involved may be quite complicated, but that is essentially what is done to arrive at norms.) Clinicians like to use standardized tests because they can come up with definite statements, such as "This child has a language age of 3 years, 6 months." This statement can be translated to mean "On this particular test, this child made the same score as the average child aged 3 years, 6 months."

There are several problems with this kind of statement. First, the statement cannot be applied to language behavior that was not on the test. If the test did not examine the child's ability to use elaborated sentences, then the clinician can make no statement concerning this ability (and should take care to make that clear to anyone, such as school officials or parents, who might make decisions affecting the child based on the clinician's findings).

The clinician may also wish to be careful about making broad statements on the basis of the performance of the "average" child. For most standardized language tests, the norms were collected using white, middle- to upper-class children in northern or midwestern cities. In other words, the language of these children is the ideal against which the language of all children is measured. The moral and esthetic implications of this situation should be obvious. At the very least, if test norms are going to be held up as performance of the average child, then children from many different language environments should be tested when the norms are established. Clinicians should realize that whenever they give a child a standardized language test, they are automatically assuming that the norms for the test are appropriate standards for comparison.

When using a language test, whether it is standardized or not, we also make the assumption that children's performance on the test is their best language performance. But, is our language-testing procedure really designed to tap the best language a child has to offer? Perhaps one example will show the necessity for asking this question. A young clinician went to a local Headstart program to do hearing tests. The child had to put on a pair of earphones and signal the clinician when he or she heard a tone by saying "now." The clinician had been screening all the city's kindergarten and first-grade children in this way, and she anticipated no problems. However, when she took the first Headstart child out to be tested, he cried and was uncooperative. The second child refused to even put on the earphones. The third child, although she didn't cry, was so obviously terrified that the clinician decided to try to find out what was going on. After talking with the teacher and several of the children, she discovered that some older children had told the group that she was there to give shots. Her strange equipment had done nothing to allay the children's anxiety. After testing the teacher and two aides in front of the class, she was able to test the children without further incident.

This clinician was lucky. She perceived that the children were not behaving normally, and she was able to find out why and alleviate the problem. But think of the ordinary language-testing situation. The clinician is faced with a child, say, a 4-year-old boy, she has never seen before. She does not know what the child has been told about why he is being tested or even whether he has been told that there will be a test. She does not know what his best language performance is, and so she cannot judge whether she is getting that performance from him. She knows that she has another patient in one hour, and besides, she has to finish this test so the child can go and have a hearing test.

Now look at this same situation from the boy's point of view. He probably has been taken away from his mother by an adult he has never seen before to a room he has never been in before. He does not know what is about to happen. He may be told something about playing a game or answering some questions, but whatever he has been told, he is acutely aware that he doesn't know the rules, that is, he doesn't know how he is expected to behave. Of all the information the child could get, this is most important. But it is this that he is least likely to have.

Let's look at the testing situation as a communication situation. The child is almost certainly unsure about what is expected and may also be frightened about being alone with a strange adult. What is the logical thing to do when you are frightened and unsure? Anybody with any sense of self-preservation will say and do as little as possible to avoid doing anything wrong. This means minimal communication. It is a rare child who can come off well in a one-to-one situation with a strange adult, and it takes an even rarer child to perform at maximum levels when there is an element of threat in the situation. Yet it is in this situation that we make the assumption that we are getting the best language performance a child has to offer. And, it is on the basis of a child's behavior in such a situation that he or she may be put in a "language enrichment" program or special class.

This brings up another problem involved in evaluating children's language development: the uses that are made of scores on language tests. Many school systems "track" children on the basis of language test scores, that is, children with low scores are put in one class and those with high scores are put in another. Apart from the questionable rationale for using language test scores to group children, one might ask what is gained by segregating children who have supposedly not developed good language from those who have. Should not the less well-developed children have the benefit of exposure to well-developed language in their peers? Is there justification for fears that "slow" children will hamper the faster children's learning? The insidious aspect of all this is that

so often a language test score becomes a substitute for an overall esti-
mate of the child's intellectual and communicative abilities in a wide
variety of situations. This often results in the horrifying spectacle of a
teacher looking at a test score and labeling the noisiest child in the class
nonverbal.

Finally, clinicians should know the basics of how speakers of nonstandard dialects sound (see Chapter 11). Children who speak nonstandard forms of English are often diagnosed as having articulation or language problems. Clinicians should be aware that tests such as the
Goldman-Fristoe Articulation Test, the Peabody Picture Vocabulary
Test, and the Illinois Test of Psycholinguistic Ability are biased toward
the speech skills of middle-class children. They should also be familiar
enough with dialects to tell the difference between dialect-appropriate
speech that is different from standard English and errors that need
therapy.

This discussion should not be taken to mean that there are no children with language problems. There are many who have obvious difficulty communicating verbally. Their problems may result from anything
from autism to delayed speech, and often it is difficult to say exactly
what the problems are. There are sensitive and well-trained clinicians
who realize the pitfalls involved in the use of standardized tests and who
are searching for some other means of describing the language problems
of such children.

Many of these clinicians look to research in communication development of normal children for a firm timetable of what communication behaviors are supposed to occur at what age. Unfortunately, research cannot provide such a timetable. Communication development unfolds at
different rates for different children. In Chapter 2 we reviewed some
behaviors that children often perform at certain ages. We repeat the caution we gave there. Do not look too closely at age levels when discussing
children's communication behavior. We challenge anyone to come for-
ward with a well-supported, reasonable description of what the "normally developing" child at age 3 years, 6 months (or any other age) is
supposed to be doing with language. If research tells us anything at all
about this, it tells us that the range of "normal" at any given age is very
broad.

Of course, this does not help the clinician who is searching for answers. Some help comes from the fact that the order in which communication behaviors emerge is fairly stable. So, for example, if a child is
making some distinctions that typically occur at a late stage of development, but missing others that typically appear early, then the missed
distinctions probably represent a problem needing clinical help. Further, in most cases there is some correspondence between the speech
milestones reported by Lenneberg (see Chapter 2) and motor development milestones. So if a child's speech sounds immature compared to
his or her motor development, there is likely cause for concern.

Supplements to Test Scores

In response to problems such as those above, careful testers should supplement standardized test data with other information. There's a wealth of information available "between the lines" in interviews with the child and parent. What tasks can the child get done? Does the child pursue discussion or shrink from interaction? Can the child "hold a conversation" with a clinician? Does the child seem to enjoy meeting people? Does the child seem to enjoy interaction with the parent? These pragmatic questions are the "big picture" in children's speech development. What a child is able to get done with communication is more important than certain problems that may be largely superficial. This type of information may seem vaguer than standardized test scores, but it can provide the clues that make diagnosis and treatment successful.

Assessment may be centered in the clinic, but it may be enhanced by incorporating data from other settings in which the child speaks and listens. What skills does a language-impaired child already have in place? That question must guide the assessment phase. Even persons who suffer extreme linguistic handicaps may have developed useful ways of getting things done with speech. An example from Frankel, Leary, and Kilman (1986) may be helpful. Adam, a 6-year-old child diagnosed as autistic, had made little progress in four years of evaluations and therapy. The child was said to be completely unresponsive. The researchers videotaped Adam at home and discovered the following accomplishments: Adam came to supper when called. Adam asked for a second helping of food (by gesture) and obtained it. Most important, when two adults at the table talked, Adam shifted his gaze away from each speaker just before that speaker finished a turn and looked at the other speaker. This showed that Adam understood the timing of the turn-taking system for conversation, though he rarely spoke himself. These observations, "discovered" in recordings from the home environment, provided clinicians with some rudimentary resources to begin therapy.

Tape-recorded data from home situations can aid diagnosis and treatment. Such data might be requested by clinicians or offered by parents. Such recordings are most useful to the extent that they are most natural, that is, representative of what usually happens in the child's world, rather than contrived for the recorder. After all, it is everyday speaking and listening that must be improved. For obtaining natural and hearable speech samples with little fuss, we especially recommend recordings made at mealtime or in other routine situations. Parents can make audio recordings at home at low cost, especially if the clinician provided the tape recorder and tape.

In what way may such recordings be put to diagnostic use? Clinicians search the data for moments in which either a communicative accomplishment or a communicative failure seems to be taking place. Repeated listening to short segments from the recording is important. A clinician can learn much more by listening twenty times to five seconds of speech than by listening twice to ten minutes of speech.

Repeated listening is aided by transcribing what is heard. The method of transcription can be simple. What is important is to note as precisely as possible what sounds are made and when pauses occur. Ask at what points is the success or failure taking place, what is accomplished in these few seconds of speech, and how are the participants interacting to accomplish this activity. Crystal (1984) emphasizes the importance of speech transcription in the diagnostic process and criticizes "loose" transcribing that fails to show details of utterances and timing. Crystal also cautions clinicians to do the transcribing themselves rather than having it done by others. The process of transcribing (because of the repeated careful listening it necessitates) turns out to be as valuable to diagnosis as is the product, or the final transcript. The final transcript may help clinicians pinpoint a problem or describe it in staff meetings, but the process of transcribing is how they find the problem. Of course, any transcribing takes time; it means more hours per case. Clinicians must educate themselves in transcribing skills, especially in techniques of phonetics and those of conversation analysis.

Throughout the diagnosis process, clinicians (and parents and teachers) should remember that every child is a dynamic organism. A diagnosis or treatment program undertaken at age 3 may be totally without basis for the same child at age 4. Diagnoses must always be regarded as tentative. Patients change, and children are sometimes needlessly burdened by the label of an outgrown disability.

TREATMENT: CHANGING SPEECH BY SPEAKING

Once a clinician has diagnosed a speech or language problem, the task is to help the child speak normally. In planning strategies to accomplish this, clinicians should keep in mind research findings about how children learn various aspects of communication behavior (see Chapter 10). For example, a syntactic problem and a problem in the use of inflectional endings require different approaches.

Clinical Strategies

Many clinicians base most of their therapy on imitation and reinforcement. These learning strategies are much less powerful than rule induction or modeling (see Chapter 10). You can try to make a child learn to talk in the same way you would teach a bird to talk (imitation reinforcement), but then you should be satisfied if the child speaks like a little parrot. If there is to be carry-over from language therapy to real-life situations, children must master rule-induction learning strategies.

We do not mean to say that all children with communication problems can learn to speak through the methods their normal peers use. We do feel, however, that normal learning strategies should be incorporated into the therapy situation wherever possible. Moreover, we do not mean to discredit all strategies based on operant conditioning or pattern practice. Especially for severely retarded or emotionally disturbed children, these techniques can be effective. But normal or near-normal communication will rarely be taught by these methods alone. To master the complexities of language, more powerful learning tools are necessary, and this learning is more likely to occur in more realistic communication situations.

Two approaches to getting children to use such strategies may be helpful. First, if Piaget is correct in saying that communication development is only one phase of general cognitive development, training in general cognitive tasks—manipulation of objects, solving puzzles, conservation tasks, and so forth—may sharpen children's learning strategies to the point that they can learn to communicate, especially if natural language use accompanies these tasks.

At this point, a second approach should come into play. The child should be led into interpersonal encounters in which language and communication skills can be used to accomplish goals—to do things that matter to the child. Some clinicians make therapy lockstep drill sessions in which children use particular linguistic forms in isolation over and over again. This approach ignores the reality that the therapy situation is also a communication situation and as such can be made a tool for learning. Children should be encouraged to use the full range of their communication skills in the therapy situation. This is, of course, much the same strategy we recommend for teaching normal children in the classroom. Children learn the most about speech by speaking and listening in ordinary interactive conversation.

Therapy as Conversation

Most clinical intervention takes place in a clinical interview, which is a kind of conversation. Sometimes we get so involved in clinical goals we forget basic practices of conversation. In the following example from Conway (1986) the child shows ample conversation skills that go unnoticed as the clinician pursues correcting a particular detail. The clinician's goal in this session is to correct a 5-year-old child's articulation of the /k/ sound. This child misarticulates many sounds, and some features are simplified in this transcript.

> EDWARD: I would just taw *[call]* the police.
> CLINICIAN: Ooh.
> E: Unless they were . . .
> C: *[Clinician interrupts.]* You would just what?
> E: I would just taw the police.

C: Just what?

E: Unless it was . . . *[pause]* just taw de police.

C: Just *what* the police?

E: Taw the police.

C: Just what?

E: Taw the police

C: Call the police. Right?

E: Yeah. ihept if it wah wah HANTA Kwas *[except if it was SANTA Klaus]. [T]*hat would be a tewible *[t]*hing.

C: Oh, a terrible thing, huh?

E: Yeah.

C: Now we're gonna do something different.

At the beginning of this scene, the child is telling what he'd do if someone robbed him, he'd "taw the police." The clinician notices the /t/ for /k/ substitution and interrupts Edward, who is trying to go on talking ("unless they were"). The clinician initiates repair ("Just what?"). Such repair initiations are usually used when someone has trouble hearing or understanding. Edward seems to judge that the clinician hasn't heard well, so he repeats his utterance. The clinician tries twice more to localize the problem in the word "call" by repeating the words around it, "just what the police?" and Edward patiently repeats his articulation mistake twice more. At length the therapist supplies the correct form. The child accepts the correction, with no particular display of attention to it, and goes on to say what he was trying to say before this repair sequence started ("unless it was Santa Klaus"). The pronunciation of "Santa Klaus," though still flawed by adult standards, contains the very feature (word-initial /k/) that the therapist is seeking to elicit, but this success goes unnoticed, or at least not acknowledged, and the therapist cuts off Edward's fascinating fantasy to begin another activity.

We want to stress that this is a good therapist working with a child who is not afraid to talk. Yet problems emerge. The big success in this story, as throughout the present volume, is that the human conversation goes on.

SUMMARY

It is important for anyone who plans to work with children whose language development is not normal to maintain a clear sense of the various stages of normal development and the processes by which normal children learn language. Approaching atypical development from this perspective should result in child-centered assessment and therapy. Recognizing that the assessment and therapy settings are essentially communication situations and that all children will learn what is made functionally important is likely to result in more successful clinical encounters.

SUGGESTED READINGS

Crystal, D. *Linguistic Encounters with Language Handicap.* Oxford: Basil Blackwell, 1984. In this slim volume a child language scholar examines the clinical process and points toward concrete solutions. The work is relevant for researchers, students, and parents.

Fey, M. E. *Language Intervention with Young Children.* San Diego: College Hill Press, 1986. Using a functionalist-interactionist perspective, Fey considers identification and intervention issues. Chapters on facilitating spontaneous talking and conversational responsiveness are particularly forward-looking and useful.

SUGGESTED PROJECTS

1. Tape record a therapy session between a clinician and child (with permission of the participants, of course). Transcribe the interaction and analyze it as a conversation. What kinds of things might the child learn about conversation from such an interaction? What does the child already appear to know about conversation?
2. Tape record an hour of clinical interaction between a language-handicapped child and an adult. Then tape this same child at home with a parent for an hour. How does the child's language use differ in the two settings? What expectations for language use are set up in each context?

Chapter
14

Children's Speech and Literacy

Writing exists only in a civilization and a civilization cannot exist without writing.
(Ong, 1967, p. 222)

*J*ohn is 8 years old and has just completed the second grade. His mother is dismayed because John's teacher has recommended that he not be promoted to third grade because he has not learned to read. John's parents cannot understand why he is having problems. He seems to be an active, normal, friendly, and talkative child. Why should he have trouble with reading?

Many children whose speaking skills appear normal fail to develop skills in reading and writing. Writing extends communication skills in many useful directions, and persons with weak literacy skills suffer limited social and professional options. No theorist disagrees that acquisition of speaking skills happens before literacy and provides the basis for literacy. Nobody denies that language development in the preliterate years is a complicated task that most children undertake seemingly without effort or prompting. Nobody can satisfactorily explain, therefore, why failures to develop literacy are widespread in spite of educators' assaults on the problem.

We cannot provide a detailed discussion of reading pedagogy, but we can briefly summarize relationships between oral language and literacy and recommend to educators and parents reading and writing programs that emphasize those relationships.

RELATIONSHIPS BETWEEN SPEECH AND LITERACY

Speech provides the verbal and linguistic structures upon which literacy is built. People speak before they learn to read or to write. Humans have been using alphabets for perhaps five thousand years, have been writing for perhaps ten thousand years, but have been speaking in ceremony, work, and conversational contexts for much longer than that. When writing began, its tie to speech was weak—humans made marks to tally quantities and the like. As pictographs developed, speech and writing became more tied to one another. The change from pictographic to alphabetic writing, perhaps the most important innovation in human communicative history, cemented the dependence of writing on the spoken word.

To describe the origin of writing in speech persuades us that speech and writing "do not abolish one another but overlie one another" (Ong, 1967, p. 9). There is a strong connection between speech and literacy, a connection teachers and parents ignore at children's peril. The best teaching methods for literacy are those based on speaking.

Ancient and medieval readers ordinarily read aloud. Silent reading was such a unique practice that observers of silent reading failed to understand it. We duplicate this practice today by teaching children to read aloud before teaching them to read silently. Reading aloud revisits the source of the written word in the spoken utterance. Although we do not accept as valuable every technique of teaching to read that involves reading aloud, we do argue the necessity of connecting speech to reading and writing. Speaking sets bases for literacy; effective reading and writing pedagogy depends upon instruction in speech. The child must build on speaking skills to acquire reading skills.

Imagine a huge tree that represents the historical record of all communication. There are many branches, representing many varieties of written and electronic media. But there is one trunk—speech, the medium par excellence from which all others grow. Speech is basic to all other communication media. If, as the child develops, speech communication fails, this failure is magnified and reflected throughout all attempts at literacy.

Perhaps the simplest way of capturing the relation between spoken language and written language is to set up a hierarchical model.

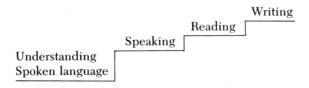

The child moves up a series of steps, each one arising from the one below. The first skill, on which all others are based, is understanding spoken language. The next skill, based on this understanding, is speaking. From speaking skills the child can move on to developing reading skills. Reading then provides a foundation for written expression.

Lundsteen (1976, p. 112) expresses the view that a child having trouble with reading or writing should "back up" a step and work on oral language skills.

Oral language is basic to writing, both draw on past experience of organizing speech in appropriate sequences, choosing words properly, and using language patterns. If a child's written composition is poor, the teacher probably needs to help him work on his oral language. Usually a child will not write better than he talks. Whether the aim is effective writing, the factor of spoken language skills sets the child's ceiling of performance.

Proponents of this view might tell a child struggling with a composition to "just write it the way you would say it." It also comes through clearly in statements such as Rubin's (1975, p. 219): "Since oral and written language are closely related, children should have many opportunities to express themselves orally, before being expected to write."

Kavanaugh (1968) calls reading "parasitic" on language. Johnson and Myklebust (1967) argue that "the visual symbol systems (reading and writing) are learned by superimposing them on auditory language." These statements, ofcourse, give rise to a logical question: Since most children are competent oral language users by the time they are 4 years old, and since written language is oral language in another form, why do so many children have trouble with literacy?

For many educators the answer to that question demands a redefinition of terms. As Olson (1977) puts it, the primary task of the child in school is to make the transition from oral language ("utterance") to written language ("text"). If reading and talking were essentially the same, there would be no need for transition. Olson and others (among them Westby, 1984; Chafe, 1982; and Wallach and Miller, 1988) see a shift from the oral style of the preschool child to a literate style in the school years. Understanding what this shift entails might give us some insight into why some children have trouble with written language.

Oral language is learned through interaction. When children learn to talk, they are taking turns with other people. Each person's turn (or utterance) is related to and built on turns (or utterances) of the other person. This leads to the development of what Wells (1986) calls *negotiated meanings.* What participants mean at any point in an interaction is a product of all of what all of the participants in the interaction have said and done. Children's utterances in an interaction are also often closely tied to an immediate, shared context that does not need to be made overt in language to be clear to the participants. Consider the following conversation between a first-grader and his mother:

ROB: Boy, Miss Johnson was crabby again today. *[Miss Johnson is his teacher. He often complains about her.]*

MOTHER: Was she yelling a lot? *[This is what Rob usually means by being "crabby."]*

ROB: Yeah. And she sent Joey to the principal again. *[The mother knows it has happened before.]*

MOTHER: Well, if you acted like Joey, I'd send you somewhere. *[Joey is well known for fighting and talking back to the teacher.]*

ROB: Yeah, well, she didn't have to yell at everybody.

MOTHER: I expect she gets tired of putting up with bad behavior sometimes, though. I'd yell too.

ROB: Me too, I guess, and maybe I'd send everybody to the principal.

This interaction is a fine example of using mutually shared information (indicated in italics) and interactive negotiation to arrive at a meaning somewhat removed from the utterance that began the interaction. Rob may not yet be capable of saying "If I had to put up with what my teacher puts up with, I'd get just as crabby as she does." This is complex role switching and complex reasoning for a 6-year-old. Yet, with his mother's help, he in fact arrives at this meaning, utterance by utterance.

The kind of language Rob will be called on to handle in school is not like this; it is not interactive, and it is not based on a common immediate context. Written language (and some oral language, such as classroom lectures) exists not as a series of utterances spoken in alternating conversational dialogue, but as a *monologue*. The reader does not have dialogue to use in determining meaning as the speaker-listener does. The reader must be able to reason on her or his own to fill in the "blanks."

Meanings in written language exist as relations between utterances (cued by words such as *therefore* and *on the other hand*) and as inferences to be made from arguments or from sequential ideas. Meanings are not negotiated; they are carried by the language of the writer. There are no gestures, facial expressions, or vocal changes to signal changes in focus or approach. There is no opportunity to ask for clarification. Clarification may be provided in the written text by the use of paraphrase, redundancy, and examples. Both the writer and the reader must come to recognize these conventions. Text is sometimes called *decontextualized;* it uses language to establish meaning, instead of depending on a shared context apart from the language. (Think back to our discussion in Chapter 11 about the difference between talking about a movie with someone who has seen it and someone who has not. The latter case calls for decontextualized language.)

Wallach and Miller (1988, p. 84) express the differences between oral interaction and reading as follows:

> Readers must engage in several levels of processing at once: they must hold in mind questions to determine if the actual text answers them, and if so, how, when, and where; they must marshal their own experiences and knowledge as a counterargument to the author's; they must withhold those of their own experiences that do not pertain to what is being proposed. . . . Finally, readers "must have learned to negotiate the world of abstractions" (Postman, 1985, p. 26). Negotiating the world of abstractions involves an understanding of and an ability to manipulate decontextualized ideas divested of whatever concrete images . . . they might have held.

As this statement suggests, the transition to literacy for children involves more than a switch from using their ears to using their eyes. Written language is not just spoken language on paper. Becoming literate involves new cognitive processes as it opens up a world of language beyond interaction.

We have presented here two ways to think about the relationship between oral and written language. The hierarchical model stresses similarities, and the divergent model, which focuses on decontextualization, stresses differences. Both points of view have a place in our thinking about children's move to literacy.

DEVELOPMENT OF LITERACY

Kroll (1981) presents a model for the transition to literacy that combines the hierarchical and divergent approaches. As he sees it, children develop literacy. They do not simply wake up one day being literate. The stages in this development can be seen in terms of changes in the relationship between oral and written language. He identifies four phases of development: preparation, consolidation, differentiation, and systematic integration.

Preparation

Children entering school, who have not yet begun to read and write, are in the preparation phase. They have developed oral language skills, but they are unable to recognize words on a page, let alone write or spell. They must learn how to translate talk into writing. Some children will already know that this can be done (although they may be unable to do it themselves); others may take some time before they grasp the basic idea that words carry speechlike messages. This understanding seems to emerge from the use of books—from being read to aloud and from browsing through books on their own. Young children, who see mostly picture books, seem to believe that the story is in the pictures. Their frequent demand that a story be read exactly the same way each time does not mean that they know the words are in the print, not the pictures.

Kroll believes that there are three important tasks for children once they realize that writing has speech meanings. They must acquire the technical skills of handwriting and spelling, practice composing by dictating to someone else, and extend their oral language skills for a variety of communicative purposes. Some educators suggest that children at this stage might learn to read most easily by reading their own writing. The children tell stories to the teacher; the teacher writes them down in their own words, perhaps using a tape recording; the teacher then gives the children their own stories as a reading lesson. In this way every word and the stories in the reading lesson are familiar to them. This allows them and the teacher to focus on the mechanical task of word recognition.

Consolidation

The consolidation stage occurs after the child has mastered some technical reading and writing skills. The major task is to strengthen the child's literacy by drawing on oral language competence. At this point the child's oral and written expression are likely to be similar; the child's written expression may, in fact, be very much like "talk written down." Kroll identifies three kinds of activity important for children in this stage: to continue to promote the development of oral language skills serving a variety of purposes, to engage in language activities in which the forms and functions of speech and writing are as similar as possible (telling and writing stories, for example), and to use talk as preparation for writing (as in class discussions prior to writing assignments).

Kroll points out that "as writing skills develop and begin to be used for conveying full and explicit messages, oral language skills are influenced" (1981, p. 47). In other words, the writing and language skills are consolidated. A reciprocal relationship between oral and written language is being established by the child.

Differentiation

In the differentiation stage the emphasis shifts to the differences between talking and writing. Children must develop those special skills that are necessary for comprehending and composing texts. They must expand their knowledge of special rules for written language and integrate these into the intact oral language system. They must learn to use language *autonomously* as well as interactively. It is in this stage that Olson's (1977) distinction between utterance and text becomes so important. Children must be freed from a dependence on utterances, where meaning depends on shared experiences and interpretations and lies primarily in the interaction of speaker, listener, utterance, and context. They must make the transition to textual literacy in which "all the information relevant to the communication of intention must be present in the text" (1977, p. 277). They must learn to signal organization through sophisticated linguistic forms for cohesion and learn the vocabulary and sentence structures necessary for expanding and making explicit textual meaning.

Kroll admits that the transition from consolidation to differentiation is a difficult one for many children. He notes that failure to differentiate the forms and functions of oral and written language may continue to plague some throughout school. Although Kroll's remarks are about writing, his conclusions seem equally true for reading. Until children can see how written language differs from spoken language, and until they are as comfortable with the conventions of written language as with those of spoken language, they will find both reading and writing difficult.

Systematic Integration

The final stage of the development of literacy is systematic integration. During this stage children become equally proficient at speaking, listening, reading, and writing, and skill in one language art is reflected in the others. The language arts become integrated.

As Kroll points out, the end of this stage, mature language use, occurs after a complex developmental journey. It will be beyond the reach of children in the age range we are concerned with here. Still, it is nice to think about it as you are struggling to help a child who still can't seem to understand that every sentence needs a verb.

DECODING AND INTERPRETING TEXT

Our theoretical discussion of the relationships between oral language and literacy can help us understand the problem of the child who is having trouble learning to read. It will guide us to possible explanations for the difficulty and provide a starting point as we think about possible solutions. Let us return to the beginning, and briefly discuss those factors that seem related to the development of literacy.

Literacy involves reading and writing. We say that a person is literate who can respond appropriately to written language. We may find it easier to think in developmental terms, however, if we broaden our sense of literacy, and say that a person is literate who can respond appropriately to a particular kind of language use. Think back to the discussion of decontextualized language, and you may begin to understand the need for this broader definition. While it is true that the use of language to establish a primary context for meaning is more frequent in writing than in talking, such language use is not limited to print. Oral monologues such as lectures, sermons, and movies are also characterized by autonomous, as opposed to interactive, meanings. The successful manipulation of autonomous or textual meaning is a complex linguistic and cognitive activity. Consider how such meanings are generated.

Assume that an intelligent 5-year-old is watching you water a plant. She sees the water fill up the saucer in which the pot sits and is fascinated by the fact that it doesn't run over right away. She asks you what keeps it from running over. You are faced with the task of explaining the surface tension of water to a child who doesn't have any formal scientific knowledge. Since you are not a coward, and the child really wants to know, you give it a try. You must first put yourself in the child's place and decide what she knows about the world and about language that you can use. Does she know what a molecule is? Has she ever stretched a rubber band until it broke? Does she understand the meaning of *tension*? The answers to these and other questions will determine the content of your explanation and the language in which you express it. This suggests two things about textual meanings: Creating them is a deliberate, conscious process, and it involves role taking, or putting yourself in the place of your audience. You decide to explain that everything in the world is made up of tiny particles, too tiny to be seen, called molecules, and that molecules like to stay together if they can. The water molecules in the saucer hang on to each other as long as possible before some of them spill over the edge. You can see the same molecule behavior if you stretch a rubber band. The rubber molecules stay together as long as they can, stretching and stretching, before some of them finally let go and the rubber band breaks. (You realize that there are flaws in your explanation, but it's the best you can do, given what you assume the child's understanding to be.)

What is the child's task like, as she tries to comprehend what you are saying? Most obviously, she will need to have the language skills necessary to follow your reasoning. It won't do you any good to use the word *invisible* unless she either knows it or is given enough information in your text to figure it out. It won't do any good for you to say that water molecules "are like" the rubber band molecules unless she has some understanding of what is means for one thing to be like another. This suggests a couple of things about the process of decoding textual meaning: The audience must be familiar with textual conventions, especially with the linguistic forms used to signal organizational ties, and the audience must be able to infer meanings that are not explicitly stated. If, at the conclusion of your explanation, the child says "Oh, you mean the water stays together until it breaks," you will know that she has successfully inferred something you never actually said—that she "got the point."

This ability to get the point of text is what distinguishes a literate from a nonliterate child, what distinguishes successful readers and writers from those with "literacy problems." Successful readers have learned to "ask themselves questions" about text in order to fill in the blanks, or check understanding. Successful child readers are learning to ask questions about where there is a gap in their knowledge of the world or in their reading skill. As we suggested, "getting the point" depends on two key abilities: to recognize and follow cohesive devices and to make inferences.

Linguistic Cohesion

In a typical utterance-by-utterance conversation, we need not necessarily attend closely to linguistic devices for signaling what is related to what. We can depend on voice, gesture, and the nonverbal context, or we can rely on other speakers to repair misunderstandings. If you look back at the conversation between Rob and his mother earlier in the chapter, you will notice that Rob ties his utterances to his mother's and to each other by using "and" or "yeah." This is perfectly adequate in the conversational context. Rob's conversation is not hard to follow. In a text, however, meaning must be made explicit. Rob would not be able to piggyback onto his mother's more sophisticated meanings. He would need to have better devices than "and" or "and then" to show the relationships among his ideas.

Halliday and Hasan (1976) use the term *cohesive devices* to refer to those aspects of language we use to indicate the connections among the elements in a text. Wallach and Miller (1988, p. 122) say, "cohesion arises at any point in a text where the meaning of some aspect of text can only be determined by reference to information contained somewhere else in the text." It is at these points that writers employ cohesive devices. The brief text presented below is filled with cohesive devices, which have been italicized to help you identify them.

> The man began to dance. *At first he* moved slowly. *Then he* began to move faster. *At that point*, a woman appeared on the stage with *him*. *She also* began to dance. *Their* movements were harmonious, *although* the music was loud and discordant. *As* the music became softer, the two *dancers* moved more slowly. *Finally* the movements and the music faded away together. *It* was over. Did you like it? *I did.*

The cohesive devices used in this text are described in Table 14.1. While we have little information about children's development of the ability to handle these language forms, Stoel-Gammon and Hedberg (1984) suggest that referential cohesion and lexical cohesion appear first in children's language, followed by conjunction, substitution, and ellipsis. While preschoolers may use some cohesive devices, it is rare to see much sophistication in this aspect of language use before age 8 or 9. This may be one area of oral language functioning that is strongly influenced by the child's exposure to reading. As the child becomes able to read more complex texts, the variety of cohesive devices to which he is exposed increases.

Inferential Meaning

One of the most notable characteristics of text is that not everything is stated overtly. Much of the meaning is carried between the lines, that is, it must be inferred. Consider the brief test below:

1. Read this paragraph:

> Fairies are little creatures who cannot be seen. These invisible creatures are often found in forests and gardens. We have one in our garden. Her footprints are there early in the morning after a heavy dew.

2. Answer these questions. In each case say whether the paragraph stated the answer or you inferred it.
  a. Are the fairies big or little?
  b. What does *invisible* mean?

Table 14.1 COHESIVE DEVICES

Reference—semantic relations achieved through continuity of reference or referring to the same thing more than once in a text
   Pronominal: Ann ate her lunch. She was hungry.
   Demonstrative: John pointed to the red balloon and said "I want that."
   Comparative: That one is mine. You can have another one.

Lexical inference—relations achieved through vocabulary selection, usually involving synonyms or repetition of words
   Synonym: This is a picture of Sue's baby. He's such a cute child.
   Repetition: We live in a city. It is a big, busy city.

Conjunction—logical relations achieved by using various connectors to show relationships between statements
   Additive: Put your toys away and pick up your clothes.
   Adversative: He was smiling, but he did not seem happy.
   Causal: The battery is missing, so the flashlight won't work.
   Temporal: After you eat lunch, we'll take a walk.
   Continuative: I will play the piano while he sings.

Substitution—relations achieved by using one word or clause in place of another to avoid repetition
   Nominal: We went to buy new shirts. The store had several on sale.
   Clausal: Can you answer the question? I think so.

Ellipsis—relations established by deleting words, phrases, or clauses
   Verbal: Who's playing? The Bears are (playing).
   Nominal: What color hat do you wear? Red (hat).
   Clausal: Who ate all the potato chips? Jerry did (eat all the potato chips).

Source: Adapted from G. P. Wallach, and L. Miller, *Language Intervention and Academic Success* (Boston: College Hill Press, 1988).

    c. Do fairies have feet?
    d. Does the writer have a garden?
    e. Is there dew in the garden?

Only question a is directly answered in the paragraph. To obtain the other information requires various levels of inference making. The easiest inference to make comes from the phrase *our garden* as an indication of the writer's ownership of a garden. The use of the word *footprints* as an indication that fairies have feet is obvious only if you know about footprints. Both of these are inferences that depend on your knowledge of word meaning. The question about dew in the garden is more complicated, demanding that the reader pull together information from several parts of the text: If the footprints are in the dew, and the footprints are in the garden, then the dew is in the garden. The use of information in the text to figure out the meaning of the word *invisible* is still another type of inferencing—a type that children must do if they are ever to figure out word meanings.

Table 14.2 presents a definition of ten types of inferences. Different kinds of text may call for different types of inferences. Only the very simplest (and the least interesting) texts make all meanings so overt that no inferring is necessary.

The process of inference making, which we have just demonstrated so laboriously, occurs with great rapidity and spontaneity in the reading and listening of skillful communicators. Some people have hypothesized that inferring is a natural part of learning for human beings, almost a consequence of the way human brain works. Researchers have demon-

---

Table 14.2 TYPES OF INFERENCE

Location—using textual clues to decide about place
  Example: We took out our math books and listened while the teacher gave the assignment. Where are we?

Agent—deciding about role or occupation of a character in the text
  Example: First she listened to the baby's heart with a stethoscope, then she checked his throat and ears. What is her occupation?

Time—deciding when something in the text occurred
  Example: The sun was blazing hot, and I felt ready to jump into the swimming pool. What time of year is it?

Action—deciding what activity is occurring
  Example: The quarterback carried the ball across the goal line as the crowd cheered. What is happening?

Instrument—deciding what tool or device is being used
  Example: Charlie played happily in the back yard, waving the nozzle around and watching the water sparkle in the sun. What is Charlie playing with?

Category—deciding about group or class membership
  Example: The chef asked for marjoram, oregano, and thyme to put into her sauce. What do you think these three things might be?

Object—deciding about the topic
  Example: After you sort it into piles, you put one pile into the machine along with your detergent. What is "it"?

Cause-effect—deciding about reasons or about outcomes
  Example: Mary looked at her bandaged hand and decided she would never play with matches again. What happened to Mary's hand?

Problem-solution—deciding about a solution or a consequence.
  Example: When she returned from vacation, Paul's houseplants were drooping and the soil in the pots felt dry. What does Paul need to do?

Feelings-attitudes—deciding about explanations for characters' actions or reactions
  Example: After the coach announced the names of the starting players, Brad turned his back and walked slowly away. How does Brad feel? Why?

Source: Adapted from D. D. Johnson and B. van Hoff Johnson, Highlighting vocabulary in inferential comprehension, *Journal of Reading, 29,* 622–625, 1986.

strated the ability in children as young as 6. They have also shown that the ability to make inferences from a text improves with age, probably as a result of more exposure to and practice with textual material. It is not until age 12 or 13 that children are completely comfortable with the meanings of expository (as opposed to narrative) texts.

In sum, we have expanded our concept of literacy to mean the ability to respond to decontextualized text, that is, the ability to decode and interpret written messages. Textual meanings are autonomous rather than negotiated, and they are often covert rather than overt. Interpreting text demands mastery of cohesive devices and inference making. These are language abilities that develop after children enter school and are brought to bear in responding to both oral and written texts.

LEARNING TO READ

It may seem strange to have come so far into a chapter about reading, writing, and speaking without having paid attention to issues of visual processing and sound-letter correspondence. However, reading and writing are primarily language activities and are only incidentally visual. There is no evidence to suggest that most children who are having trouble learning to read are having visual problems or problems related to distinguishing one letter from another. The idea that being able to read is dependent on some set of visual discrimination, auditory discrimination, and sequencing skills is an old-fashioned belief growing out of the concept of "reading readiness" developed early in this century. Tests of reading readiness continue to be used in our schools, and the concept of readiness governs much reading instruction, in spite of the fact that as early as the 1930s Gates and his associates demonstrated that readiness tests were of little value in predicting which children would be good readers.

Reading is not only the result of an accumulation of discrete skills that must be taught to a child. As Reid (1981) points out, reading is largely the result of a normal developmental process in which the child is an active learner. In this way reading is like oral language. Throughout this book we have emphasized the active role of the child as a language learner—selecting and organizing experience and attributing meaning to the world. According to current theory (Schwartz, 1977; Goodman, 1980; Hiebert, 1978; Reid, Hresko, and Hammill, 1981), reading is a result of the same kind of learning process. Reid summarizes this position saying, "Early reading originates in the same kind of adaptive behavior that motivates all other kinds of learning and is closely related to the development of oral language" (1981, p. 66).

As current research shows, nearly all children can recognize some words prior to starting school. Store names, street signs, cereal labels, and other frequently encountered words are readily recognized by most preschoolers. In a study of 1,000 children aged 3 to 7, not one child failed to identify the McDonald's sign (Reid et al., 1981). In addition, many children begin school knowing that we read from left to right and from top to bottom of a page, knowing that a story is conveyed by the print rather than by the pictures in a book, and able to follow along as familiar stories are read to them. In short, children seem to have a natural tendency to try to make print meaningful by using their oral language skills. They come to recognize words and groups of words that have particular meaning for them.

Then they start to school and are taught names of letters and sound groups. They learn to segment the stream of meaning into physical units called words. They learn that, when reading, they cannot say just any word that conveys the meaning, but only the right word.

There are two current theoretical positions about what happens to the child's reading at this point. One group of researchers (Gibson, 1970, 1976; Liberman, Liberman, Mattingly, and Shankweiler, 1978) believe that children must learn to combine letters into units appropriate for speech, and that good readers are better than poor readers at mapping sounds onto letters and groups of letters. Another group (Smith, 1975; Goodman, 1976) believe that children read by relating meaning directly to printed symbols without any necessity for breaking words down into sounds and letters. The first group advocate teaching through phonics to focus on sound, and the second group advocate teaching through whole word language experience to focus on meaning. Regardless of the teaching method advocated, both groups seem to have arrived at similar views of the learning process involved:

> The need for a concept of readiness evaporated. Children did not develop a series of skills whose later metamorphosis enabled them to read. They began learning to read (learning about the vocabulary and strategies and processes of reading) through trial and error, through selecting, guessing, testing, and generating categories and systems of words and knowledge— just as they were organizing their oral language experiences. . . . There is no readiness different from reading itself and reading is primarily cognitive and linguistic and not visual and perceptual" (Reid, 1981, p. 70).

When we encounter children who are having trouble learning to read or write, we will of course want to check for vision or hearing difficulties that might not have been suspected earlier. Certainly, a child who cannot see well enough to distinguish letters on a page or a child who cannot hear well enough to distinguish "fit" from "sit" will have problems. Also, there are some children whose brains do not seem to handle visual input as other children's do. These children may routinely reverse letters and words and demonstrate other perceptual difficulties. It should be emphasized that this is a small group, that not all children having trouble learning to read demonstrate such problems, and that some children with visual or aural perceptual problems do not have trouble with written language.

Most children who encounter significant difficulty with reading, writing, and spelling are neither visually nor aurally impaired. They will probably be labeled "learning disabled" by the schools, which is shorthand for saying that the child's academic achievement doesn't match up to what we would expect given the child's intelligence and that the problems are not due to mental retardation, emotional disturbance, or environmental deprivation. There is some controversy about whether "learning disabilities" are the result of neurological impairments. In the end, it probably doesn't matter, since we attempt to work with the child's problems regardless of their cause. Specific strategies for helping children who are having problems with written language are beyond the scope of this book. However, there are some facts related to language learning and language use that are relevant in this context.

TRAINING GROUND FOR LITERACY

Throughout this book we have attempted to present a consistent approach to children's language—an approach enabling us to talk about both oral language and written language from the perspective of the child as an active learner. Our focus on the child should not be taken as an indication that the language-learning environment is insignificant, however. At this point it is appropriate to ask what is the best kind of environment for learning about written language? How can we give a child the best start for this aspect of language?

The most obvious answer is to expose the child to as much oral and written language as possible. Children who see their parents reading books, magazines, and newspapers and who see their parents using writing to convey meaning will have a great appreciation for the uses of print in our society. They will have a positive attitude about reading and writing and are likely to ask about print in the environment.

We can do a great deal to influence children's literacy by reading stories to them. When we read to children, we are providing pleasurable experiences with print; they learn that books are fun. But there is much more. Children who hear stories are exposed to textual language with its autonomous and covert meanings. They hear the cohesive devices they might not be exposed to in conversation. They get practice with inference making as they think about the story. Their ears grow accustomed to the sounds and rhythms of writing. They learn to hear the structure of stories. In fact, Wells (1986), in his large-scale study of children's language development, found that the single best predictor of a child's success in school was parents' reading to the child at home. It is impossible to overemphasize the importance of this activity.

Beyond this, it is also helpful to expose children to a wide variety of communication situations. They need to learn that language can be used to meet many diverse purposes, and they need to hear stylistic variations across contexts and functions. Interaction is critical for the young child learning language, but it is not the only linguistic context, and children need to learn about other contexts. Not only listening to stories, but also telling stories, perhaps for someone else to write down; using language to direct and organize pretend play; helping in the kitchen as someone else follows a recipe; looking for signs as someone navigates a trip, whether across the country or around the neighborhood—all these are ordinary events that serve as training grounds for literacy. They are important not only in the preschool years, but also after children have started school. If there is any validity to the idea of "readiness training" for literacy, it can be found in activities of this sort.

There are two kinds of people in the world, people who read for fun and people who read only to get tasks accomplished. The people who belong to the first group are the people you see on airplanes or hallways curled up with a novel, a book about current events, or a book of poems. You hear them discussing recent books with other readers, trading and lending books, and so on. These are, not surprisingly, some of the best readers and writers. These are people who have the literacy habit—people who read every day because they enjoy the experience whether they are reading to pass the time, to satisfy their curiosity about the world around them, or to challenge their minds. The best way to get children to be effective readers is to help them find what's exciting for them to read. Reading is not only useful and enjoyable, it makes the reader smarter. Literacy creates and transforms the reader. And in changing each reader, it creates and transforms the world in which we all live.

SUMMARY

Language use does not always involve speaking. Sometimes it involves reading and writing. The child's ability to create and respond to written language is an outgrowth of speaking, since the child brings to the encounter with print all that he or she has learned about talking. It is also true, however, that reading and writing demand new language skills.

In particular, literacy demands that a child decode and interpret textual meanings, which are different from the negotiated meanings of conversation. Textual meaning is conveyed through cohesion and inferencing. These language abilities develop during the elementary school years.

The best preparation for literacy comes from the preschool environment in which a child is exposed to a variety of printed messages, is read to regularly, and is exposed to a wide variety of communication situations.

SUGGESTED READINGS

Harst, J., C. Burke, and V. Woodward. Children's language and world: Initial encounter with print. In J. Lange and M. Smith-Burke (eds.). *Reader Meets Author: Bridging the Gap.* Newark, Del.: International Reading Association, 1982. These authors do a wonderful job of illustrating the natural processes children go through as they begin to read the print in their environments.

Calkins, L. M. *Lessons from a Child: On the Teaching and Learning of Writing.* Portsmouth, England: Heinemann Educational Books, 1983. This book is written out of the author's wide experience with young children. It is filled with examples of children's early writing and their thoughts about it.

SUGGESTED PROJECTS

1. Tape record children at different ages (say, 5 through 10) telling a story based on a wordless storybook. You should leave the child alone with the book and the tape recorder when you do this. After you have transcribed the stories, look for developmental changes. You might focus on cohesive devices, on the child's ability to include all relevant information, or on some other variable that interests you.

2. Make up several short inference tests like the one in this chapter. Give these tests to children at different ages or to children at a single age level classified as good or poor readers. Describe the differences you observe in their ability to make inferences from a text.

Bibliography

Alland, A. *Evolution and Human Behavior.* New York: Natural History Press, 1967.

Allen, R., and K. Brown (eds.). *Developing Communication Competence in Children.* Skokie, Ill.: National Textbook, 1976.

Ardrey, R. *The Territorial Imperative.* New York: Atheneum, 1966.

Austen, J. L. *How to Do Things with Words.* London: Oxford University Press, 1962.

Bakeman, R., and J. V. Brown. Behavioral dialogues: An approach to the assessment of mother-infant interaction. *Child Development 48,* 195-203, 1977.

Barrera, M. E., and D. Maurer. Discrimination of strangers by the three-month-old. *Child Development 52,* 558-563, 1981.

Basso, K. To give up on words: Silence among the Western Apache. In P. Gigliali (ed.), *Language and Social Context.* New York: Penguin, 1970.

Bates, E. Pragmatics and sociolinguistics in child language. In D. Morehead and A. Morehead (eds.), *Language Deficiency in Children.* Baltimore: University Park Press, 1976.

Bates, E., L. Camaione, and V. Volterra. The acquisition of performatives prior to speech. *Merrill-Palmer Quarterly 21,* 205-216, 1975.

Bates, E., and B. MacWhinney. Functionalist approaches to grammar. In E. Wanner and L. Glietman (eds.), *Language Acquisition: The State of the Art.* New York: Cambridge University Press, 1982.

Bates, R. *A Study in the Acquisition of Language.* Unpublished doctoral dissertation, University of Texas, Austin, 1967.

Bateson, G. A theory of play and fantasy. *Steps to an Ecology of Mind.* San Francisco: Chandler, 1972.

Bauman, R. *The Development of Competence in the Use of Solicitational Routines: Children's Folklore and Informal Learning.* (Working Papers in Sociolinguistics, No. 34). Austin: University of Texas Folklore Center, 1976.

Bernard, R., and M. Sontag. Fetal receptivity to tonal stimulation: A preliminary report. *Journal Of Genetic Psychology 70,* 205-210, 1947.

Bever, T. The cognitive basis for linguistic structures. In J. R. Hayes (ed.), *Cognition and the Development of Language.* New York: Wiley, 1970.

Bigelow, A. *Infants' recognition of their mothers.* Paper presented at the biennial meeting of the Society for Research in Child Development, New Orleans, March 1977.

Bloom, L. Why not pivot grammars? *Journal of Speech and Hearing Disorders 36,* 40-50, 1971.

Bloom, L., P. Lighttown, and L. Hood. Structure and variation in child language. *Monographs of the Society for Research in Child Development 40,* 1975.

Bowerman, M. Discussion summary—Development of concepts underlying language. In R. Schiefelbusch and L. Lloyd (eds.), *Language Perspectives—Acquisition, Retardation, and Intervention.* Baltimore: University Park Press, 1974.

Bowerman, M. *Word meaning and sentence structure: Uniformity, variation, and shifts over time in patterns of acquisition.* Paper presented at the Conference on Early Behavioral Assessment of the Communicative and Cognitive Abilities of the Developmentally Disabled, Seattle, Wash., 1976.

Bowerman, M. The acquisition of word meaning: An investigation in some current conflicts. In N. Waterson and C. Snow (eds.), *The Development of Communication.* New York: Wiley, 1976.

Braine, M. D. S. The ontogeny of English phrase structure: The first phase. *Language 39,* 1-13, 1963.

Branigan, G. Some reasons why successive single word utterances are not. *Journal of Child Language 6,* 411-421, 1979.

Brenneis, D., and L. Lein. "You fruithead": A sociolinguistic approach to children's dispute settlement. In S. Ervin-Tripp and C. Mitchell-Kernan (eds.), *Child Discourse.* New York: Academic Press, 1977.

Brown, R. *Words and Things.* New York: Free Press, 1958.

Brown, R. *Psycholinguistics.* New York: Free Press, 1970.

Brown, R. *A First Language: The Early Stages.* Cambridge, Mass.: Harvard University Press, 1973.

Brown, R., and U. Bellugi. Three processes in the child's acquisition of syntax. *Harvard Educational Review 34,* 133-151, 1964.

Brown, R., C. Cazden, and U. Bellugi. The child's grammar from I to III. In J. Hill (ed.), *1967 Minnesota Symposia on Child Psychology.* Minneapolis: University of Minnesota Press, 1969.

Brown, R., and C. Hanlon. Derivational complexity and order of acquisition in child speech. In J. R. Hayes (ed.), *Cognition and the Development of Language.* New York: Wiley, 1970.

Browne, G. Y., H. M. Rosenfield, and F. D. Horowitz. Infant discrimination of facial expressions. *Child Development 48,* 555-562, 1977.

Bruner, J. S. From communication to language—A psychological perspective. *Cognition 3,* 255-287, 1975a.

Bruner, J. S. The ontogenesis of speech acts. *Journal of Child Language 2,* 1-20, 1975b.

Bruner, J. S. *Child's Talk: Learning to Use Language.* Oxford: Oxford University Press, 1983.

Burling, R. *English in Black and White.* New York: Holt, Rinehart and Winston, 1973.

Cairns, R. B. Beyond social attachment: The dynamics of interactional development. In T. Alloway, P. Pliner, and L. Krames (eds.), *Attachment Behavior.* New York: Plenum, 1977.

Caron, A., R. Caron, R. Caldwell, and S. Weiss. Infant perception of the structural properties of the face. *Developmental Psychology 9,* 385-399, 1973.

Cazden, C. *Environmental Assistance to the Child's Acquisition of Grammar.* Unpublished doctoral dissertation, Harvard University, Graduate School of Education, Cambridge, Mass.,1965.

Cazden, C. The neglected situation in child language research and education. In F. Williams (ed.), *Language and Poverty.* Chicago: Markham, 1970.

Cazden, C. *Child Language and Education.* New York: Holt, Rinehart and Winston, 1972.

Chafe, W. Features distinguishing spoken and written language. In D. Tannen (ed.), *Spoken and Written Language.* Norwood, N.J.: Ablex, 1982.

Chase, W. P. Color vision in infants. *Journal of Experimental Psychology 20,* 203-222, 1937.

Cherry, L., and M. Lewis. Mothers and two-year-olds: A study of sex differentiated aspects of verbal interaction. *Developmental Psychology 12,* 278-282, 1976.

Chomsky, C. *The Acquisition of Syntax in Children from 5 to 10.* Cambridge, Mass.: MIT Press, 1969.

Chomsky, N. *Language and Mind.* New York: Harcourt Brace Jovanovich, 1968.

Chomsky, N., and M. Halle. *The Sound Patterns of English.* New York: Harper & Row, 1968.

Clark, E. What's in a word? On the child's acquisition of semantics in his first language. In T. E. Moore (ed.), *Cognitive Development and the Acquisition of Language.* New York: Academic Press, 1973.

Clark, E. Some aspects of the conceptual basis for first language acquisition. In L. Lloyd and R. Schiefelbusch (eds.), *Language Perspectives—Acquisition, Retardation, and Intervention.* Baltimore: University Park Press, 1974.

Clark, E. Strategies for communicating. *Child Development 49,* 953-959, 1978.

Clark, H. Language use and language users. In G. Lindzey and E. Aronson (eds.), *Handbook of Social Psychology.* Reading, Mass.: Addison-Wesley, 1983.

Clark, R. What's the use of imitation? *Journal of Child Language 4,* 341-358, 1977.

Clark, H. and Clark, E. *Psychology and Language.* New York: Harcourt Brace Jovanovich, 1977.

Cohen, L. B., J. S. DeLoache, and R. Pearl. An examination of interference effects in infants' memory for faces. *Child Development 48,* 88-96, 1977.

Condon, W. S., and L. S. Sander. Neonate movement is synchronized with adult speech, interactional participation, and language acquisition. *Science 183*, 99-101, 1974.

Conway, M. Is Pragmatics Useful for Speech Therapy? Paper delivered at Western Speech Communication Conference, 1986.

Cooper, W. E. Selective adaptation to speech. In F. Restle et al. (eds.), *Cognitive Theory*, vol. 1. Hillsdale, N.J.: Erlbaum, 1975.

Cromer, R. F. The development of language and cognition: The cognition hypothesis. In B. Fass (ed.), *New Perspectives in Child Development*. Harmondsworth, England: Penguin, 1974.

Crystal, D. *Linguistic Encounters with Language Handicap*. Oxford: Basil Blackwell, 1984.

Dale, P. S. *Language Development: Structure and Function*, 2nd ed. New York: Holt, Rinehart and Winston, 1976.

DeStefano, J. S. (ed.). *Language, Society and Education*. Columbus, Ohio: Jones, 1973.

Dore, J. Holophrases, speech acts and language universals. *Journal of Child Language 2*, 21-40, 1975.

Dore, J. Conversation and preschool language development. In P. Fletcher and M. Garman (eds.), *Language Acquisition*. Cambridge: Cambridge University Press, 1979.

Dore, J. Holophrases revisited: Their logical development from dialog. In M. D. Barrett (ed.), *Children's Single Word Speech*. New York: Wiley, 1985.

Dore, J. The development of conversational competence. In R. Schiefelbusch (ed.), *Language Competence: Assessment and Intervention*. San Diego: College Hill Press, 1987.

Dore, J., M. Franklin, R. Miller, and A. Ramer. Transitional phenomena in early language acquisition. *Journal of Child Language 3*, 13-28, 1976.

Edelsky, C. Acquisition of an aspect of communicative competence: Learning what it means to talk like a lady. In S. Ervin-Tripp and C. Mitchell-Kernan (eds.), *Child Discourse*. New York: Academic Press, 1977.

Eimas, P., E. R. Siqueland, P. Jusczyk, and J. Vigorito. Speech perception in infants. *Science 171*, 303-306, 1971.

Ervin, S. Imitation and structural change in children's language. In E. Lenneberg (ed.), *New Directions in the Study of Language*. Cambridge, Mass.: MIT Press, 1964.

Fantz, R. L. Visual perception and experience in early infancy. In H. Stevenson, E. Hess, and H. Rheingold (eds.), *Early Behavior: Comparative and Developmental Approaches*. New York: Wiley, 1967.

Ferguson, C., and C. Farwell. Words and sounds in early language acquisition: English initial consonants in the first fifty words. *Language 51*, 419-439, 1975.

Flavell, J. *Communication and the Development of Role-Taking Skills in Children*. New York: Wiley, 1968.

Franke, C. Uber die erste Laustufe der Kinder. *Anthropos*, 12, 663-676, 1912.

Frankel, R., M. Leary, and B. Kilman. Building social skills through pragmatic analysis: Assessment and treatment implications for children with autism. In D. Cohen and

A. Donellan (eds.), *Handbook of Autism and Disorders of Atypical Development.* New York: Wiley, 1986.

Furth, H. *Piaget and Knowledge.* Englewood Cliffs, N.J.: Prentice-Hall, 1969.

Gardner, R. A., and B. Gardner. Teaching sign language to a chimpanzee. *Science 165,* 664-672, 1969.

Garvey, C. Requests and responses in children's speech. *Journal of Child Language 2,* 41-63, 1975.

Garvey, C. The contingent query: A dependent act in conversation. In M. Lewis and L. Rosenblum (eds.), *Interaction, Conversation and the Development of Language.* New York: Wiley, 1977.

Garvey, C. Contingent queries and their relations in discourse. In E. Ochs and B. Schieffelin (eds.), *Developmental Pragmatics.* New York: Academic Press, 1979.

Garvey, C., and G. Berninger. Timing and turn-taking in children's conversations. *Discourse Processes 4,* 27-57, 1981.

Gates, A. I., and G. Bond. Reading readiness: A study of factors determining success and failure in beginning reading. *Teachers College Record 37,* 679-685, 1936.

Gibson, E. J. The ontogeny of reading. *American Psychologist 25,* 136-143, 1970.

Gibson, E. J. Learning to read. In H. Singer and R. Ruddell (eds.), *Theoretical Models and Processes of Reading.* Newark, N.J.: International Reading Association, 1976.

Goffman, E. *Forms of Talk.* Philadelphia: University of Pennsylvania Press, 1978.

Goodman, K. Reading: A psycholinguistic guessing game. In H. Singer and R. Ruddell (eds.), *Theoretical Models and Processes of Reading.* Newark, N.J.: International Reading Association, 1976.

Goodman, Y. Roots of literacy. In M. Douglas (ed.), *Forty-fourth Yearbook of the Claremont Reading Conference.* Claremont, Calif.: Claremont Reading Conference, 1980.

Goodwin, M. H. Aggravated correction and disagreement in children's conversations. *Journal of Pragmatics 2,* 657-677, 1983.

Goodwin, M. H. The serious side of jump-rope: Conversational practices and social organization in the frame of play. *Journal of American Folklore 98,* 315-330, 1985.

Gumperz, J., and D. Hymes (eds.). *Directions in Sociolinguistics.* New York: Holt, Rinehart and Winston, 1972.

Haaf, R., and C. Brown. Infants' response to face-like patterns: Developmental changes between 10 and 15 weeks of age. *Journal of Experimental Child Psychology 22,* 155-160, 1976.

Hall, E. T. *The Silent Language.* Garden City, N.Y.: Doubleday, 1959.

Halliday, M. A. K. *Learning How to Mean: Explorations in the Development of Language.* New York: Arnold, 1975.

Halliday, M. A. K., and R. Hasan. *Cohesion in English.* London: Longman, 1976.

Hargan, D. Learning to tell jokes: A case study of metalinguistic abilities. *Journal of Child Language 8,* 217-224, 1981.

Hayes, A. Interaction, engagement, and the origins and growth of communication: Some constructive concerns. In L. Feagans et al. (eds.), *The Origins and Growth of Communication.* Norwood, N.J.: Ablex, 1984.

Hiebert, E. H. Preschool children's understanding of written language. *Child Development 49*, 1231-1234, 1978.

Holt, J. *How Children Learn.* New York: Pitman, 1967.

Hopper, R. Communicative development and children's responses to questions. *Speech Monographs 38*, 1-9, 1971a.

Hopper, R. Expanding the notion of competence. *The Speech Teacher 20*, 29-35, 1971b.

Horgan, D. Rate of language acquisition and noun emphasis. *Journal of Psycholinguistic Research 10*, 629-640, 1981.

Horn, T. (ed.). *Reading for the Disadvantaged.* New York: Harcourt Brace Jovanovich, 1970.

Howe, C. J. The meanings of two-word utterances in the speech of young children. *Journal of Child Language 3*, 29-48, 1976.

Hymes, D. *On Communicative Competence.* Philadelphia: University of Pennsylvania Press, 1970.

Hymes, D. Introduction. In C. Cazden, V. John, and D. Hymes (eds.), *Functions of Language in the Classroom.* New York: Teachers College Press, 1972.

Iwamura, S. *The Verbal Games of Preschool Children.* London: Croom Helm, 1980.

Jaffe, J., D. N. Stern, and J. C. Peery. "Conversational" coupling of gaze behavior in prelinguistic human development. *Journal of Psycholinguistic Research 2*, 321-329, 1973.

Jakobson, R., and M. Halle. *Fundamentals of Language.* The Hague: Mouton, 1956.

Johnson, D., and H. Myklebust. *Learning Disabilities.* New York: Grune & Stratton, 1967.

Kagan, J. The growth of the "face" scheme: Theoretical significance and methodological issues. In J. Hellmuth (ed.), *The Exceptional Infant.* Vol. 1, *The Normal Infant.* New York: Brunner/Mazel, 1967.

Karmiloff-Smith, A. *A Functional Approach to Child Language: A Study of Determiners and Reference.* New York: Cambridge University Press, 1979.

Kavanaugh, J. F. (ed.). *Communicating by Language: The Reading Process.* Bethesda, Md.: National Institute of Child Health and Human Development, 1968.

Keenan, E. O. Conversational competence in children. *Journal of Child Language 1*, 365-380, 1974.

Kessel, F. *The Development of Children's Comprehension from 6 to 12.* Unpublished doctoral dissertation, University of Minnesota, Minneapolis, 1969.

Klima, E. S., and U. Bellugi. Syntactic regularities in the speech of children. In J. Lyons and R. Wales (eds.), *Psycholinguistics Papers.* Edinburgh: Edinburgh University Press, 1966.

Kroll, B. M. Developmental relationships between speaking and writing. In B. Kroll and R. Vann (eds.), *Exploring Speaking-Writing Relationships: Connections and Contrasts.* Urbana, Ill.: National Council of Teachers of English, 1981.

Labov, W. The logic of nonstandard English. In F. Williams (ed.), *Language and Poverty*. Chicago: Markham, 1970a.

Labov, W. *The Study of Nonstandard English*. Urbana, Ill.: National Council of Teachers of English, 1970b.

Labov, W., et al. *A Study of the Nonstandard English Used by Negro and Puerto Rican Speakers in New York City* (Final report, U.S. Office of Education Cooperative Research Project No. 3288). Washington, D.C.: U.S. Office of Education, 1968.

Laffey, J., and R. Shuy (eds.), *Language Differences*. Washington, D.C.: International Reading Association, 1973.

Lee, L. *Developmental Sentence Analysis*. Evanston, Ill.: Northwestern University Press, 1974.

Lehiste, U. *Suprasegmentals*. Cambridge, Mass.: MIT Press, 1970.

Lenneberg, E. The natural history of language. In F. Smith and G. Miller (eds.), *The Genesis of Language*. Cambridge, Mass.: MIT Press, 1966.

Lenneberg, E. *Biological Foundations of Language*. New York: Wiley, 1967.

Lewis, M. M. *Language, Thought and Personality in Infancy and Childhood*. New York: Basic Books, 1963.

Lewis, M. M. Infants' responses to facial stimuli during the first year of life. *Developmental Psychology 2,* 75-86, 1969.

Liberman, I. Y., A. M. Liberman, I. G. Mattingly, and D. Shankweiler. Orthography and the beginning reader. In J. Kavanaugh and R. Venezky (eds.), *Orthography, Reading, and Dyslexia*. Baltimore: University Park Press, 1978.

Lieberman, P. *Intonation, Perception, and Language*. Cambridge, Mass.: MIT Press, 1967.

Lieven, E. V. M. Conversations between mothers and young children: Individual differences and their possible implications for the study of language learning. In N. Waterson and C. E. Snow (eds.), *The Development of Communication*. New York: Wiley, 1978.

Linden, E. *Silent Partners*. New York: Times Books, 1986.

Lock, A. (ed.). *Action, Gesture and Symbol: The Emergence of Language*. New York: Academic Press, 1979.

Martlew, M., K. Connolly, and M. McCloud. Language use, role, and context in a five-year-old. *Journal of Child Language 5,* 81-100, 1978.

Maurer, D., and P. Salapetek. Developmental changes in the scanning of faces by young infants. *Child Development 47,* 523-527, 1976.

May, F. *Teaching Language as Communication to Children*. Columbus, Ohio: Merrill, 1967.

McNeill, D. Developmental psycholinguistics. In F. Smith and G. Miller (eds.). *The Genesis of Language*. Cambridge, Mass.: MIT Press, 1966.

McNeill, D. *The Acquisition of Language*. New York: Harper & Row, 1970.

McReynolds, L. V., and D. A. Huston. A distinctive feature analysis of children's misarticulations. *Journal of Speech and Hearing Disorders 36,* 155-156, 1971.

McTear, M. Towards a model for analyzing conversations involving children. In P. French and M. Maclure (eds.), *Adult-Child Conversations*. London: Croom Helm, 1985.

Mehler, J., and T. Bever. Cognitive capacity of very young children. *Science 161,* 141-142, 1967.

Michael, G., and F. Willis. The development of gestures as a function of social class, education and sex. *The Psychological Record 18,* 515-519, 1968.

Miller, J., R. Chapman, M. Branston, and J. Reichle. Language comprehension in sensorimotor stages 5 and 6. *Journal of Speech and Hearing Research 4,* 1-12, 1980.

Moffett, J. *Teaching the Universe of Discourse.* Boston: Houghton Mifflin, 1968.

Morris, C. *Signs, Language, and Behavior.* Englewood Cliffs, N.J.: Prentice-Hall, 1946.

Naremore, R., and R. Dever. Language performance of educable mentally retarded and normal cildren at five age levels. *Journal of Speech and Hearing Research 18,* 82-95, 1975.

Nelson, K. Concept, word, and sentence: Interrelations in acquisition and development. *Psychology Review 81,* 267-285, 1975.

Nelson, K. Facilitating children's syntax acquisition. *Developmental Psychology 13,* 101-107, 1977.

Newson, J., and E. Newson. Intersubjectivity and the transmission of culture: On the social origins of symbolic functioning. *Bulletin of the British Psychological Society 28,* 437-446, 1975.

Ninio, A., and J. Bruner. The achievement and antecedents of labelling. *Journal of Child Language 5,* 1-15, 1978.

Ochs, E., and B. Schieffelin (eds.). *Developmental Pragmatics.* New York: Academic Press, 1982.

Oller, D. K., L. Wieman, W. Doyle, and C. Ross. Infant babbling and speech. *Journal of Child Language 3,* 1-12, 1976.

Olney, R., and E. K. Scholnick. Adult judgments of age and linguistic differences in infant vocalization. *Journal of Child Language 3,* 145-156, 1976.

Olson, D. R. From utterance to text: The bias of language in speech and writing. *Harvard Educational Review 47,* 257-281, 1977.

Ong, W. J. *The Presence of the Word.* New Haven, Conn.: Yale University Press, 1967.

Peters, A. Language learning strategies. *Language 53,* 560-573.

Phillips, J. Syntax and vocabulary of mothers' speech to young children: Age and sex comparisons. *Child Development 44,* 182-185, 1973.

Piaget, J. *The Child's Conception of the World,* Trans. Marjorie Wordon. New York: Harcourt Brace Jovanovich, 1928.

Postman, N. *Amusing Ourselves to Death.* New York, Viking Penguin, 1985.

Postman, N., and C. Weingartner. *Teaching as a Subversive Activity.* New York: Dell (Delacorte Press), 1969.

Premack, D. Language in chimpanzees? *Science 169,* 808-822, 1971.

Pulaski, M. A. S. *Understanding Piaget*. New York: Harper & Row, 1971.

Quine, W. Speaking of objects. In J. Fodor and J. Katz (eds.), *The Structure of Language*. Englewood Cliffs, N.J.: Prentice-Hall, 1964.

Ratner, N., and J. Bruner. Games, social exchange, and the acquisition of language. *Journal of Child Language 5,* 391-401, 1978.

Reid, D. K. Child reading: Readiness or evolution? *Topics in Language Disorders 1,* 61-72, 1981.

Reid, D. K., W. P. Hresko, and O. D. Hammill. *Test of Early Reading.* Austin, Tex.: Pro-Ed, 1981.

Rees, N. Learning to talk and understand. In T. Hixon, L. Shriberg, and J. Saxman (eds.), *Introduction to Communication Disorders.* Englewood Cliffs, N.J.: Prentice-Hall, 1980.

Rogers, S. Self-initiated corrections in the speech of infant-school children. *Journal of Child Langauge 5,* 365-371, 1978.

Sacks, H. Button, button, who's got the button? *Sociological Inquiry 50,* 318-327, 1980.

Sacks, H., E. Schegloff, and G. Jefferson. The simplest systematics for the organization of turn-taking for conversation. *Language 50,* 696-735, 1974.

Salus, P. *Linguistics.* Indianapolis: Bobbs-Merrill, 1969.

Sanches, M., and B. Kirshenblatt-Gimblett. *Child Language and Children's Traditional Speech Play* (Penn-Texas Working Papers in Sociolinguistics, No. 5). 1975.

Schaffer, H. R. (ed.). *Studies in Mother-Infant Interaction.* London: Academic Press, 1977.

Schegloff, E., G. Jefferson, and H. Sacks. The preference for self-correction in the organization of repair in conversation. *Language 53,* 361-382, 1977.

Schiefelbusch, R., and L. Lloyd (eds.). *Language Perspectives—Acquisition, Retardation, and Intervention.* Baltimore: University Park Press, 1974.

Schiff, L. *A Study of Proxemics for Elementary Education.* Unpublished master's thesis, University of Illinois, Chicago, 1973.

Schmerling, S. F. *Aspects of English Sentence Stress.* Austin: University of Texas Press, 1976.

Schwartz, R. M. Strategic processes in beginning reading. *Journal of Reading Behavior 9,* 17-26, 1977.

Serbin, L. A., and K. D. O'Leary. How nursery schools teach girls to shut up. *Psychology Today,* December 1975.

Shore, D. *The Effects of Close Proximity in a Dyadic Interview Situation.* Unpublished master's thesis, University of Illinois, Chicago, 1971.

Silberman, C. *Crisis in the Classroom.* New York: Random House, 1970.

Sinclair, J., and R. Coulthard. *Towards an Analysis of Discourse: The English Used by Teachers and Pupils.* London: Oxford University Press, 1975.

Sinclair-de-Zwart, H. Developmental psycholinguistics. In D. Elkind and J. Flavell (eds.), *Studies in Cognitive Development.* New York: Oxford University Press, 1969.

Skinner, B. F. *Verbal Behavior.* Englewood Cliffs, N.J.: Prentice-Hall, 1957.

Slobin, D. I. The acquisition of Russian as a native language. In F. Smith and G. Miller (eds.), *The Genesis of Language.* Cambridge, Mass.: MIT Press, 1966.

Slobin, D. I. Cognitive prerequisites for the acquisition of grammar. In C. A. Ferguson and D. I. Slobin (eds.), *Studies of Child Language Development.* New York: Holt, Rinehart and Winston, 1973.

Smith, F. (ed.). *Psycholinguistics and Reading.* New York: Holt, Rinehart and Winston, 1975.

Snow, C. Mothers' speech research: From input to interaction. In C. Snow and C. Ferguson (eds.), *Talking to Children.* London: Cambridge University Press, 1977.

Spelt, D. K. The conditioning of the human fetus in utero. *Journal of Experimental Psychology 38,* 338-346, 1948.

Spitz, R., and K. Wold. The smiling response: A contribution to the ontogenesis of social relations. *Genetic Psychology Monographs 34,* 57-125, 1946.

Stoel-Gammon, C., and N. L. Hedberg. *A Longitudinal Study of Cohesion in the Narratives of Young Children.* Austin, Tex.: Third International Congress for the Study of Child Language, 1984.

Sugarman, S. The development of preverbal communication. In R. Schiefelbusch and J. Pickar (eds.), *The Acquisition of Communicative Competence.* Baltimore: University Park Press, 1984.

Trevarthen, C. Descriptive analyses of infant communicative behavior. In H. R. Schaffer (ed.), *Studies in Mother-Infant Interaction.* London: Academic Press, 1977.

Trevarthen, C., and P. Hubley. Secondary intersubjectivity: Confidence, confiding and acts of meaning in the first year. In A. Lock (ed.), *Action, Gesture and Symbol: The Emergence of Language.* New York: Academic Press, 1979.

Tyack, D., and R. Gottsleben. *Language Sampling Analysis and Training: A Handbook for Teachers and Clinicians.* Palo Alto, Calif.: Consulting Psychologists Press, 1974.

U.S. Riot Commission. *Report of the National Advisory Commission on Civil Disorders* (Kerner Commission). New York: Bantam Books, 1968.

Wallach, G. P., and L. Miller. *Language Intervention and Academic Success.* Boston: College Hill Press, 1988.

Wells, G. *Learning Through Interaction: The Study of Language Development.* Cambridge: Cambridge University Press, 1981.

Wells, G. Influences of the home on language development. In A. Davies (ed.), *Language and Learning at School and Home.* London: Heinemann, 1982.

Wells, G. *The Meaning Makers.* Portsmouth, England: Heinemann, 1986.

Wertsch, J. From social interaction to higher psychological process: A clarification and application of Vygotsky's theory. *Human Development 22,* 1-22, 1979.

Westby, C. Development of narrative language abilities. In G. P. Wallach and K. Butler (eds.), *Language Learning Disabilities in School-Age Children.* Baltimore: Williams & Wilkins, 1984.

Whorf, B. *Language, Thought and Reality.* Cambridge, Mass.: MIT Press, 1956.

Wilkinson, L., and K. Rembold. The communicative context of early language development. In S. Kuczaj (ed.), *Language Development.* Vol. 2, *Language Thought and Culture.* Hillsdale, N.J.: Erlbaum, 1982.

Williams, F. (ed.). *Language and Poverty.* Chicago: Markham, 1970.

Williams, F., R. Hopper, and D. Natalicio. *The Sounds of Children.* Englewood Cliffs, N.J.: Prentice-Hall, 1977.

Williams, F., and R. C. Naremore. On the functional analysis of social class differences in modes of speech. *Speech Monographs 36,* 77-102, 1969.

Wood, B. S. *Communication and Children.* Englewood Cliffs, N.J.: Prentice-Hall, 1976.

Woolf, P. H. The natural history of crying and other vocalizations in early infancy. In B. M. Foss (ed.), *Determinants of Infant Behavior,* vol. 4. London: Methuen, 1966.

Index